Understanding Contemporary Social Problems through Media

Understanding Contemporary Social Problems through Media

Roberta Goldberg

Paradigm Publishers

Boulder • London

Copyright © 2014 by Paradigm Publishers

Published in the United States by Paradigm Publishers, 5589 Arapahoe Avenue, Boulder, CO 80303 USA.

Paradigm Publishers is the trade name of Birkenkamp & Company, LLC, Dean Birkenkamp, President and Publisher.

Library of Congress Cataloging-in-Publication Data

Goldberg, Roberta.
  Understanding contemporary social problems through media / Roberta Goldberg.
    pages cm
  Includes bibliographical references and index.
  ISBN 978-1-61205-633-3 (hardcover : alk. paper)
  ISBN 978-1-61205-634-0 (paperback : alk. paper)
 1. Social problems—21st century. 2. Social action—21st century. 3. Applied sociology.
4. Technology—Social aspects. I. Title.
  HN18.3.G65 2014
  361.1—dc23
                                                                          2013045741

Printed and bound in the United States of America on acid-free paper that meets the standards of the American National Standard for Permanence of Paper for Printed Library Materials.

18 17 16 15 14 1 2 3 4 5

To Ray, Alex, and Danny
With love

Contents in Brief

Contents in Detail

Figures, Tables, Boxes, and Photographs

Figures

Tables

Boxes

🎥 Movie Picks

🌐 Web Exercises

📖   Reading Room

☞   Fast Facts

🖥 ## Watch Online

ⓘ ## Information

Photographs

Preface

> **The primary task of a useful teacher is to teach h[er] students to recognize 'inconvenient' facts...**
>
> **Max Weber**

There are almost as many different approaches to the study of social problems as there are books on the topic. One common feature of most social-problems texts is that they survey a very wide range of problems with little opportunity for examining issues in depth. This book differs from most others because its purpose is to provide opportunities for a deeper immersion into some of the major crises facing us today. In selecting the topics for this book, I asked these questions: What are the most serious problems today's students will face as they move through the twenty-first century? What do they understand about these problems? Where do they see themselves in relation to these problems? What can sociology offer to help students understand their lives in relationship to these crises?

This book focuses on some of the most pressing contemporary issues, those that have already set the tone for the twenty-first century and that, I contend, are significant enough to be considered social crises. A quick look at the table of contents reveals that we will explore problems associated with the environment, the developing world, health, terrorism, and technology. For the purposes of this book, then, social problems are those concerns society faces today that are major causes of turmoil and conflict for individuals and the larger society. These crises are pervasive and interconnected. Considering these problems as crises implies an immediacy for understanding and addressing them that is explored further in Chapter 1.

We will use basic sociological principles including the sociological imagination, sociological theories and concepts, and attention to inequality to explore these timely issues. A unique feature of the book is that it connects directly to various media, especially film and the Internet, to help students develop a fuller and up-to-date understanding of these social issues and to give them an opportunity to explore significant issues using technologies in which they are already immersed. A companion website, described below, links the book's topics to films, readings, and exercises presented in each chapter.

Two abstract yet useful observations come to mind in selecting the topics for this book. First is the sense that the world is getting smaller. Obviously, this is not a scientific observation but a social one, in which we sense that we are affected by and affect events that take place almost anywhere in the world. A few concrete examples: When we read about melting glaciers we learn that seemingly contradictory effects of flooding and water shortages can result, depending on where we live. Our experiences with hurricanes at home and tsunamis abroad are tied to global changes in climate and are not isolated events. A visit to the gas pump raises the issue of sustainable energy, peak oil, and new forms of energy as a global phenomenon that affects all nations. The 2010 earthquake in Haiti exemplifies the confluence of our almost instantaneous exposure to the crisis and our need to understand the aftermath exacerbated by poverty and politics. Wars in geographically remote parts of the world impact us directly, perhaps because of a commitment to aiding refugees and new waves of immigrants, or because of inserting our military into conflicts to preserve economic or strategic interests. Understanding our role in world political strife is complicated by our direct experiences of terrorism. In the area of health, the spread of HIV/AIDS is both an issue for those stricken with the disease and a problem that must be tackled domestically and globally through medical research and public policy. The rapid changes in technology help us connect to the world and, at the same time, threaten our privacy. The problems explored in this book demonstrate the notion that the world is getting smaller, and we must understand how these issues impact us individually and socially.

The second useful observation is that time seems to move faster and faster. What gives us this sense in the twenty-first century are the tremendous advances in technology that enable us to function twenty-four hours a day and retrieve information at the push of a button allowing us to learn about world events almost instantaneously. The pace of modern life challenges our ability to absorb information and interpret that information in ways that are useful. Instant news and weather; cultural, economic, and political shifts shown in real time in disparate locations like Greece or Syria or Libya; blogs and online videos—all have the effect of channeling huge amounts of information to us at a furious pace. Indeed, the very topics chosen for this book are those that change rapidly and that, without outside sources of information, will be old news before the reader finishes this book. The technology provides information but does not distinguish between fact and fiction. Indeed, fictional representation of social issues may enhance or detract from our understanding of these problems. Thus the book recommends various media sources, including both documentary and fiction films and a range of Internet sources, to explore the problems as they develop into the future. Application of sociological concepts and theory will help students sort through the massive amounts of information and make sense of the crises we face.

This book is organized into two parts. Part I provides an overview of the sociological concepts and theories through which the topics in the rest of the book are examined. For students already familiar with basic sociology, this section will be a good refresher. For students new to sociology, it will provide a basic introduction to the discipline. In Chapter 1, beginning with the sociological imagination, students learn to apply their personal experiences to the larger social world. Basic sociological concepts are reviewed. The macro theories of functionalism and conflict theory help provide a framework through which students can analyze why social problems exist in the present social framework and how they are experienced by individuals. The micro field, including symbolic interaction, helps students see how communication among people impacts, and is impacted by, the crises they experience. Social construction theory is introduced to help students understand the significance of culture and history in defining social problems. Finally, the role of media in presenting and exploring social problems is addressed. Many students are quite savvy about utilizing media; this section will help them learn to evaluate the sources of information and the role media plays in defining their world.

Chapter 2 focuses on social inequality, particularly social class, gender, race, and ethnicity. These concepts are basic to sociological analysis as frameworks around which social problems are analyzed, and they are also understood as sources of problems in themselves; Chapter 2 is therefore devoted to both the analytical and problematic aspects of inequality. Inequality is a vital concept with which we understand the relative position of people in society and the social dynamics that take place across institutions. Inequalities of class, gender, race, and ethnicity are expressed in nearly every aspect of modern society, including those to be discussed in the second section of this book. Examining ways in which these forms of inequality intersect is an important tool in analyzing social structures and interaction.

Part II contains a chapter on each of the crises described above: the environment, the developing world, health, terrorism, and technology. Each chapter includes an overview of the topic, a discussion of its significance as a social crisis, the application of relevant sociological theories and concepts, and recommendations for use of outside media sources to enhance understanding. Film recommendations, additional readings,

and web-based exercises are included to enhance learning. In the epilogue we consider the practical application of the knowledge gained in learning about the crises. An end-of-book Glossary facilitates quick access to definitions of terms used in the book.

How Media Is Utilized in This Book

Several years of teaching sociology by using film and the Internet have convinced me of the value of using multiple sources of knowledge to enhance learning. Thus, this book was conceived as a multimedia approach vastly different from most social-problems texts. It will work best if it is accompanied by a selection of the many chapter assignments related to online sources of information and recommended films to provide opportunities for innovative exploration and analysis. Links are found on the companion website. Not only are the recommended media sources widely available, students are extremely comfortable with these media as they are immersed in them daily. Indeed, students may want to add their own media suggestions.

There are several explicit contributions to learning when these media sources are used in tandem with the written text. First, movies, whether documentary or fiction, add alternative dimensions for understanding social issues. Each chapter includes "Movie Picks" suggestions that add rich and often riveting content to help bring the text to life. The films can be shown in full or in part during class or as outside assignments. A number of films and film clips are online for easy access or are available through college libraries or commercial movie sources. Many of the recommended films will evoke strong reactions from students while also asking them to view the content sociologically and critically. For instance, the documentary *Invisible Children* recommended in Chapter

4 helps students explore the differences between their own lives and those of vulnerable children caught up in an intolerable war. The combination of graphic images and the dedication of the young filmmakers never fails to raise provocative questions while also encouraging introspection and analysis.

A second important contribution made by using media, especially the Internet, is the ability to stay current on the issues presented in this book. Students and instructors will find an abundance of online material on each of the topics in this book. Scientific findings, research reports, statements by political advocacy groups, and policy updates can be found in each chapter through the "Reading Room," "Web Exercise," and "Watch Online" features that can be accessed through the book's companion website.

The use of a variety of media with this book allows for a dynamic process and invites active student participation. For example, the study of terrorism can be enhanced by the latest information on conflicts across the globe. A discussion of health reform can encourage students to access the most current information on the political status of the current law, as well as provide guidelines for their personal access to health care and insurance.

Utilizing these resources can also take the reader in new directions, with interconnections between topics and opportunities to examine issues in greater depth. Indeed, this book may be of special value in film and media courses with its emphasis on major social issues as an organizing framework for the study of film and other media. Finally, this book is not intended to be a comprehensive text on social problems, but the resources it suggests to readers are a useful jumping-off point for those who want to examine issues beyond those raised in the book.

Information P.1
Using the Companion Website

www.paradigmpublishers.com/resources/goldbergmedia.aspx

Each web exercise and reading room recommendation, and many of the films in this text, are also listed in the companion website. Students can easily link to these directly through the website. Occasionally a link disappears or moves, so the companion website will be updated regularly with new or alternative links. Check the website for updates when assigning exercises or readings.

Acknowledgments

I am grateful to many people who helped at various stages of the writing process, as well as friends and family who cheered me on as this project progressed. It wasn't easy and your support was invaluable! First, I want to thank Dean Birkenkamp at Paradigm Publishers for believing in this book and for his good advice and his support in seeing the book to completion. Laura Esterman was also a great help in preparing the manuscript and Jason Barry equally so with preparing the photos. Karl Yambert was an amazing copy editor, and saved me from myself in countless ways. Dennis Gilbert was one of the first people to encourage me to write this book before I even saw its potential; thank you, Dennis. I also want to thank Dave Repetto, who helped me through the early stages of this project.

My colleagues at Trinity Washington University were a great source of support throughout. Special thanks to my sociology colleagues, Roxana Moayedi and Konia Kollehlon, who sustained me intellectually and personally. Roxana, especially, was always there to keep me balanced. Other Trinity colleagues who were instrumental in helping me stay on track, providing good advice, giving me the time and space to do this work, and simply just being there, include Pat McGuire, Virginia Broaddus, Liza Child, Mary Lynn Rampolla, Minerva San Juan, Jackie Padgett, Kathleen McGinnis, Lori Shpunt, Susan Farnsworth, and Janet Stocks. Great colleagues, all. I am also grateful to our intrepid faculty services staff, Cassandra Boston and LaWander McFarland. This book evolved out of a course I developed called Social Criticism through Film, and I sincerely want to thank all the students who have taken this course. Their enthusiasm for the topics and the use of media were an inspiration and kept me motivated. Thanks especially to two students who assisted with some of the research: Sandra Villegas and Waseme Berry.

Friends were so vitally important throughout. Special thanks to Pat Sellner with whom I spent many therapeutic evening walks that got me out of my self-absorption. Tammy and Martin Trocki, Clara Raju, Joann Albert, Sarah Berger, Rick Frederick, and Debi Leekoff are great friends and family who gently asked me about my progress, even when it appeared I was going nowhere and who distracted me with food, books, and fun.

My sons, Alex and Danny, the Millennial Generation personified, were the main inspirations for this book. I wanted to understand (and to help them understand) what their futures might be like as young adults facing the twenty-first century, immersed in media and sorting through the many challenges they will face in their lifetimes. They cheered me on, gave me good advice as digital natives, and inspired me. Finally, to my husband, Ray, my in-house computer guru, artist, and provider of space (literal and figurative), you patiently put up with my ups and downs. I couldn't have done it without you!

PART I

UNDERSTANDING SOCIAL PROBLEMS AS SOCIAL CRISES

THE BASICS

CHAPTER 1

A Sociological Look at Social Crises

Figure 1.1 The Sociological imagination.
Source: April Milne

I have watched my children grow up under the pall of 9/11 and the wars in Iraq and Afghanistan. They watched Hurricane Katrina on television. Oil prices, the economy, and their health care are mysteries about which they have little understanding and seemingly no control. The information technology they are so adept at using brings them information so rapidly that it is hard to digest. As a parent and a sociologist, I am amazed at the problems their generation faces, and I try to imagine how these problems look to them. Similarly, I look at my students, eager to face the world, but burdened by their time and place. How do they make sense of their world?

While there are many social problems worthy of examination, this book focuses on some of the most significant social crises we face in the twenty-first century. What constitutes a social crisis? Several components help us define a social problem as a crisis. First, a crisis constitutes both an immediate and a long-term challenge that, left unaddressed, is likely to have significant negative consequences for large numbers of people. Natural disasters such as earthquakes and floods come to mind. But crises are also man-made. The impact of war, oil spills, disease, and terrorism are examples of crises we address in this book. There is a need to examine these problems, but also to understand that solving them means committing resources both immediately and over the long term.

Second, people will experience crises differently depending on geographic location, cultural factors, political dynamics, or unequal access to resources. For example, responses to flooding in the American Midwest will differ from responses to flooding in Pakistan based on available resources and other economic and political considerations. The 2010 earthquake in Haiti resulted in a great humanitarian crisis, while the 2011 earthquake in Japan layered a nuclear crisis on top of human suffering. It was not only the natural disaster that determined the outcomes in these two countries. The degree of development and wealth, the sources of energy, and the overall social dynamics of each society were major factors in determining the impact of the earthquakes. The global nature of these crises means they cannot be addressed solely by local solutions, and that a solution in one area may not be appropriate in another. Cooperation within and between nations is required to address the problems adequately. The need for cooperation contributes to the complexity of the crises and recognizes that any crisis may be experienced and understood differently in different social locations. It is important that individuals learn more about these crises in order to address them directly in their own lives, hence their relevance to today's college students. These are not just distant problems but matters that affect people in their everyday lives. Sociology is uniquely able to connect personal experiences to larger social issues by applying the sociological imagination, discussed later in this chapter and throughout the book.

In Part II of this book we explore five specific social problems that fit the definition of social crisis. They are among the most pressing concerns we face, though not the only ones. Within each crisis we focus on specific issues that are not intended to represent the full range of the problem but rather to provide concrete examples of the nature of each problem and how it impacts individuals and society. Briefly, the social problems addressed in the book are

- *The environmental crisis:* focus on climate change and energy issues.
- *Conflicts in the developing world:* focus on global inequalities, child soldiers, human trafficking, and genocide.
- *Health and health care:* focus on obesity, HIV/AIDS, and health-care reform.
- *Terrorism:* focus on the aftermath of 9/11 and the ramifications of the responses to terrorism.
- *Technology:* focus on issues of privacy and identity.

Among the characteristics that these topics share is that they are fluid. The conditions affecting the crises addressed in this book can change rapidly. Political, economic, and social factors create a dynamic situation in which keeping up with information is a challenge. Nearly every problem covered in this book has been impacted by recent and sometimes unanticipated events. Consider these:

- The oil spill in the Gulf of Mexico in 2010 has shaped our understanding of the relationship of oil to energy and natural habitats.
- The "Arab Spring" of 2011 had a significant impact on global politics and economics and has spilled over into violent conflicts, most notably in Syria.
- The unresolved political debate about health-care reform raises important questions about the future of health care in the United States.
- Our understanding of terrorism has been impacted by the killing of Osama bin Laden in 2011 and the unprecedented growth of national and international security programs.

- The growth of international cyberattacks demonstrates how technology can supersede traditional political dynamics globally.

By applying sociological concepts and theories we have a basis for analysis that can be applied to these problems even as they continue to evolve.

The remainder of this chapter introduces the sociological perspective through concepts and theories, starting with the sociological imagination. Sociological research methods are introduced as well. We also look at the role of media in our culture and how media affects our exposure to and understanding of our social world. Chapter 2 then addresses social inequalities that impact the experiences people have in relation to these crises.

Developing a Sociological Perspective

Most of us see the world around us through our individual experiences. How we see our place in the world and the decisions we make

Figure 1.2 Components of a sociological perspective.
Source: Raymond Lee

accordingly are colored by these experiences. Consider these concerns: As a college student you may wonder if you have enough money to stay in college. Or perhaps you experience discrimination because of your race or ethnicity or your sex. Will you drive or take public transportation to school or work? Do you know anyone who has died in a war or in a terrorist attack? Are you HIV-positive or do you know someone who is? Have you ever had your identity stolen? These are personal problems, but they have their origins in social situations. Although individuals may have various ways of dealing with these problems, there is a social context to each that takes them out of the purely personal into the larger social world. If you do not examine your personal problem in relation to social forces, you miss an opportunity to address the problem in an effective way. If you do not reflect on the problems of others, even if you don't experience them yourself, you also miss an important component of sociological thinking. This is one of the most difficult tasks college students must master. Your own experience may or may not seem unique, or may or may not look like the experiences of others. Either way, you must reach beyond your comfort zone to think sociologically. It is important to understand that everything you experience personally has a social context that is bigger than you, and sociology can help you gain that perspective.

The Sociological Imagination

One of the classic books in sociology, *The Sociological Imagination* by C. Wright Mills (1959), helps us explore the connections between our individual experiences and the larger social world. Mills demonstrates how sociology can help us tie our personal problems to social circumstances and events. To use the **sociological imagination**, Mills asks us to look at how structural changes in

Web Exercise 1.1
What Is the Sociological Imagination?

Read "Chapter One: The Promise" from *The Sociological Imagination* online (https://socialsciences.nsula.edu/assets/Site-Files/The-Promise.pdf).

- Briefly summarize the ideas in your own words.
- Describe a personal problem you face and explain how you can apply the sociological imagination to better understand your situation.
- Does this exercise change your perspective on the problem? Why or why not?

Access the live/updated links at http://www.paradigmpublishers.com/resources/goldbergmedia.aspx

society impact our individual lives and the lives of others. Developing a global view of history will help us see the context in which we must make decisions that may be life altering. If we cannot do that, we will likely have the experience that our "private lives are a series of traps" (Mills 1959, 3). These traps may seem inescapable, and our own fault, because of our inability to perceive the greater circumstances that shape our lives. Mills challenges our tendencies to see our lives as purely psychological experiences overwhelmed by forces out of our control. Thus sociology enables us to step out of our personal cocoons and connect our personal lives to larger social structures and historical trends. This process helps us understand that individuals alone are not entirely responsible for the circumstances of their lives. When we understand the role social forces play in our lives, we get closer to being able to influence those social forces in hopes of bettering our own lives and those of others. We will use the sociological imagination throughout this book to help us understand our own experiences in the context of the larger crises around which this book is formed.

What Is Culture?

Culture is a way of experiencing and seeing the world from the perspective of the people

sharing it, a society. The essence of social experience is culture, and while cultures differ from society to society, all cultures share some common characteristics as they meet the needs of their members. There are two basic types of culture: **material culture** and **non-material culture**. Material culture refers to tangible aspects of the lives of people in a society. It emerges from the ways in which people meet basic needs for food, shelter, and overall sustainability. Housing, clothing, forms of transportation, food, and technology are some of the most important aspects of material culture. Non-material culture is more abstract. It represents ideas about the world around us. What we think of as justice, honor, morality, religion, and beauty—our values and attitudes, along with the skills and knowledge necessary to meet our needs—make up our non-material culture. For example, in American society the preference for driving cars over taking public transportation links material culture (cars) and non-material culture (the values regarding individual choices about transportation). As gas prices soared in the United States through the first decade of the twenty-first century, many people curtailed travel, which in turn impacted businesses. If prices remain high in the long term, there may be a shift in the values placed on automobiles over public transportation. As we will see in Chapter 3, transportation preferences and related technologies have a profound effect on the global environmental crisis that we face today.

Not only is culture shared among a group of people, it must be passed down from generation to generation for a society to thrive. The cumulative knowledge, skills, and values gained from previous generations are taught to newer generations. But culture is not static, so what is passed to each generation builds on previous experience and is also affected by new experiences. We do not have to "reinvent the wheel" each generation, but we can add to our knowledge about wheels and create better ones that fit the needs of each successive generation. If the generational link is disrupted through civil conflict, extreme poverty, or natural disaster, challenges to accumulated knowledge and values become serious problems. Societies must also address problems that have grown over time to a point of crisis. War and epidemics come to mind. How each society responds to a crisis is tied to its culture—its technological and scientific knowledge, its capacity to use resources to address the crisis, and the values it holds that influence how resources are distributed. For example, we will see in Chapter 5 how the AIDS epidemic is experienced differently in different societies. Cultural values regarding sexual behavior or the practices of IV (intravenous) drug use provide a social context through which people understand AIDS and respond to it. The trends in infection, education, and treatment vary largely because of cultural differences. Moreover, in some parts of the world where AIDS has left many children orphans, we see a direct effect of the loss of the generational link so important to maintaining culture. When examining the crises presented in this book, we must try to understand the cultural context through which societies address each crisis. Since these crises cross borders, the opportunities for cultural misunderstanding are abundant, so exploration into how a crisis is experienced in different cultures is important in enabling us to comprehend the crisis adequately.

A sociological perspective on culture utilizes some additional important concepts that enable us to understand why people act the way they do. We categorize social action according to the **norms** of society, the expected behaviors of the people who share a culture. In every culture there are expectations that range from demanded behaviors called **mores,** which include written laws and unwritten requirements to which people are expected to strictly adhere, to more flexible expectations, called **folkways**. For example, in the United States there are laws that prohibit sex between closely related people, but much of the rest of sexual activity is quite liberal compared to some other societies. Thus, adult sexual practices within and outside of marriage may be considered customs, or folkways, giving Americans a fairly open set of norms from which to choose. In more conservative societies, restrictions on sexual behavior would fall more rigorously into the area of demanded behaviors, or mores. Penalties, or **negative sanctions,** for violating mores can be quite severe. Further complicating our understanding of culture is that different norms may apply to men and women and to people of different statuses or ranks in society. We will see in Chapter 4 that gender inequality is significant when discussing child soldiers and human trafficking. Understanding sexual practices and attitudes about gender in those contexts enables us to better understand the inequalities that make women and girls especially vulnerable.

Additional components of culture include **subcultures**, which, although adhering to a society's overall normative expectations, may add other layers of expectations that are specific to that group but that are not in opposition to the expectations of the larger society. Subcultures may include religious or ethnic groups, occupations, youth culture, and so forth. Keeping with the example of sexual practices, within some religions sex outside of marriage is prohibited, while among the subculture of American college students it is widely practiced. **Counter-cultures** oppose the norms of society by creating their own set of norms in opposition to, and marginalizing themselves from, the mainstream. In some cases society responds by criminalizing their activities. Extremist groups that advocate terrorism would be considered countercultures in most countries with stable regimes. Not all countercultures are extreme, however. For example, in American culture, although marijuana use is outlawed at the national level (at least for now) and is not considered normative, those who support and participate in the recreational use of marijuana and argue for decriminalization might be considered a counterculture. Indeed, in the 1960s and 1970s, the term *counterculture* was popularized when referring to young adults who challenged laws against marijuana use along with outspoken opposition to the war in Vietnam.

Culture and Mass Media

There are many references to media sources throughout this book, including film, news and entertainment outlets, and the enormous variety of material found on the Internet. These are valuable sources of information and are vital to our understanding of the complexity and timeliness of the issues presented in this book. We cannot accept these sources at face value, however. The media has a powerful influence on society, and it is important to examine its role sociologically. We will first look at how mass media is part of culture. Then we will explore how media outlets are organized as corporate entities, how that organization impacts what is seen and heard, and how access to media differs according to social location. Last, we examine how we use the media to gain understanding of the problems discussed in this book.

We are well aware of the explosion of media sources available to us and the rapid changes in related technologies. Newspapers are transforming before our eyes from traditional print to web-based news, if they are to survive at all. Television and radio have expanded to stations too numerous for most of us to count. Films come in forms ranging from expensive studio-based productions to homemade curiosities shown on the Internet. Anyone can blog, set up a Facebook page, or produce a video for mass consumption.

In the view of sociologists, mass media both reflects the culture from which it comes and helps define that culture in the first place. Through increasingly complex technology, we generate and absorb a great deal of information and entertainment. This technology also makes it possible to blur (at least virtually) traditional national borders and cultural barriers so that people great distances apart may be exposed to the same media sources. How people in different cultures interpret what they experience through media may differ, but access across great geographic distances has grown dramatically.

Cultural diffusion, exchanging goods and knowledge across cultures, has existed since the first human societies came into contact with one another, and mass media today is one of the most important contributors to cultural diffusion. Today, because media technology allows for rapid transmission across the globe, the influx of new ideas and experiences can be unnerving, or worse, threatening. The concept of **cultural lag** helps explain the gap between access to information through new technologies and the response to that information. For example, when people in conservative cultures access cable television or websites that present sexually provocative images typical of Western media, there may be a rejection of both the images and the culture from which it comes. Alternatively, Americans may be intolerant of cultural practices regarding sex or gender from other societies. Such reactions may reflect deep cultural or religious positions that challenge intercultural understanding. More broadly speaking, significantly different political orientations are presented through the Internet every day, and although exposure to different points of view can be enlightening, it may not be understood or approved of by those outside the culture from which it comes, especially if there are political implications that question the status quo. Periodically, non-Western nations challenge large Internet and technology companies regarding access to audiences in their countries, as was the case in China and Saudi Arabia in 2010. During the upheavals in the Middle East in 2011, access to electronic sources of information was periodically curtailed. The "Arab Spring" demonstrated that even when formal news reporting was restricted during political demonstrations, communications made their way around the world, providing information crucial to understanding those significant political events. Even in America's relatively open culture, there is discomfort with some media presentations as well as disagreement about its significance. The advances in media technology often move faster than the ability to absorb it into any culture. The result can be confusing or even destabilizing, providing valuable information while also challenging the status quo.

Among sociologists there is little doubt that mass media has emerged as a major social institution because it is woven so deeply into the social fabric. It is an important part of our social structure and serves a variety of functions, including disseminating information and entertainment as well as selling products. A few statistics can demonstrate the penetration of mass media into our lives. According to Nielsen (2012a), the average American spent thirty-four hours a week watching television in 2012. Increasing numbers of households have a variety of devices with which to watch shows and movies, play games, and access the Internet, so overall in 2012 an average in excess of forty-one hours per week was spent on these devices (Nielsen 2013b). Nielsen (2013a) also reported that 208,703,000 Americans used the Internet in January 2013. Social-networking sites also beckon us. Nielsen (2012b) reports that visiting social-media sites increased by 63 percent between 2011 and 2012, with Facebook, the most popular, accessed by 152.2 million viewers.

The Internet is an especially vibrant and vital system of communication that is much more interactive than other media and that has seemingly endless sources of information. Indeed, searching for statistics on Internet usage, I posed the question (online, of course), "How many Internet websites exist?" This inquiry generated 278 million sources from which to choose. As of June 2012, there were a reported 2,405,518,376 Internet users, over 34 percent of the world's population (Internet World Stats 2012).

The distribution of Internet use is uneven globally. More than three-fourths of North Americans (78.6 percent) use the Internet, while African usage is 15.6 percent. Although Asia has only a 27.5 percent usage rate, there are 1,076,681,059 users in Asia, a far greater number than any other region of the world, giving them a 44.8 percent share of global usage, followed by Europe (21.5 percent) and North America (11.4 percent). The smallest shares of Internet use are Latin America/Caribbean (10.6 percent), Africa (7 percent), the Middle East (3.7 percent), and Oceania/Australia (1 percent) (Internet World Stats 2012). This unequal access to the Internet has important implications for how information is distributed across the globe.

What can these statistics tell us about the importance of mass media? First, as part of culture, it represents both the material culture (hardware, software, and related technology) and the non-material culture (communication skills, the value of sharing

Movie Picks 1.1
Merchants of Cool

The PBS *Frontline* video *Merchants of Cool* (http://www.pbs.org/wgbh/pages/frontline/shows/cool/view/) depicts the influence of media on youth culture and the connections between media owners, merchandisers, and their messages to youth. Most interesting is how this media machine exploits the youth market by seeking new trends in youth culture and turning them into corporate profits.

Mixed-Media Extra

View additional material on the *Merchants of Cool* website, especially "Some Themes in this Report."

Thinking Sociologically

- From a sociological perspective, how do media empires connect to their audiences?
- Does culture drive media or does media create culture?
- How does media influence your choices of music and clothing?

Access the live/updated links at http://www.paradigmpublishers.com/resources/goldbergmedia.aspx

---

information and ideas, and the presentation of news and entertainment across a wide spectrum of people). Since its inception the Internet has influenced a new generation of people, including today's college students, in creating and validating new forms of communication, both written and oral. In observing the rapid acceptance of the Internet and its likely future domination as a form of communication, it becomes apparent that, although mass media largely reflects cultural experiences and beliefs, it also helps create them.

Organization and Ownership of Media

It may appear that mass media consists of freewheeling activity in which citizens everywhere equally participate, yet there are structural underpinnings that are important in understanding the role media plays in our economy and our culture.

Media outlets for the most part are owned by large corporations, and as such they play an important role in the economy and in shaping what we see and hear in the news and in entertainment. One might think that with the proliferation of cable television with hundreds of stations available, ownership would diversify. The opposite has been the case. Moreover, ownership across the range of types of media is consolidated into a few large corporations. Whether called "The Big Five" (Khan 2003) or "The Big Ten" (Miller 2002), it is evident that media owners are vastly rich and influential. Mark Crispin Miller's 2002 analysis of the domination by a few corporate owners demonstrates the importance of corporate control over media. As an example of the breadth and depth of corporate control, we can look briefly at AOL and Time Warner, which merged in 2001 and subsequently broke up in 2009. At that time, the merger was the largest in history (Hoberman 2009). Khan (2003) reported that AOL Time Warner had

Web Exercise 1.2
What's My Connection to the Media Empire?

List the five television programs you watch most often along with the station on which you view it. Identify the corporate owner of each network by using the link on this book's companion website, "Who Owns the Media?"

- What other types of media do those corporations own?
- What is the revenue of each corporate owner?
- Do you think the owners of these networks influence the content of what you watch?
- Explain.

Access the live/updated links at http://www.paradigmpublishers.com/resources/goldbergmedia.aspx

revenues over $40 billion in 2002, including holdings in the Internet, television stations, music companies, and magazines. Other large media corporations have similar holdings: radio stations, network and cable television stations, film studios, newspapers, and book publishers, among others.

While the names at the top may change in the ever-evolving media empires, the consolidation of ownership has shaped our understanding of the world and how significantly news and entertainment have been impacted. The question of media ownership and its impact on what we see and hear is significant and there is much discussion of the need for an informed citizenry. Critics do not necessarily agree on the extent of the damage done to democracy by media giants, however. Miller argues that, despite the appearance of variety in programming, news has simply become another form of entertainment in the competitive drive for profit: "The news is, with a few exceptions, yet another version of the entertainment that the cartel also vends nonstop" (Miller 2002). Miller goes on to argue that the result is a loss of freedom and democracy as journalism must take a backseat to company profits. Similarly, Khan argues that the control over media by these few corporation leads to little real choice for viewers, and points out

the importance of an informed public: "The First Amendment rests on the assumption that the widest possible dissemination of information from diverse and antagonistic sources is essential to the welfare of the public" (Khan 2003). Sociologists Gamson and Latteier (2012) argue that despite the concentration of media in a few hands, and the potential danger in that, there is more diversity than one would expect. Their study "Do Media Monsters Devour Diversity?" argues that the media is not the monolith described by critics. Rather it is more complex, with variety in the areas of format, diversity, and ideas. There is no question that the media is owned by a small group of powerful corporations, and it is worth watching how they evolve in the coming decades.

Keeping a critical eye toward the complexity of mass media and its enormous influence today, this book offers many opportunities to enhance learning through the use of media, primarily film and the Internet. Our culture is deeply immersed in mass media, and it can be a useful tool in exploring the ideas in this book.

Culture as a basic sociological concept helps us understand the structural and interpersonal components of society, and will be applied throughout this book. Concepts

Movie Picks 1.2
Weapons of Mass Deception

Weapons of Mass Deception critically examines the role of mass-media news coverage of the war in Iraq (http://www.youtube.com/watch?v=07VyQimMonM#t=57). The film argues that, by providing "coverage" rather than "journalism," mass-media news led the nation to believe weapons of mass destruction existed in Iraq, when that was not the case.

Thinking Sociologically

- How did news programming and reporting change in the aftermath of 9/11?
- Was the media influential in convincing the public of the need to go to war?
- Is the news affected by the limited range of media ownership?

Access the live/updated links at http://www.paradigmpublishers.com/resources/goldbergmedia.aspx

alone do not explain behavior, social trends, or differences in how people connect to society. For that we turn to sociological theory, to help explain how and why people act in a social context, as part of groups and as whole societies.

Sociological Theory

In any academic discipline the purpose of theory is to provide a framework for analyzing what is being studied. In sociology the great thinkers of the nineteenth and twentieth centuries developed theories that provide insight into how societies are structured and how people interact within and between societies. These theories enable us to organize our ideas about social experience and provide a context for research.

The earliest sociological theories emerged at times of social upheaval, from the Enlightenment to the Industrial Revolution and the growth of modern capitalism. Just as we try to sort through the social problems we face today, these scholars saw their world as rife with problems needing to be understood and solved. They drew primarily from philosophy and the natural sciences for their orientation and

developed a unique discipline that we now call sociology.

Macro Theory

From the classic thinkers, especially August Comte, Herbert Spencer, Karl Marx, Emile Durkheim, and Max Weber, emerged two distinct modern sociological theories: structural functionalism and conflict theory. These are considered macro theories, or structural theories, as they address the significant structures that make up our social world. These structural theories are the backbone of modern sociological theory today. These theories are used to examine the topics in this book, so a synopsis of each theory is useful.

Structural functionalism, also called functionalism, developed from the early analyses of social phenomena by Comte, Spencer, and Durkheim. As its name suggests, the theory examines the structure of society and how different parts function, both of these factors being useful in understanding social life. Drawing from a natural-science model, functional theory likens society to an organism with interdependent parts, much like a living being. Essential to social structure are the basic **social institutions**: the family, religion, education, economics, and political institutions are like organs that keep society alive and functioning. Just as hearts, lungs, brains, and so forth are necessary for the physical survival of an organism, so too are these social institutions necessary for social survival. These institutions make up the structure of every society, though how institutions are shaped and how they function vary from society to society and over time. In recent years sociologists have suggested additional institutions that have emerged in modern society: mass media, science, the military, technology, and health each have important functions in society today and permeate modern life.

A sociologist's bookshelf.
Source: Roberta Goldberg

Functional theory argues that social change occurs when something interferes with the normal equilibrium of society and part of society becomes dysfunctional. In order to regain the balance necessary for social institutions to function properly, change must occur. Thus, social dynamics are a result of the correction of imbalances that are considered abnormal deviations from societal equilibrium. Thus, structural functionalism describes the framework of social structure and the mechanisms by which different parts of that structure work to serve social needs. When examining the crises presented in this book, our analysis will be aided by attention to how social institutions work in the context of these crises.

Criticism of functionalism is based on its limited ability to incorporate social change as fundamental to society. For example, if the institution of the family functions well to reproduce members of society, why, then, do family structures and functions change over time? Are changes in fertility and marriage patterns a sign of dysfunction or simply the effects of ongoing social dynamics? We

explore this topic further in Chapter 7 as we discuss the application of reproductive technology to social experience. Because functional theory argues that change occurs when there is social dysfunction, critics regard this as a simplistic way of viewing change, arguing that social change is an ongoing, normal part of social life, rather than occurring only when society is dysfunctional. These critics find themselves more comfortable with conflict theory, discussed next.

Conflict theory derives in large part from the writings of Karl Marx and Max Weber, classical thinkers widely read by philosophers, economists, political scientists, and sociologists alike. Marx and Weber lived in a tumultuous time. They observed the rise of modern capitalism during the Industrial Revolution in nineteenth-century Europe. Like other thinkers of that era, they asked essential questions about the direction society was taking.

It is difficult to describe Marx's thinking in a few paragraphs, but the essentials are found in his understanding of the inevitable conflicts that arise from the unequal distribution of resources and power that emerged with the growth of industrial capitalism. Marx believed that all of human history was a result of the changes created by the inequalities that emerged from particular social configurations of any historical era, and for him this new form of capitalism marked an especially dynamic stage of human history. A crisis created from the extreme inequalities brought about by modern capitalism would, according to Marx, dramatically alter social conditions and relationships—so much so that major conflict and upheaval could not be avoided. Marx saw these conflicts culminating in the destruction of capitalism through revolution and the rise of a more egalitarian society.

What did Marx see in the rise of capitalism that was so significant? He argued that the industrialization that spanned Europe and North America in the nineteenth century was revolutionary in many ways. It transformed cities as large numbers of people moved from the countryside to look for work in new industries. Industrialization brought new divisions of labor, more complex and requiring different skills than ever before in history. For Marx, these changes were a result not just of industrialization but of the rise of modern capitalism in which a small number of people owned and controlled the major sources of industrial wealth, while large numbers of people worked for wages in the factories, mines, and mills of the capitalists. There was a new dynamic between people based on the relations between capitalists who owned the industries and members of the working class who labored for them. New technologies restructured work and decision-making, and new sources of wealth generated large profits as production was enhanced by those technologies. Marx argued that economic power enabled a small group, the "ruling class," to dominate politically so that capitalism was supported by and defended by political power structures. At the same time, the working class was exploited by the dynamics of their relationship to capitalism. Because of the inequality inherent in this situation, Marx argued that conflict was inevitable and he predicted that a workers' revolution

would overthrow capitalism and replace it with communism.

Conflict theory today utilizes Marx's notion that inequalities based in the distribution of resources result in social conflict that sooner or later must be confronted and resolved. Resolution of one conflict gives rise to others as long as inequalities exist, thus we see the ongoing dynamics of social life. Chapter 4 discusses how unequal distribution of resources between the least developed nations and the developed world help define the conflicts that are driving the crises in these poor nations. Similarly, in Chapter 5 we see how unequal access to health care creates disparities in treatment of diseases such as AIDS and conditions such as obesity. Political discourse about health reform exposes conflicts that reflect these inequalities.

Max Weber also observed the effects of capitalism on social life and so, too, contributed to the development of modern conflict theory. He agreed with Marx that the social classes arising out of industrial capitalism created a new, modern dynamic not seen before in history and potentially full of conflict. Beyond that agreement, Weber's outlook veered away from Marx's predictions of revolution in important ways. In his analysis of the new social classes created by capitalism, Weber predicted that social change would not result in a complete overhaul of society and a new form of economy, but rather would create incremental change serving the needs of specific groups within their social networks. Factors associated with occupation and status would contribute to a range of different responses to capitalism that would preclude the revolution that Marx anticipated. Further, Weber argued that modern capitalism was not universal but tied to the particular social history of Europe, specifically the confluence of Protestantism and capitalism.

Weber also addressed one of the most important social developments in modern

Reading Room 1.1
Classical Theory

To read more about classical sociological theory, select additional information on Marx or Weber or other theorists linked on this volume's companion website. Consider the following:

- How is sociological theory different from common sense?
- How do you think sociological theory can help you understand major events of our time such as the crises covered in this book?

Access the live/updated links at http://www.paradigmpublishers.com/resources/goldbergmedia.aspx

society: **bureaucracy**. He anticipated the dominance of bureaucracy over other forms of social organization as crucial to the functioning of the modern world. Although he understood the inevitability of bureaucracy, he also saw that it depersonalized social interaction and limited creativity. A modern analysis of Weber's theory of bureaucracy can be found in George Ritzer's *The McDonaldization of Society 6* (2011). Behemoth organizations, whether they be mass-media corporations, fast-food restaurants, military organizations, or health-care systems, strive for efficiency and predictability among other characteristics but often produce harmful outcomes. Fast-food restaurant chains have had enormous global success because they can deliver a highly desirable product, but as we will see in Chapter 5, they have also contributed to dangerous levels of obesity.

Modern conflict theory incorporates the essentials of Marx's and Weber's ideas regarding the relevance of inequality to the problems facing society today. It assumes that social change is a constant, brought on by inequality that is always found in all societies, rather than an episodic response to occasional dysfunction, as portrayed by functionalist theory. When we examine the crises in Part II, we will see how conflict theory addresses the challenges presented by each of these crises. Using conflict theory will help us understand the relative position of people as

they are impacted by crises of the environment, health care, access to technology, and so forth. Chapter 2 goes into greater depth regarding the most deep-seated inequalities in society today by examining class, gender, race, and ethnicity.

Micro Theory

Where structural theories examine the large-scale workings of society, we also must pay attention to how people perceive themselves and communicate with one another. Social interaction is the subject of **symbolic interaction theory**. Symbolic interaction theory studies how we use language and other forms of communication to reflect who we are, give meaning to our circumstances, and meet our social needs. Symbolic interaction is deeply embedded in culture. Oral and written language, gestures, and other symbols are important representatives of each human culture and provide the social context of meaning. In the twenty-first century, technology has driven new forms of communication, most recently the rapidly expanding use of texting and Twitter, which have in a few short years influenced the shape of language and the reach of electronic communication. Beyond language, the meaning we give to clothing, ritual symbols, jewelry, and other forms of material culture represent who we are as members of society and as individual participants in society.

George Herbert Mead argued that this micro approach to understanding society is a significant sociological theory. An important component of symbolic interaction theory developed by Mead is the concept of "self." The "self" represents how we see ourselves in relation to the world around us. Charles Horton Cooley demonstrated the importance of the "looking-glass self," that is our ability to see ourselves as others see us. We look in a mirror, literally and figuratively, to imagine how we present ourselves to the world around us. What you choose to wear, how you conduct yourself in a job interview, what you say to your professor or fellow students in class, your political preferences—all reflect your "self." You do not stand outside of social influence. Your "self" is a reflection of the choices you make in a social context. The period of history in which you live, your family circumstances, your generational experiences, and your economic resources, for example, are all reflected in your "self." In other words, even as an individual you make decisions large and small that reflect your social circumstances.

Symbolic interaction theory recognizes that society is a context, but that individuals also make independent decisions to act within that context, thus the "self" is a significant participant in society. In some ways this concept is reflected in the sociological imagination. Both concepts enable you to see yourself in the larger social picture. The concerns you have, the choices you make, and your view of the world are part of your sociological imagination and how you see your "self." Decisions you make give you **agency**, the ability to direct your personal life in society. As you study the crises later in this book, reflect on your personal actions as a participant inside or on the periphery of these crises. When you think about your reaction to climate change, global conflicts, terrorism, and other crises, you will consider your role both in how you might be affected and in how you might respond to these crises. Symbolic interaction theory provides students with tools to see themselves as actors on the social stage.

Social construction of reality theory offers an important perspective as well. Indeed, looking back at the definition of social crises offered at the beginning of this chapter, one could easily argue that defining social problems as crises depends at least in part on the perspective of the people experiencing it, the moment in time, and the culture of a particular group. What is perceived as a crisis by one group in one period of history may be seen quite differently by another group or in another time or place. Certainly the crises covered in this book were not always perceived as crises, and for some, they still are not. For example, scientific evidence about climate change notwithstanding, the debate endures about whether it is a crisis at all, and, if so, if it is a crisis created by human activity or natural climate cycles.

Structural conditions alone cannot explain how people interpret these problems, so we must try to understand the changes in perspectives over time and from one society or group within a society to another. Social construction theory can help us do that. For example, later in this book we examine HIV/AIDS as it is experienced in different parts of the world. A quick examination of its spread in the United States demonstrates the usefulness of social construction theory. When it first was recognized as a new disease, AIDS quickly gained a stigma as a "gay cancer" acquired through sexual activity between men. That stigma contributed to a limited understanding of the disease and thus how it was addressed medically and socially. Early responses to the disease were woefully inadequate and contributed to widespread misunderstanding, limited medical care, and lack of support for those infected. This was a social construction that hurt the ability to

Movie Picks 1.3
Lord of the Flies

Lord of the Flies (either the 1963 or 1990 version) depicts the breakdown of society when boys stranded on an island are forced to create their own society for survival. It presents an intense exploration of responses to the disruption of social order. This film is useful for the application of many sociological concepts.

Thinking Sociologically

- Consider how culture can develop from chaos and how inequality leads to power struggles.
- How has reality been constructed as the boys try to create a working society?
- What unique symbols are developed as this new society emerges?
- Which sociological theory most effectively explains the dynamics of the events depicted in the film?

Access the live/updated links at http://www.paradigmpublishers.com/resources/goldbergmedia.aspx

control its spread and help those infected. Without the use of social construction theory, understanding HIV/AIDS would be limited to examining data without a social context. Social construction theory examines our perceptions of the problems we face and how social circumstances help define them. It recognizes people as agents of, and active participants in, the development of social experiences.

The concepts and theories introduced in this chapter enable us to see a wide range of experiences through a sociological lens. As you read this book you may find a new perspective on the world around you, and a new way of interpreting those experiences.

Sociological Research: An Overview

Theories by themselves are interesting intellectual exercises, but in sociology and other social sciences they do not stand alone. Research is based on theory and in turn new theory is created from research findings that include both quantitative and qualitative data. Using properly gathered data to analyze social issues is the lifeblood of sociological research. How else can we know about social life beyond our individual experiences? Research helps us understand the experiences of groups, social trends, and attitudes, which we could not do without gathering and assessing data. Throughout this book a variety of research findings are presented as evidence for evaluating the scope and significance of the important crises we face. As we see in later chapters, some of these findings are connected to natural sciences, such as environmental science or medical research. Other findings show social patterns across cultures in response to political and economic change or technology. In all cases, we could not understand the world around us without research.

Values and Social Research

If you have studied the scientific method in your science classes, you have the general idea of how sociological research is conducted. While the methods will seem familiar, the subject matter is quite different. Early theorists like Comte and Spencer modeled sociology on the natural sciences, arguing that the study of society was as much a science as biology or physics. However, studying human beings in their social habitats—that is, in society—is a difficult task, as it is impossible to establish appropriate laboratory settings typical of the natural sciences. Social-science research must take into account the fact that social experiences cannot be studied outside of the social framework in which they exist. In addition, as scientists, it is difficult for sociologists to remove their own expectations as social beings from the research process. Both of these conditions present obstacles to objectivity. These concerns have been part of sociological research from the earliest attempts at creating the science of society.

Max Weber wrote about the desire for value-free sociology, arguing that although it was impossible to be completely value-free, much of the subjectivity could be eliminated by acknowledging the role of values in research and then removing those values in the collection and analysis of data. Sociologists acknowledge that social values are present from the early decision about what to study to the final interpretation of results.

Before we judge these limitations too harshly, though, consider how even natural scientists choose their research topics. Personal passions or experiences often guide scientific research. For instance, medical researchers often point to an early personal experience with the medical problems of a family member that gave them an interest in particular research. Further, even results from laboratory-based natural science can be interpreted differently. Thus, the interpretation of scientific data can lead to different conclusions. Climate change, which is explored in Chapter 3, is a case in point. Much data deriving from precise, objective measures indicate that the earth is warming, yet the evidence has not convinced everyone of climate change or its source. Interpreting data on climate change has important social ramifications for how energy is produced and distributed. Another example, this time taken from the chapter on health, has to do with obesity. Medical researchers have agreed upon a medical definition of obesity that is based on body measurements. They have conducted research that statistically points to the risk of certain diseases associated with obesity. The measures are objective and the correlations between body mass index and health problems are clear. Why, then, does the issue of obesity remain a debate? Differing social perceptions of obesity and the related values assigned to it are examples of the social interpretations of scientific data. Further, understanding how trends in obesity determine the cost of treating those diseases linked to obesity impacts decisions about the distribution of health care. Thus, we see that values play an important role in selecting a research topic and in interpreting results in all sciences. And as the above examples demonstrate, there are many overlaps between sociology and natural sciences. In all scientific research, therefore, it is important to eliminate as much subjectivity as possible in order to have meaningful results and to acknowledge the role that values play in choosing topics to study and in interpreting results.

Conducting Research

When sociologists conduct research, a number of decisions must be made. Of course, the first decision is what to study. A research question or thesis statement clarifies the goals of the research. Once that is accomplished, the research project is designed. Large-scale projects such as attitude surveys

Information 1.1
ABCs of Sociological Research

- Ask a research question.
- Design the research project. Will it be qualitative or quantitative?
- Decide on the best methods for gathering data.
- Gather the data.
- Analyze the data.
- Interpret and share the findings.

or the national census are typically quantitative surveys in which a great deal of data are gathered and statistically analyzed. We see examples of quantitative research every day in marketing research, political polls, and even college freshman surveys. The methods by which these data are gathered enable the researcher to look at a number of variables in the quest to better understand social behavior. Smaller-scale research is also important. In-depth interviews with a small number of respondents can give the qualitative researcher greater insight into social experiences that otherwise could not be gleaned from surveys. The decision about what kind of research to conduct is a reflection of the initial research question. In all cases, the research project must be well thought-out and designed in such a way that the data collected reflect the research question and is objective in design. It is at this stage that values cannot play a role or the research will be worthless. The design of the research and the gathering of data, whether quantitative or qualitative, require studious attention to detail and objectivity. Once the data are gathered, it is important to understand it. Analysis of the data determines the conclusions drawn from the research and ties it back to the theories from which the research is derived. As in all sciences, the next step is to share the findings with others to add to the body of knowledge in the discipline. Without the sharing of findings, science becomes stagnant.

Looking Forward

The sociological tools introduced in this chapter are basic to any discussion of social problems. The sociological imagination enables you to see yourself in the larger social world, whether it be the family, your campus, the work environment, politics, or global events. Utilizing the concepts and theories provides a sociological lens through which you can interpret and analyze social experience. Research provides important information gained through a formal process to understand social experience. The value of sociological research is particularly important as a way to better understand the volatile problems of the twenty-first century. As you explore these problems and utilize the variety of media presented in this book, it is all the more important that your understanding is grounded in respected research and that you apply appropriate research findings to the crises we will be examining.

In the next chapter, we examine social inequality, a major focus of sociology that connects to the specific crises presented in Part II. Each of these crises has important social components that can be better

Reading Room 1.2
Sociological Research

A number of websites provide more details about sociological research methods. Several of these are linked on the companion website. In exploring more about research methods, consider these ideas:

- How is sociological research similar to or different from other types of research?
- As you study the social crises in this book, think about how you might design a research project to learn more about one that is important to you.

Access the live/updated links at http://www.paradigmpublishers.com/resources/goldbergmedia.aspx

understood by applying the sociological imagination and the basic concepts, theories, and research method presented in this chapter.

Web Watch

A number of sociology websites are found online, and many relevant videos appear on youtube.com. In fact there are over 10,000 YouTube entries for sociology, ranging from class lectures to student presentations. Websites include advocacy organizations, critical articles, and sites for downloading videos, along with outlets for all major newspapers and television stations. A selection of these sites can be found on this book's companion website. Following are a few good places to start:

The American Sociological Association: http://www.asanet.org/
The Society Pages: Social Science That Matters: http://thesocietypages .org/
The Sociological Cinema: Teaching and Learning Sociology through Video: http://www.thesociologicalcinema .com/
Sociological Images: http:// thesocietypages.org/socimages/

CHAPTER 2

What Makes Us Unequal?

Pedestrians walking by homeless man on sidewalk.
Source: AlbeStock.com

In the first decade of the twenty-first century the United States endured a serious economic recession. Unemployment was up, housing sales were down. Foreclosures were up, spending was down. Homelessness was up and, curiously, profits were up. The stock market plunged, surged, and plunged again. A bailout of the auto industry and of banks "too big to fail" provided a political backdrop to a suffering economy and many confused and distressed citizens. The Great Recession was not confined to the United States. Global economies are so intertwined that almost every region of the world was impacted by economic problems. Who suffered the most? Who the least? How was the pain distributed? These are compelling questions with complex answers. When large numbers of people lose jobs or families lose their homes, these are individual problems brought on by social conditions. From individuals to small businesses to large corporations, everyone is affected. While the recession hit us all, not all people were affected the same way. Those with savings could weather the loss of income for a while, as could many families with more than one source of income.

Although the recession was a painful event for all, inequality is distributed unevenly, and is especially painful to people at the bottom. It is important to understand the interplay of class, gender, race, and ethnicity as components of economic well-being in examining inequality. It is the goal of this chapter to lay out the larger picture of the dynamics of inequality that are built into society in order to understand not just the recession but the overall picture of inequality in our time.

The study of **inequality** is one of the most important areas of sociology. While inequality may take somewhat different forms in different societies, sociologists agree that it is central to understanding modern social life. The recent recession described above is an extreme expression of the inequalities that have existed throughout modern society. Since inequality is deeply embedded in all societies it is important to tie it to the crises examined in this book. In Part II we will focus on specific crises that affect all of us, and on the inequalities, so pervasive in society, that make the experiences of these crises markedly different for people with greater or lesser access to the resources that provide cleaner air, distance from war, better health, protection from terrorism, and beneficial technology. With these crises in mind, this chapter provides an overview of inequality in the United States and globally.

Sociologists use the term **social stratification** to describe the inequalities that exist in society, and we use it interchangeably with *inequality*. An unequal or stratified society is often represented as a hierarchy portrayed as a pyramid or ladder, with people ranking from top to bottom based on the values given to specific social phenomena—primarily access to resources and the power that results from that access. Those with the most resources are found at the highest layers while those with the least are found at the bottom of the hierarchy. Depending on a variety of circumstances, the middle layers may be large or small, and they have moderate access to resources and power.

Sociologists argue that inequality derives from social structure. Although some inequality may stem from individual initiative, luck, or other non-structural factors, the foundation of inequality is social, residing especially in those economic and political institutions that contribute to the distribution of jobs, wealth, and income that are tied to differences in access to resources, consumption patterns, and lifestyle. Inequality is a social problem because the structure of a society limits the experiences of some people while enhancing those of others. Inequality reflects differential access to resources, power, and other experiences by virtue of one's social position, and it raises the potential of conflict between groups competing for those resources. Sociologists agree that the most significant inequalities in modern society reside in these basic areas: social class, gender, race, and ethnicity. Although there are debates about their relative importance and their connection to each other, there is agreement that these are the most overarching components that contribute to our understanding of the inequalities in society today. They thus are our focus in this chapter. Inequality is also tied to other factors, especially age, sexual orientation, and disability, which should be kept in mind, though these are not covered here. The remainder of this chapter provides a sociological overview of the sources of stratification emphasizing class, poverty, gender inequality, and racial and ethnic inequality. Although the focus is primarily on inequality in the United States, we also briefly explore global inequalities. In Part II of this book we apply our knowledge about inequality to twenty-first century crises in the environment, the developing world, health care, terrorism, and technology.

Web Exercise 2.1
Income Differences

Watch the video *The L Curve* (www.youtube.com/watch?v=woIkIph5xcU) showing a graphic representation of income distribution in the United States. Also see "The L Curve" website (http://www.lcurve.org/). Based on their incomes, compare the life chances people at the midpoint to those at the top.

- Where does your family fit on the graph?
- How might income inequality set the stage for other types of inequality?
- Can you think of other ways to represent income inequality graphically?

Access the live/updated links at http://www.paradigmpublishers.com/resources/goldbergmedia.aspx

Information 2.1
What Are Your Life Chances?

What is the chance in your lifetime that you will ...

- Finish college?
- Have access to good health care?
- Have a job that provides financial security?
- Buy a home?
- Go to a gallery, the theater, or Europe?

OR

- Drop out of school?
- Be poor?
- Be unemployed?
- Be homeless?

Life Chances

Max Weber, a classical theorist introduced in Chapter 1, described inequality through the concept of **life chances.** He argued that a person's resources and access to experiences will vary according to factors built into the social structure and thus are predictable.

Sociologists examine the factors that determine life chances. There are important social components that can predict the relative life chances of different groups of people, thus we look beyond individuals to how a society's structure contributes to access to the resources and the experiences described in the box "What Are Your Life Chances?" Social scientists compile vast quantities of data that measure the degree of access people have to resources that impact their life chances. This research demonstrates the importance of social forces in predicting life chances: the categories of social class, gender, race, and ethnicity are especially significant in determining the likelihood of having opportunities for education, health, good jobs, decent housing, and a secure life, among other things. We examine each of these in the rest of the chapter.

Social Class Inequality

Social class is considered the most fundamental component of stratification in modern society. If you read enough sociology textbooks you will come across several different ways of categorizing social classes. The simplest—a three-class grouping consisting of upper, middle, and lower classes—represents the most basic understanding of social class. Sociological discussions of class typically present a more nuanced, detailed categorization, breaking each of the three major classes into smaller and more complex units. In his book, *The American Class Structure in an Age of Growing Inequality*, Dennis Gilbert (2011) suggests a useful diagram to help us see the various components of social class as shown in Figure 2.1.

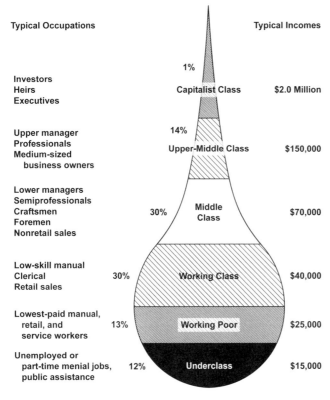

Figure 2.1 Gilbert-Kahl model of class structure.
Source: Dennis Gilbert/SAGE Publications

In this diagram Gilbert uses the categories of occupation and income to place Americans in six classes. The source of income in each category is important. At the highest level, much income derives from investments and other assets. In the middle, the major source of income comes from the work one does, and income varies according to the type of job held. People at the bottom of the class structure derive income from low-level jobs, sporadic employment, and public assistance. The diagram's shape shows the relative size of each class.

Subjective factors, referred to as prestige or social status, are also important in shaping social inequality. They include how people see themselves and their neighbors, as well as lifestyle factors. We look at such subjective factors more closely later in the chapter. The combination of objective and subjective factors demonstrates the complexity of social

stratification. The film *People Like Us* (see Movie Picks 2.1) shows how that complexity is borne out in the everyday lives of people.

Sociologists agree that in modern capitalist societies one's social class position is determined by several interconnected factors. Income, wealth, and occupation are the most directly measurable elements that help us understand social classes. Education is tied closely to these factors, especially income. We will examine each of these briefly and then explore the most significant problem of social class—poverty—which according to Gilbert's model characterizes 25 percent of the population. Status factors including inequalities of gender, race, and ethnicity are very much intertwined with social class and are discussed as well.

Income is compensation mostly earned through a job. Other sources of income include interest, dividends, and government sources such as Social Security and public assistance. We focus here on the two major occupational sources of income: wages, which are based on hourly work, and salaries, which are based on yearly income. These different sources reflect the main types and levels of occupations available in the job market, with salaried positions typically receiving higher pay and better working conditions and benefits, while wage work is found in lower-paying and less-secure jobs. These reflect important differences in the occupational structure discussed later in this chapter.

According to the US Census Bureau (2012b), the median household income in the United States in 2011 was $50,054. Statistics on median income do not tell us the full story about the *distribution* of income, especially the gap between those earning

Movie Picks 2.1
People Like Us

People Like Us: Social Class in America documents Americans' experiences of social class. From old-money social scions to poverty-burdened families, the film explores many facets of social class. A long movie (two hours), it can be watched in segments that are clearly defined for ease of selection.

Mixed-Media Extra

Visit the PBS film's companion website (www.pbs.org/peoplelikeus/), which provides information on the segments as well as additional stories, games, and sample stories from the film.

Thinking Sociologically

- Compare the life chances of the people interviewed in the film.
- Why do so many people define themselves as middle class when their circumstances are so different?
- In addition to money and jobs, what symbols of class are presented in the film?
- How is social class seen in both objective and subjective terms?
- Why do you think Americans are reluctant to talk about social class?
- Does the movie help you figure out your social class position?

Access the live/updated links at http://www.paradigmpublishers.com/resources/goldbergmedia.aspx

top salaries and the rest of the workforce. The disparity in income between those earning the highest incomes and the lowest is enormous. "Income at the top 5 percent of households—those making $180,000 or more—was 3.58 times the median income, the highest since 2006" (AP 2009). The gap has grown over time and it even appears to have grown with the economic recession that started in 2007–2008.

As we can see in the box "Fast Facts: The Widening US Income Gap," the income gap is significant. The data show that the gap grew dramatically in the latter half of the twentieth century and sustained a large gap into the twenty-first century, even with the Great Recession. This income gap shows greater income increases at the top levels of the class structure compared to those at lower levels.

Education is an important component of stratification. Income is impacted by the level of education a person achieves and in turn contributes to educational success. According to the Bureau of Labor Statistics, in 2012 the full-time median weekly earnings for a person with a bachelor's degree were $1,066, compared to $652 for someone with only a high-school education. The comparative unemployment rates for the same two groups were 4.5 percent and 8.3 percent, respectively. Even more extreme, employees with a doctoral degree or professional degree earned more than three times that of someone who did not graduate high school (US Department of Labor 2013a). Those with the highest incomes have the resources to provide better educational opportunities for their children through strong public schools, private schools, tutoring, and selective colleges, thus perpetuating income security for the next generation. Figure 2.2 shows that, despite increases in income for all education groups in the twenty-first century, the gap

Fast Facts 2.1
The Widening US Income Gap

- Gap between corporate CEO's and average worker's pay (Domhoff 2013, 16):
    - 1960: 42 times higher
    - 2005: 411 times higher
    - 2007: 344 times higher
- Recession gap between richest 10 percent ($138,000+) and poorest ($12,000) (AP 2009):
    - 2007: 11.2 times higher
    - 2008: 11.4 times higher

between educational levels has remained consistent over time and the greatest income increase is among those with a college education.

The increasing costs for attending college, especially the rising tuition rates, will likely have serious consequences for new generations of students who may not be able to afford college. Although tuition rates have soared, income has not, so many potential students are squeezed out of the possibility of a college education at the same time the value of that education has increased. According to *Measuring Up*, a report by the National Center for Public Policy and Higher Education, college tuition and fees increased 439 percent between 1982 and 2006 while median family income rose only 147 percent. For the lowest-income families the cost of a four-year college education was 55 percent of median income in 2008, whereas for upper-middle-class families it was 16 percent of median income (Callan 2008, 8).

Wealth is another important indicator of inequality. It can be measured in a number of ways, but for our purposes personal wealth includes assets, such as bank accounts and stock and real-estate investments, minus debt. Wealth can be acquired through inheritance, investments, and savings. The disparities of wealth are even greater than the disparities of income, with those in the top 1 percent owning 35.4 percent of privately held wealth in the United States in 2010. The bottom 80 percent held only 11.1 percent of the

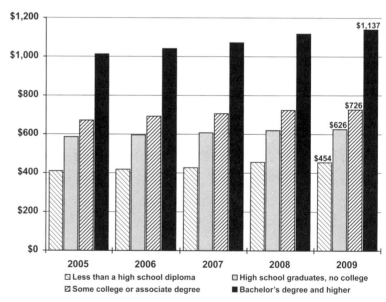

Figure 2.2 Median usual weekly earnings of full-time wage and salary workers 25 years and older by educational attainment, 2005–2009 annual averages.
Source: US Department of Labor 2010

nation's wealth (Domhoff 2013, 3). Personal wealth is linked to corporate wealth. The vast wealth earned by corporations translates to personal wealth for those most benefiting from those corporations: CEOs, investors, and owners. The poor, on the other hand, have no significant wealth; when they are unable to work, they have no nest egg on which to rely.

Wealth is also reflected in **political power**. People with the most wealth have the greatest influence and power. From supporting political campaigns to lobbying for projects they support, wealthy individuals and corporations have much greater political influence than average citizens, and the poor have the least power. Political decisions regarding the crises discussed later in this book such as climate change, health care, and responses to terrorism are impacted by well-financed lobbies and interest groups with the financial means to dominate political discourse. In Chapter 1, we discussed that a small number of wealthy, powerful media corporations can largely determine the information to which we are exposed. They not only define to a great extent what we understand to be news and entertainment, but there are few alternative news sources with the power to challenge those media representations. With the "message" controlled by major corporations, it is difficult for average citizens to be well-informed and to influence the political process.

Social-class differences reflect trends in **occupations**, the jobs people hold. The most significant occupational trend in the United States since the mid-twentieth century is away from industrial production to a post-industrial society. Today's growing occupations include a variety of jobs that provide information, systems of communication, and services. Although some of these occupations are well-paid professional positions (teachers, nurses, and computer programmers to name a few), many of them are low-level, low-paid positions held by people at the bottom of the class structure. Jobs held by restaurant workers, home-health aides, data-entry clerks, and domestic workers are examples of the types of jobs at the low end of the service sector. Workers most at risk for poverty fill many of these jobs. Because higher-level jobs require educational preparation that is often not available to the poor, there is little chance that those with limited resources will be able to move into a job enabling them to rise above poverty.

Different kinds of jobs not only provide a range of incomes but also different levels of job security, opportunities for advancement, and benefits such as health insurance, sick leave, and vacation time. A good way to understand the differences between types of

---

 Reading Room 2.1
Statistics on Inequality

To find more information about American inequality read the following:

- William Domhoff's article, "Wealth, Income, and Power" (2013), at WhoRulesAmerica .net, which provides detailed statistics on and analyses of the distribution of wealth and income in the United States, with comparisons to other countries.
- "Inequality Data and Statistics" at Inequality.org (n.d.) for additional information on economic inequality in income, wealth, race, and health.

Access the live/updated links at http://www.paradigmpublishers.com/resources/goldbergmedia.aspx

Web Exercise 2.2
What Do I Want to Be When I Grow Up?

Visit the website for the US Bureau of Labor Statistics "Occupational Outlook Handbook 2012–13" (www.bls.gov/ooh). You will find employment projections up to 2020 by occupation, education, and industry. After exploring the site, find an occupation of personal interest to you.

- What are the projections for that occupation?
- Given your education and other social factors, what are your chances of getting a job in that area?
- Use your sociological imagination to explore the connection between your personal work goals and the structural factors that may enhance or impede your ability to work in that field.
- Consider the jobs you have held as a student. What are the projections for that occupation? How do those projections differ from your career goals?

Access the live/updated links at http://www.paradigmpublishers.com/resources/goldbergmedia.aspx

jobs, income, and opportunity is to see the job market as two distinct sectors referred to as the **dual labor market.** Generally, the **primary sector** provides the highest pay, most security and autonomy, and best benefits. It also requires the most formal education. The **secondary sector** is the reverse: lower pay, less security and autonomy, and lower benefits. Less education is required, though employees may get specialized training for certain jobs. In general there is more expansion of jobs in the secondary sector than the primary sector, making it harder to break into primary sector occupations. (See Table 2.1.)

The economic recession in the first decade of the twenty-first century impacted jobs in both sectors of the job market, yet those working in the secondary sector suffered more severe consequences because of the large-scale trends in job loss, the workers' smaller nest eggs, and their lower educational levels, which limited their access to new careers. Further, in the post-recession economy, secure, well-paying jobs will require workers to learn advanced skills through post-secondary education.

Income, wealth, and occupation are the most identifiable factors in determining inequality. Those with the least resources are considered poor, and we now turn to gaining a better understanding of poverty as a social problem.

Table 2.1
Occupational Sectors

Primary Sector Jobs	Secondary Sector Jobs
Higher pay: salaried	Lower pay: hourly wage
Higher job security	Lower job security
Clear career ladder	Little opportunity for advancement
College education or more	High-school education, training
More benefits	Fewer benefits
Less job growth	More job growth
Professional, managerial, administrative	Clerical, service, industrial

Watch Online 2.1
"A Town in Crisis"

Watch the *60 Minutes* segment, "A Town in Crisis" (`http://www.cbsnews.com/video/watch/?id=4752321n&tag=related;photovideo`). This story depicts the impact of the economic recession on the lives of working people in Wilmington, Ohio, as a local employer lays them off.

Thinking Sociologically

- Which social classes are represented in the story?
- Which occupational sector suffered the greatest loss of jobs?
- How have the job losses affected other areas of the lives of those unemployed?
- What are the structural factors that changed the life chances of the people in the story?

Access the live/updated links at `http://www.paradigmpublishers.com/resources/goldbergmedia.aspx`

Poverty

Measuring Poverty

How do we know when someone is poor? **Poverty** may be defined generally as the lack of resources necessary to meet basic needs; however, as we will see, it's definition depends on many factors. Poverty as it is understood by social scientists and policy makers can be measured in any of several ways, and there is a great deal of debate about these methods and their implications. The US government has defined poverty in a very specific way since guidelines were first developed in the 1960s. Each year the **poverty threshold** is determined by calculations by the US Census Bureau, based on a formula originally developed by the Social Security Administration and tied to the cost of food. This threshold determines the guidelines used by the government to draw a **poverty line** below which people are determined to be eligible for public

Some of the poor might call a cold hard bench home.
Source: Department of Housing and Urban Development

assistance, though assistance varies by state. According to the US Census Bureau (2013), the poverty threshold for a one-person household in 2012 was $11,945; for a family of four it was $23,681. The official poverty rate in the United States was 15 percent, representing 46.2 million people (US Census Bureau 2012c).

Many social scientists argue that the government's current definition of poverty is not an accurate representation of the reality of poverty, and they suggest other methods of determining thresholds. In early 2010, the Commerce Department began the process of reconfiguring the definition of poverty by including expenses not formerly included. It is expected that the new calculations will show a higher poverty rate than is indicated by the current measures. This new calculation will no doubt be controversial as it works its way through political discourse (Goldstein 2010, A02). Any new definition of poverty and the criteria for measuring it requires recognition of lifestyle variables that are difficult to determine and about which there is likely to be disagreement.

A close examination of poverty data shows that poverty rates vary by race, ethnicity, age, and family status. Based on percentages, whites are least likely to be poor, whereas blacks and Hispanics are about twice as likely as whites to be poor. However, in absolute numbers, whites make up the largest number of poor because they make up most of the population. Children under eighteen are more likely to be poor than any other age group. As for family status, dual-headed families are much less likely to be poor than single-headed families, and those families headed by black and Hispanic women are the most likely to be poor (Gilbert 2011, 224). Another way of stating who is likely to be poor is to look at which groups have a greater or lesser risk of being poor, as Table 2.2 shows. Later in this chapter we explore aspects of the social structure that contribute to this uneven distribution of poverty by sex, race, and ethnicity.

 Web Exercise 2.3
Calculating Poverty

Visit the website for the government agency Health and Human Services (HHS) for information on the poverty guidelines (aspe.hhs.gov/poverty/13poverty.cfm). Read the guidelines and the rates for the current year.

For a visual representation of poverty, watch the US Conference of Catholic Bishops "Take a Tour of This Forgotten State" video (http://old.usccb.org/cchd/povertyusa/tour.htm). Next explore the Economic Policy Institute's Basic Family Budget Calculator (www.epi.org /resources/budget). Compare (1) the poverty line for a family of four on the HHS website to (2) the budget for a family of four in your state or region.

- What is the difference between the two numbers (the poverty line and the basic family budget)?
- Does the family budget for your region seem realistic?
- How would you describe the people who are above the poverty threshold but below the basic budget? Where do they fit in Figure 2.1 shown earlier in this chapter?
- What can explain the gap between the poverty threshold and a basic family budget?
- Which figure—the poverty line or the basic family budget—is the more accurate representation of poverty?

Access the live/updated links at http://www.paradigmpublishers.com/resources/goldbergmedia.aspx

Table 2.2
Poverty Risk

Higher Chance of Poverty	Lower Chance of Poverty
Blacks and Hispanics	Whites
Children under 18	Adults
Single-headed families	Dual-headed families
(mostly headed by women)	

How poverty is determined has important implications for the provision of government assistance such as TANF (Temporary Assistance for Needy Families, or welfare), food stamps, Medicaid, education benefits, child-care subsidies, and other forms of government support. Since welfare reform in the 1990s, important changes have taken place in determining how and to whom welfare is distributed. Among the most significant changes were work requirements and limits to funding for multiple children in a family. A report by the Urban Institute (2006) describes some of the most important changes brought about in the decade after welfare reform. Caseloads significantly declined, welfare recipients went to work in larger numbers, and incomes increased in this time period, when the economy happened to be strong. At the same time, most of the jobs acquired by those who left welfare were low paying, and many did not provide health insurance. In addition, there was a population of "hard-to-serve" welfare recipients who had major barriers to being able to work and thus were unable to successfully reduce their need for assistance. Poor health, being out of the workforce for many years, and caring for a disabled child were among the characteristics of this group. The study found that child poverty was reduced in the 1990s only to rise again by 2004. Much of this change reflected changes in the economy that hurt the poor.

Poverty and the Great Recession

The recent economic recession has had a significant impact on the experience of poverty.

 Movie Picks 2.2
Ending Welfare as We Know It

The film *Ending Welfare as We Know It* documents the effects of changes in welfare policies in the late 1990s. Following six women whose welfare status changed under the new law, it becomes apparent that the new policy had the effect of removing the safety nets that these women and their families relied upon.

Thinking Sociologically

- What will be the effect of welfare reform over time on women such as those in the film?
- Will they ever be in a position to support themselves and their families?
- Does society have any responsibility for people who cannot support themselves?

Access the live/updated links at http://www.paradigmpublishers.com/resources/goldbergmedia.aspx

Following are some important observations from the first decade of the twenty-first century:

- A Brookings Institute study reports, "Nearly one in five children under age 18 lived in poor families in 2008" (Isaacs 2010, 1).
- The recession had the effect of increasing the welfare rolls in recent years in some states. The impact of the recession on the poor is complex, as various factors impact the qualifications for eligibility. In some states with high unemployment, welfare rolls may have stayed the same or decreased due to changes in qualifying income thresholds or in the availability of unemployment compensation. Nonetheless, Florida, Maryland, Ohio, and California are among the states in which the number of welfare recipients increased between 10 and 30 percent between 2008 and 2009 (Murray 2009).
- The food stamp program, easier to qualify for than TANF, has seen the greatest increase. Those receiving food stamps increased 24 percent (Isaacs 2010).

The effects of poverty are multiple. With few resources and limited job opportunities, the poor often face much more dire outcomes when dealing with some of the same problems that others with more resources also encounter. In Part II of this book we examine a number of areas in which the poor suffer terrible consequences for their inadequate access to resources. For example, health care and insurance are important to all classes, but, health-care reform notwithstanding, the present crisis of access to these resources has its most dramatic effect on the poor. The poor also are more likely to suffer effects of environmental damage, especially from storms and flooding, and they have less access to the technology so vital to modern life.

Social Status

Our discussion of social class so far has emphasized the position people hold by objective measures such as income and wealth. These are not the only factors that contribute to inequality, however. Along with objective measures, we also have subjective factors that contribute to stratification. In sociology these are referred to as **social status**, a person's social rank or **prestige**. Status is associated with social class, but is not the same thing. The two main types of status are **ascribed status** and **achieved status**. Ascribed status refers to the status a person is born with or that is not altered by social circumstances: sex, age, race, and ethnicity are important ascribed statuses. Achieved status is acquired by people due to some actions on their part. Some major achieved statuses include occupation, education, marriage, parenthood, and home ownership. As we will see later, the relationship between ascribed and achieved status has important implications for inequality.

Status and the Great Recession

The recession described in the beginning of this chapter has impacted the achieved statuses of many Americans. For instance, according to a survey conducted by the Pew Research Center (2010), 32 percent of respondents were unemployed at the time of the survey or were unemployed in the thirty months since the recession began. Around one-fourth of respondents either had pay cuts or a reduction in working hours. Such large-scale changes in social position have an important impact on individuals and society and of course are reflected in the objective measures of income and wealth.

Reading Room 2.2
"How the Great Recession Has Changed Life in America"

This detailed report by the Pew Research Center (2010) looks at the effects of the recession on Americans (http://www.pewsocialtrends.org/2010/06/30/how-the-great-recession -has-changed-life-in-america). On the right side of the page, "Report Materials" provides "interactive" graphics also titled "How the Great Recession Has Changed Life in America." It examines the effects of the recession on work, housing, spending, retirement, and other aspects of stratification. It compares findings across the categories of age, education, race, and political affiliation.

- What relationships do you find between ascribed and achieved status in the findings?
- What aspects of life chances are determined by factors such as personal action, economic trends, age, and race?
- What do the findings regarding political affiliation tell us about people's experiences in the recession?

Access the live/updated links at http://www.paradigmpublishers.com/resources/goldbergmedia.aspx

Interestingly, ascribed status plays a role in what respondents believed was in store for them in the future. The survey found that 57 percent of whites were optimistic about improvement in their "financial situation" while 74 percent of Hispanics and 81 percent of blacks were optimistic.

In the next section we turn to examining the importance of ascribed status as an influence on stratification, specifically gender, race, and ethnicity—those statuses we are born with and with which we live out our lives. They have profound effects on our position in society and are directly related to inequality.

Gender Inequality

Biological differences between men and women are important, and no one disputes their respective contributions to reproduction. The roles of women and men in conception and birth along with the distribution of hormones that contribute to differences in size and strength are the starting point for understanding gender differences, but they do not automatically imply inequality. Sociologists make an important distinction between sex and gender to distinguish between biological parameters and social experiences. **Sex** is defined as the biological attributes that determine whether someone is male or female and the related reproductive roles of each sex. **Gender** defines the social roles that result from the social interpretation of those biological attributes. Thus, while sex is understood as a biological identifier, gender is much more fluid and is subject to cultural interpretation.

The Social Construction of Gender

Gender roles vary throughout history and across cultures. As a social construct, gender can be best understood as a social interpretation of biological roles that fits the needs of social institutions and serves to maintain social order. For example, gender is reflected in the ways in which societies prepare children to socially affirm their biological

Figure 2.3 Male/Female symbols.
Source: Raymond Lee

identity. **Gender socialization** takes place in families, schools, religious institutions, and the broader culture, teaching girls and boys to take on their culturally assigned roles, thus ensuring stability in carrying out reproductive and social roles that follow from conception to birth to parenting and the wider social expectations of each sex. Once a child's sex is identified, gender roles are reinforced with dress, color, personal interaction, toys, and other such attributes that are culturally identified with each sex. Beyond the family, the social construction of gender defines the parameters for men and women in other important spheres of society: politics, the economy, religion, and education. Thus, gender is tied to the structural elements of society that reinforce gender roles throughout social institutions as well as the symbolic representations and interactions expected of each sex.

Though there is no apparent inequality inherent in the biological attributes of either sex, gender assignment leads to vastly different consequences for women and men and results in unequal access to resources and important differences in the value society places on each sex. In other words, there is nothing in our respective reproductive roles that implies greater or lesser power or value. Rather, social expectations are imposed on those roles that give men greater power over resources, devalue women, and contribute to the dependency of women on men. These

differences can be seen in most areas of social life from the broadest occupational patterns and income distribution, to the most personal and intimate patterns of domestic abuse and sexual exploitation. On both the macro and micro levels these patterns point to women as holding less value in society than men, and they persist over time and through virtually all societies. It could be argued that the source of **patriarchy**, the dominance of men over women, may have originated with the earliest reproductive roles played by men and women—that is, with the biological factors of pregnancy, childbirth, and infant dependency on mothers combining to restrict the participation of women in wider society. However, the persistence of male dominance has less to do with biological roles and more to do with maintaining male social control (despite social change), the rigidity of gender roles, and the social expediency of curtailing women's power. Thus the social construction of gender creates structural barriers to gender equality, which then reinforce traditional gender constructs despite the many gains women have made today in improving their social position. Mass media contributes to these cultural assumptions about gender by perpetuating stereotypes that devalue women through programming and advertising.

Gender and the Workplace

One of the most important areas of gender inequality is in work and income. In examining the different experiences of women and men in this arena, we can better understand the structural limitations placed on women by virtue of their limited access to economic resources. Significantly, gender inequality is found in job segregation and a narrowing but persistent income gap. Although nearly half of the workforce is women, they tend to hold jobs that have less prestige, fewer career ladders, and lower incomes. Women are thus more heavily represented in the secondary sector of the labor market than the primary sector. The US Census Bureau (2012b) reports that in 2011 women in the United States earned 77 percent of what men earned overall.

Regardless of the patterns of job segregation, in full-time, year-round work, women lag behind men in pay. At every educational level women earn less than men, and the higher the level of education, the less equal the pay between men and women. For example, in 2011 women with a high-school diploma earned 76.9 percent of men's earnings, while those with at least a bachelor's degree earned 74.9 percent of men's earnings (US Department of Labor 2012, 9). According to Fairfield (2009), women typically are paid less than men even in the same occupations, as demonstrated in Web Exercise 2.4.

As we can see by the discussion in this section, gender factors into inequality in several important ways. Reproductive expectations, patriarchy, socialization, media representation, and limits on economic well-being all contribute to assumptions about gender differences that point to different life chances for men and women. As an ascribed status, gender is universally one of the most important indicators of inequality. Along with inequalities associated with class, race, and ethnicity we begin to understand the complex relationships between objective and subjective measures of inequality.

Inequalities of Race and Ethnicity

The Social Construction of Race and Ethnicity

Defining race and ethnicity sociologically is more complicated than it may seem. These

---

 Movie Picks 2.3
Killing Us Softly IV

Mass-media representations of women often reflect traditional gender constructs, even today. Watch *Killing Us Softly IV*, the most recent of four critical explorations of how women are portrayed in advertising. Earlier versions of the film (I–III) can be found online.

Mixed-Media Extra

A companion study guide by the Media Education Foundation explores gender in media extensively along with relevant exercises (http://www.mediaed.org/assets/products/241/studyguide_241.pdf).

Thinking Sociologically

- What are the major themes and symbols used by advertisers to portray women?
- Are these representations realistic?
- To whom do the advertisements appeal?
- How are men portrayed in advertising?
- How have these representations reinforced or challenged traditional gender constructs?
- What are the implications for gender inequality in the way women are portrayed in the media?
- In what ways can students address gender inequality in media?

Access the live/updated links at http://www.paradigmpublishers.com/resources/goldbergmedia.aspx

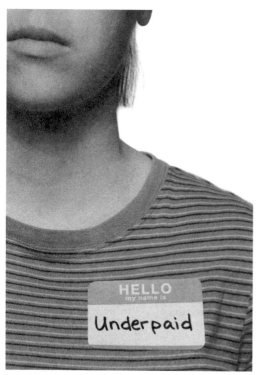

Women are paid less than men across most
occupational categories.
Source: ThinkStockPhoto.com

example of how these concepts are defined
than to look at the categories created by the
US Census Bureau over time. The Census
began in 1790 and almost every ten years
thereafter race and ethnic categories have
been redefined to reflect structural and cultural dynamics, especially regarding slavery
and its aftermath, industrialization, immigration, and the status of Native Americans.
Historically there was a great deal of cross-
over between what was understood as race
and what was understood as ethnicity in any
given census year. Once the categories were
created for census-taking, the identification
of a person's race or ethnicity was left up to
the census taker or the person being counted,
but there was no attempt to apply an objective biological measure.

Defining Race

The history of the Census demonstrates that
there is no useful scientific measure of our
genetic heritage that can categorize humans
into specific biological races. In fact, scientists point out that as much genetic difference is found *within* racially defined groups
as *between* them, especially because once-
geographically isolated communities have
diversified over time with contact outside

are related but different concepts. Like
gender, much of what we understand about
race and ethnicity derives from experiences
associated with culture and history and thus
is socially constructed. There is no better

Web Exercise 2.4
Income and Gender

To examine gender differences in pay, explore the *New York Times* interactive graph "Why Is
Her Paycheck Smaller?" (http://www.nytimes.com/interactive/2009/03/01
/business/20090301_WageGap.html?_r=0; Fairfield 2009).

- In which kinds of jobs is the wage gap smallest? greatest?
- Given what you know about gender inequality, what are the structural barriers that
  contribute to unequal wages between women and men in the same occupations?
- To what extent does the social construction of gender contribute to income inequality?

Access the live/updated links at http://www.paradigmpublishers.com/resources/goldbergmedia.aspx

Reading Room 2.3
"Race and the Census"

Read "Race and the Census: The 'Negro' Controversy" by D'Vera Cohn (http://www.pewsocialtrends.org/2010/01/21/race-and-the-census-the-%E2%80%9Cnegro%E2%80%9D-controversy/). This article provides an excellent overview of how the Census Bureau historically defined race and ethnicity.

- From your point of view does the Census help or hurt our understanding of race and ethnicity?
- Have your views on race have changed over time? What influenced you in making those changes?
- Should the Census collect data on race? Should sociologists?

Access the live/updated links at http://www.paradigmpublishers.com/resources/goldbergmedia.aspx

their communities. This means that race can best be understood as a social construction. Yet, the average American will argue that observable biological characteristics such as skin color, hair texture, or facial characteristics define race. Sociologists point out that these physical variations are used to solidify socially important racial categories. Without the historical and cultural significance of race, though, these biological variations would be socially meaningless. Despite the absence of significant genetic differences, race remains one of the most important social phenomena in America, and is an essential source of social inequality.

The absence of a biological measure of race leaves us to wonder if races even exist. Sociology is especially helpful in understanding this seeming contradiction between scientific and social understanding. The concept of race is important because of the long association of race with slavery, one of the most defining experiences in American history, and the subsequent experiences of discrimination both in law and in practice. For over three hundred years the institution of slavery involved the buying and selling of Africans and their descendants and the exploitation of their labor for the economic

benefit of slaveholders and the country's agricultural economy. This system was broken by the Civil War, but the association of people of African heritage with the institution of slavery and the acceptance of their domination by the majority population persists to this day. People of African heritage have been identified by the general physical characteristics of people from that continent, but also by a variety of assumptions about them that helped make slavery more palatable to the population at large. The social construction of race as Americans understand it today is linked to the history of slavery and to the prejudice and discrimination that followed in the century and a half since its demise.

Today, even though scholars agree there is no significant genetic difference between racial groups, socially recognized biological "markers" of race such as skin tone continue to convey its importance to society. Because of the social consequences of slavery and the resulting history of discrimination, race remains an important category that is reflected in inequalities today despite the lack of real biological parameters. Given these qualifications we can sociologically define race as follows: a **race** is a group of people whose geographic origins may

Watch Online 2.2
Faces of America with Henry Louis Gates, Jr.

Watch *Faces of America with Henry Louis Gates, Jr.*, a four-part series on genes and identity at PBS (http://video.pbs.org/program/faces-of-america/). Using "genealogy and genetics to explore the family histories of 12 renowned Americans," this series raises interesting questions about how we understand who we are and it challenges biological definitions of race. Also see the interactive companion website (http://www.pbs.org/wnet/facesofamerica/).

Thinking Sociologically

- Is it important to know your genetic origins? Why or why not?
- How would knowing them change your understanding of yourself?
- How would knowing your genetic origins impact your relationships with other people?
- Why do you think Americans are interested in family history and genetic connections?
- Does the science of genetics inform us about race?

Access the live/updated links at http://www.paradigmpublishers.com/resources/goldbergmedia.aspx

indicate certain physical characteristics and whose unique historical experiences tie them to specific identities of importance to the society in which they live. Race, then, is a social construction that varies from society to society and changes over time. Based on this definition the experience of race in the United States is one of inequality. For Americans, race has become one of the defining characteristics of one's place in society, and the racial distinctions of "black" and "white" are the most often cited in discussions of race, and the most conflict laden. By looking at only these two races—understandable given our history—we often neglect the complexity of the racial and ethnic tapestry and thus limit our understanding of race as a social phenomenon. The experiences of Asians and Native Americans are also important to our understanding of race in our history and culture but are often left out of serious discussions of race. Race alone does not address the inequalities experienced by groups of people according to their heritage. We now turn to a discussion of ethnicity.

Defining Ethnicity

Ethnicity is a category that represents a group of people who share a cultural heritage, including a place of geographic origin and language. It may also include other cultural attributes associated with social institutions such as family lifestyle and shared religious practices. Ethnic groups are often considered **subcultures**, groups within the larger culture that share special attributes, in this case their ethnic identity. How ethnicity is defined changes under various circumstances, and it is important to recognize that each society has its own understanding of ethnicity based on its particular history and culture. We will see in Chapter 4 some examples of the importance of ethnicity to conflicts in the developing world.

As descendants of immigrants, many Americans have at least one ethnic heritage that they claim based on their ancestry outside of the United States. The acknowledgment of one's ethnicity may be represented in descriptions such as "Italian–American" or "Mexican-American," demonstrating a connection to an ethnic identity along with nationhood. These identities can also be complicated by various racial identities within ethnic groups. Historically, patterns of ethnic inequality in the United States can be traced to the timing of immigration, the reasons for immigration, and the economic and political conditions here that create opportunity, animosity, or fear. At different points in American history, patterns of immigration have ignited reactions that attempt to exclude particular groups from immigrating or achieving citizenship. Today there is no better example in the United States than the conflicts that arise over immigration across the border from Mexico. Immigration from a variety of Latin American countries has changed the ethnic landscape of the United States, and Hispanics are now the fastest-growing ethnic group in the country. Among the recent controversies are a recent law in Arizona aimed at curtailing immigration, and challenges to the Fourteenth Amendment to the US Constitution, which grants US citizenship to all people born within the United States. Alternatively, the DREAM Act proposes to grant permanent residency status to young immigrants who came to the United States illegally but who have lived most of their lives and attended school in the United States. These controversies go to the heart of what it means to be American and the right to claim one's ethnicity as acceptably American. Ethnic status has important implications for access to resources and opportunities for jobs, housing, and education, as is discussed later in this chapter.

Experiencing Racism

Racism refers to beliefs or actions that reinforce inequality by being directed at a group or individuals based on their race alone. **Ethnocentricity** refers to a sense of superiority of one racial or ethnic group over another group. For the purposes of discussion, both concepts are referred to here as *racism*. Two important dimensions of racism are prejudice and discrimination. **Prejudice** is a belief or set of beliefs directed toward a group. For the purposes of this chapter, it refers to beliefs about racial and ethnic groups, though more broadly it may include groups based on age, sexual orientation, or obesity, for example. Prejudicial beliefs are usually negative, though not always, and are unrelated to any real or individual traits. These beliefs usually take the form of **stereotypes**, which associate whole groups or members of the group with such beliefs. **Discrimination** is an act that singles out a group or an individual member of a group for unequal treatment. Prejudice and discrimination may go hand in hand, with people who are prejudiced acting in a discriminatory manner toward a group, but they need not go together. One might harbor a prejudicial attitude toward members of a certain group, for example, but not take any discriminatory action based on that feeling.

One of the most important social structural aspects of racism is **institutional discrimination**, also known as **institutional racism**. In this case, it is not necessarily prejudice that leads to unequal treatment, but rather practices that have been established over time that discriminate even in the absence of overt racism. In other words, institutional discrimination is built into the fabric of society by a combination of historical experience, cultural practices, and long-term overt prejudice and discrimination—so much so that even as overt racism diminishes, discrimination may continue. We can see institutional racism in the patterns of many social institutions. In education, for example, the persistent gap in achievement, whether measured by test scores or graduation rates, demonstrates important differences that hurt opportunities for students on the basis of their race or ethnic group. Patterns of disease and treatment are also impacted by institutional discrimination, as is environmental degradation. In the case of health, there are important racial differences in the rates of obesity, AIDS, and cancer, for example, not necessarily because of conscious discrimination, but because of a variety of cultural patterns and social practices such as access to nutritious affordable food, attitudes about AIDS, and access to health care, which is especially difficult for the poor and immigrants. Employment patterns and pay differences are another example of institutional discrimination. In these examples, individual prejudice may play a role, but it is important to recognize that racial patterns in many social institutions are embedded in practice and difficult to change.

The Intersections of Class, Race, Ethnicity, and Gender

The examples above of institutional discrimination point to one of the most significant complexities of inequality. Racial inequality is intricately tied to class inequality, particularly the effects of poverty. Furthermore, gender plays an important role in the dynamics of inequality as well. In order to fully understand unequal life chances, we need to study the connection between class, gender, race, and ethnicity. Let's first look at some basic differences between racial and ethnic groups in the areas of income and wealth.

Race, Ethnicity, and Social Class

According to the Bureau of Labor Statistics, weekly median income for specific racial and ethnic groups in 2011–2012 was as follows: Asians, $920; whites, $792; blacks, $621; and Hispanics, $568 (US Department of Labor, 2013c). There are also significant disparities

in wealth and poverty among racial groups. The most recent data from the Census Bureau (n.d.) show that in 2007 the median family net worth for white families was $170,400, whereas for non-white families (including Hispanics) it was $27,800. Not surprisingly, given the above statistics, the poverty rate among non-whites is higher than for whites, as seen in Table 2.3.

Table 2.3
Poverty Rates by Race and Ethnicity

Non-Hispanic Whites	9.8%
Asians	12.3%
Hispanics	25.3%
Blacks	27.5%
All Races	15.0%

Source: US Census Bureau (2012a)

The data demonstrate that racial and ethnic disparities in income and wealth contribute to an overrepresentation of blacks and Hispanics among the poor, thus limiting their life chances to a greater degree than for whites and Asians. The connection between class, race, and ethnicity has mostly to do with the availability and distribution of jobs and income, and the different patterns of employment, geography, and history experienced by people in different racial and ethnic groups. Overt discrimination on the basis of race or ethnicity is still an important factor as well. Untangling these complex interrelationships is complicated by political and economic trends.

Of course we know that poor people are found in every race and ethnic group, just as each group is represented in the middle and upper classes. How then can we develop a clearer understanding of the relationship of class to race and ethnicity? For instance, how does class position impact racial or ethnic identity? Do wealthy and middle-class people of specific racial or ethnic backgrounds have more in common with other members of their group, or with the upper and middle

Reading Room 2.4
Race and Class

Sociologist William Julius Wilson has dedicated much of his scholarship to understanding the linkages between race and class. Read the transcript of an interview with him on the PBS website, "The First Measured Century" (http://www.pbs.org/fmc/interviews/wilson.htm). His analysis of the connections of race and class to history, the economy, and culture help us understand the complexity of these relationships sociologically.

Access the live/updated links at http://www.paradigmpublishers.com/resources/goldbergmedia.aspx

classes of other races? Do the poor of any race or ethnic group have more in common with each other or with their own race or ethnic group, regardless of class differences? Much of the research in this area points to growing class similarities across racial and ethnic categories. Class has become a greater indicator of well-being than race or ethnicity, impacting such social patterns as education, housing, marriage, and consumption.

Gender, Race, and Class

Having addressed the intersection of race, ethnicity, and class, we now explore how gender contributes to our analysis. We have already discussed important gender differences that influence unequal access to resources derived from a long history of patriarchy. These differences become more nuanced when we look at gender through class and race or ethnic prisms. Women and men in different social classes have different expectations and outcomes in relation to marriage patterns, parenting, occupations, and income. Additionally, differences among ethnic groups and races, with their particular social and historical patterns, indicate variations on gender stratification.

There are many ways in which we can examine this intersection. Table 2.4 shows the comparative income data for the first quarter of 2013, clearly indicating the

intersection of race, ethnicity, and gender. Note that men outearn women in each respective race and ethnic group and white and Asian men outearn both other men and all women.

Educational achievement is an important factor in income. Generally, the higher the educational level, the higher the income for all groups, but there are additional important differences of sex and race that demonstrate that education is not much of an equalizer. A study done by the National Committee on Pay Equity in 2002 found the following:

• The higher the level of educational achievement, the wider the gap between white men and white women. In 2001, for high-school graduates, the gender wage gap was $10,000, but for those with a college degree, the gap was more than $15,000.

Table 2.4
Weekly Median Income by Sex, Race, and Ethnicity, First Quarter 2013

Race	Male	Female
White	$888	$723
Black	$666	$597
Hispanic	$593	$531
Asian	$1,058	$831

Source: US Department of Labor, Bureau of Labor Statistics (2013b)

Movie Picks 2.4
Two Nations of Black America

Two Nations of Black America (PBS *Frontline*) explores the complex dynamics of race and class. Henry Louis Gates Jr. discusses the relationship between race and class, especially the rise of the black middle class. Also see the companion website (http://www.pbs.org/wgbh/pages /frontline/shows/race/).

Thinking Sociologically

- As more African Americans move into the middle class, is there a single black community?
- Which is more important today in determining life chances, race or class?

Access the live/updated links at http://www.paradigmpublishers.com/resources/goldbergmedia.aspx

- When comparing white men to black and Hispanic men at the level of high-school graduates, the gap is around $7,000; it doubles at the college-graduate level.
- The gap between white women, black women, and Hispanic women is smaller than that between women and men, and remained between $2,000 and $4,000.

Thus, being a white man is a distinct advantage over all blacks and Hispanics, regardless of educational achievement, and is most clearly advantageous when comparing incomes with women of all races (National Committee on Pay Equity 2002).

Although sex and race income differences are important, so too are family patterns. Marriage, childbearing and child-rearing, household structure, and the rise of dual-income families are some of the patterns that reflect gender-based issues impacting inequality. Perhaps there is no better example of the importance of gender than its impact on poverty. Cawthorne (2008) reports that in all racial and ethnic categories women are poorer than men. Among women the majority of the poor are single women

without dependents (54 percent) followed by single women with dependents (26 percent). While this statistic may seem counterintuitive, women's poverty is compounded by a number of factors. For instance, 13 percent of women over 75 years old are poor, and there is a high rate of poverty among women suffering domestic abuse.

Another example of the intersection of gender and other factors of stratification is in the area of immigration. The challenge to the Fourteenth Amendment mentioned earlier is both an immigration issue and a gender issue. Questioning the right of citizenship for children born on American soil also questions the patterns of pregnancy and birth among foreign-born women.

Intersections in the Great Recession

The recession in the first decade of the twenty-first century and the programs for economic recovery play out in the intersection of class, gender, and race as well. It is too early to know the long-term effects of the recession but we can observe how the recession and its recovery will affect taxes,

Web Exercise 2.5
Gender and Poverty

Read Cawthorne's 2008 article "The Straight Facts on Women in Poverty" (http://www
.americanprogress.org/issues/2008/10/pdf/women_poverty.pdf). Consider the relative
status of poor women compared to men. Find additional statistics on the poverty rate of
women of various racial and ethnic groups.

- What are the major social reasons why women have a higher poverty rate than men?
- What do you conclude about the life chances of women who are most likely to be poor?

Access the live/updated links at http://www.paradigmpublishers.com/resources/goldbergmedia.aspx

programs to help the poor and the elderly, housing, and jobs, all of which will have an impact on the life chances of people. Although social class is central to our understanding of these changes, they are experienced differently depending on one's race, ethnicity, and gender.

Careful analysis of the inequalities of class, gender, race, and ethnicity in the United States demonstrates that we live in a highly complex and interconnected system of stratification within our national borders. We have an important relationship with the rest of the world with which we become more intertwined every day, so any consideration of inequality must take into account the stratification that exists in the larger world. We now turn our attention to global inequality.

Global Inequality: An Introduction

The study of inequality around the world includes the same basic concepts we have already applied in this chapter, though there are important considerations not yet touched upon. Understanding how resources are distributed globally is a huge task, but it can be made easier if nations and regions are categorized according to basic principles of inequality tied to specific historical experiences. Access to valuable natural resources, coupled with contact between more and less fully developed political and economic entities, are the keys to understanding global inequality. In Chapter 4 we examine some of the more significant outcomes of these relationships. Here, we provide a basic introduction to global inequality.

Reading Room 2.5
"Gendering the Birthright Citizenship Debate"

This article by Michelle Chen (2010) shows how debates about ethnicity and the rights to citizenship are also important gender issues (http://www.huffingtonpost.com/michelle-chen /gendering-the-birthright-_b_687794.html). How women in these situations are described in this and other cases historically is important to our understanding of the overall picture of inequality.

Access the live/updated links at http://www.paradigmpublishers.com/resources/goldbergmedia.aspx

Watch Online 2.3
"Color Lines: Race and Economic Recovery"

Watch "Color Lines: Race and Economic Recovery" (http://www.youtube.com/watch?v
=LaM6iI-eCdk) for an examination of how the economic recovery impacts the poor, especially
women of color.

Thinking Sociologically

- Does the economic recovery help the poor find work?
- What has been the effect of the recession on people receiving public assistance?
- What is the relative importance of gender and race as the economy recovers?

Access the live/updated links at http://www.paradigmpublishers.com/resources/goldbergmedia.aspx

Categorizing Development

Keeping in mind the rapid changes that are
taking place globally as once-distant regions
come closer through trade, media, and travel,
we can use criteria tied to dimensions of
development to help us sort through the
differences in the distribution of resources
and consequent political power worldwide.
Scholars and international organizations
offer similar, but not identical, categories
to represent a country's relative position
regarding its access to and use of resources.
These categories represent nations that are
at different stages of development in relation to agricultural, industrial, and post-
industrial economies. The relative health of
an economy impacts the daily lives of citizens
in the types of work performed and living
standards, or life chances. Although there

Hard labor and low pay are typical in developing regions of the world.
Source: ThinkStockPhoto.com

are inequalities of wealth and political power in all societies, the distribution of these inequalities differs in important ways. Terms such as *most developed countries*, *developing* and *least developed countries*, and *industrialized* and *industrializing countries* are commonly used to describe global inequalities.

Understanding global inequality necessitates categorization, but it must be remembered that today all economies are interconnected and that economic and political inequalities in one region can impact others quite profoundly. Categories are neither mutually exclusive nor sufficient to fully appreciate the complexity of global inequality, but they are a start. Given these parameters, the following categories will help us understand the basics of global inequality among nations:

1. **Highly industrialized** and **post-industrialized nations** have strong capitalist economies and stable political systems that are mostly democratic. Some manufacturing takes place in these countries, but much of the economy is based on post-industrial information-processing and service industries. These nations include the countries of Western Europe, the United States, Canada, Japan, and Australia (referred to as "the West") as the most influential representatives of this category.

2. **Mid-level industrialized** and **rapidly developing nations** have transforming economies aided by strong ties to Western capitalist nations. Some of these nations have emerging democratic political structures but overall less-stable political systems than the highly industrialized nations. China and India are the best examples of these countries, but we can also include Russia and other nations once part of the Soviet system that ended in the late twentieth century.

3. **Developing** and **least developed nations** are primarily agricultural but are beginning to industrialize. There is a great deal of poverty throughout this sector. They have weak governments and heavy investments from abroad to develop and extract natural resources and influence economic and political stability. Internal civil wars, inability to respond effectively to natural disasters, and weak infrastructures mark this group. Much of Africa, parts of Asia and the Middle East, as well as Haiti and some other countries in the Caribbean and Latin America represent this category.

Global Inequality and Political Power

A brief historical overview will help explain the ways in which economic and political change have enabled some nations to develop substantial economic wealth and political stability even as others remain in weakened economic and political positions. Starting with the rise of trade and subsequent colonization by Western European nations as they made contact with Africa, the Middle East, Asia, and the Americas in the fifteenth century, we can see a pattern of exploitation of natural resources and local labor for the growing wealth of Europe. By controlling geographic areas as both economic and political colonies, valuable natural resources were extracted and wealth was gained by the colonial powers while the loss of these resources created poverty and dependence over time among the local populations. In the last century, formal colonial rule ended in most of the world, but the exploitation continued largely by forcing newly independent nations into political relationships with the West that enabled the economic exploitation to continue. This process discouraged democracy, and thus we see regimes in neocolonial relationships friendly to Western

Web Exercise 2.6
Life in the Least Developed Countries (LDCs)

Read "About LDCs" at the website of the United Nations Office of the High Representative for Least Developed Countries (http://www.unohrlls.org/en/ldc/).

- What criteria are used to determine if a country is included in this list?
- What social conditions are most important in understanding the life chances of people living in these countries?
- Do you think that citizens of these countries would agree with the UN definition and criteria for LDCs?

Access the live/updated links at http://www.paradigmpublishers.com/resources/goldbergmedia.aspx

nations, resulting in the continued extraction of resources and labor at the expense of democracy and equality. In Chapter 4 we see these countries referred to as *fragile states* and *failed states*, indicating their tenuous political and economic circumstances.

Today the interdependent relationships between nations at different points in development are complex. For example, in Chapter 3 on the environmental crisis, we see how the West's dependence on oil shapes its relationship to oil-rich regions both economically and politically. While the highly industrialized and post-industrial nations are the largest users of oil at present, China and India are rapidly developing their own needs for oil as their economies grow. The intersection of the sources of this natural resource, the need for it in disparate parts of the world, and the environmental impact of its extraction and use converge to make for a complicated set of relationships verging on crisis and needing serious attention. Oil is just one of many natural resources caught up in a complex web of global enterprise and local suffering. The diamond trade, for example, has contributed to war and destabilization in parts of Africa. The value of diamonds on the global market has encouraged the exploitation of local populations and war over access to this

resource. The desire for other precious metals used in the latest technology is having a similar effect in regions where those metals are mined.

These global dynamics lead to extremes of inequality between nations and also among groups within nations. Generally, a small group in power dominates the politics and economies of developing nations. Class differences are significant, with a few wealthy citizens, large numbers of poor, and a small middle class. Gender inequality is exacerbated by traditional roles of male dominance. Ethnic disputes fester and sometimes erupt into war based on religious, ethnic, or territorial conflicts and control over resources. These conflicts are at least in part the legacy of colonial rule that was imposed by the West but that was never eliminated after the colonizers left. In order to retain control over local economies and resources, neocolonial relationships supported corrupt political regimes, often at the expense of democratic efforts on the part of these newly independent nations. As the global economy evolves, these economic and political inequalities persist.

As described in this book's preface, it seems the world is getting smaller, so understanding the global nature of inequality helps us see the intersection of cultures, economies, and politics that will be prominent

Watch Online 2.4
Diamonds of War

"Diamonds of War: Africa's Blood Diamonds," a National Geographic Special, documents the relationship between the highly valued natural resource of diamonds and civil war in Sierra Leone (http://www.youtube.com/watch?v=aaqQjIzIbiY). Known as *conflict diamonds* because they help finance the war, the diamonds are part of a web of complex relationships between the developed and least developed worlds.

Thinking Sociologically

- Explore the impact on local populations of the extraction of valuable natural resources.
- In the United States, diamonds are a symbol of enduring love. Apply symbolic interaction theory to compare the different meaning diamonds have in our society and among the miners in African diamond mines.

Access the live/updated links at http://www.paradigmpublishers.com/resources/goldbergmedia.aspx

throughout the twenty-first century. Sociology can provide an important framework for understanding inequality internal to our own society and in relation to the larger world. Your sociological imagination can link your personal experiences to the larger world to show how much you are a part of this dynamic, whether inequality is on your campus, in your hometown, or thousands of miles away.

Looking Forward

As we move into Part II of this book, we will use this understanding of inequality to ask related questions:

- What is the impact of the extraction of natural resources on the environment for people living nearby and globally?

Movie Picks 2.5
Slumdog Millionaire

Slumdog Millionaire is an award-winning fictional depiction of the clash between classes in India and the cultural influence of the West. Poverty and dreams of a better life are interwoven with corruption and danger.

Thinking Sociologically

- What are the life chances of an Indian child born in a slum?
- How are gender and ethnic inequality depicted in the film?
- What Western influences are present?
- In your view, what level of development is represented in the film? How can you tell?
- What are some examples of cultural diffusion found in the film?

Access the live/updated links at http://www.paradigmpublishers.com/resources/goldbergmedia.aspx

- How does extreme poverty impact life chances?
- How does inequality contribute to conflicts in disparate parts of the world?
- How do families, especially women and children, the most vulnerable populations, fare under extreme conditions?
- What are the implications for health care, especially when diseases such as HIV/AIDS threaten to undermine communities and economic well-being?
- How can obesity and the hunger associated with poverty coexist?
- How is terrorism connected to inequality?
- What role does technology play in increasing or decreasing inequality?

Web Watch

In addition to the web resources found in this chapter, many other websites provide information on all aspects of inequality. US government websites can be very useful for the most recent data on various indicators of inequality. The website FedStats.gov provides a portal to government agencies by topic interests. The US Census Bureau updates poverty statistics every year. Along with searching the websites listed on this book's companion website, it is worth doing independent searches (such as on websites suggested in Chapter 1) to stay updated on topics in sociology as well as other disciplines. Here are some websites that provide data and address issues of inequality:

FedStats: www.fedstats.gov
Inequality.org: www.inequality.org
The PEW Charitable Trusts: www.pew.org
US Census Bureau: www.census.gov
US Department of Health and Human Services: www.hhs.gov
US Department of Labor: www.dol.gov
US Department of Labor Bureau of Labor Statistics: www.bls.gov

PART II

TWENTY-FIRST-CENTURY CRISES

CHAPTER 3

Crisis in Our Environment

Fossil Fuels and Climate Change

Deepwater Horizon Fire.
Source: US Coast Guard photo

On April 22, 2010, an explosion on an oil rig in the Gulf of Mexico sent millions of gallons of oil spilling into the waters of the Gulf. Eleven workers were killed and the oil rig sank. Somewhere between 5,000 and 60,000 barrels a day spilled for months. By all accounts, this was a historic environmental disaster and its effects are expected to last for many years. In 5,000 feet of water, it was one of the deepest offshore wells ever built, making the challenge of capping the well especially difficult because of its depth. Inadequate technology and inexperience at working at that depth contributed to the delays in capping the well. The consequences of the spill promise to be dramatic in both the short term and long term, and to raise important questions about the demand for oil, the extent to which oil companies will go to find this increasingly scarce resource, the safety of offshore drilling, and the environmental effects on a fragile ecology, a fishing-dependent economy, tourism, and wildlife. There are important social and political ramifications resulting from this spill, from the effects on local culture and politics to larger questions about dependency on oil for much of our energy, transportation, and industry.

The environment is in crisis. Although the oil spill in the Gulf of Mexico was dramatic, it was not unprecedented. It is but one example of environmental destruction caused by human activity that is both avoidable and inevitable. There have been many oil spills, including one in the Yosemite River in the summer of 2011, and there will be many more. Natural disasters can also take a toll beyond the immediate destruction they cause. In the spring of 2011, a devastating earthquake and tsunami flattened a large coastal area of Japan. The most frightening and likely long-lasting effect was the ensuing crisis at several partially destroyed nuclear reactors. With leaking radiation and the loss of a major source of energy, it is one of the most dramatic and important environmental disasters of the new century. As we will see in this chapter, the consequences of human behavior on the environment, especially climate change and the depletion of fossil fuels, have been profound.

The Environmental Crisis as a Social Problem

We are in a period of increased awareness of the impact human societies have on the natural environment. Sociology makes an important contribution to understanding the role humans play in the causes and consequences of this environmental crisis. Questions about the ability to sustain modern consumption patterns in light of finite resources are being asked throughout our social institutions. From board rooms to churches, from families to schools, and across diverse parts of the world, a greater awareness of the human impact on the environment has grown. Environmental problems are both local and global in nature, affecting all aspects of society from small groups and communities to complex national and international entities. Most

scientists agree that these physical changes have been created by human activity. The changes can be resolved only by addressing both the physical nature of the problems and the social and political dynamics that both created them and are necessary to solve them. Thus the topic is especially suitable for sociological analysis. Sociologists also recognize that there are important differences globally in the use of resources and in the relative contributions of nations to climate change. Attention to environmental issues is therefore tied to national and international political systems and economies. From the most personal decisions we make about conducting our daily lives to the global distribution of fossil fuels and other sources of energy, this is a crisis that will play out through this century.

The field of environmental sociology is a relatively new subdiscipline that addresses this complex interaction between the physical environment and social experience. It is especially useful in that it examines the social causes of the changes in the physical environment as well as the subsequent awareness of environmental problems and the attempts to resolve them. The American Sociological Association's section on Environment and Technology addresses the link between the science of the environment and the need to study the crisis in social terms on its website. It sums up the issues:

Radiation, genetically-modified crops, toxic waste, biodiversity loss, climate change. Facing the challenges of the twenty-first century requires more than sound scientific understanding and technological solutions. Too often missing from the debate is knowledge of the complex social, economic, and political relationships that drive society in destructive directions. Environmental Sociology brings together the tools of social sciences and applies them to these key issues of our day. (American

Web Exercise 3.1
What Is Environmental Sociology?

Visit the website of the American Sociological Association Section on Environment and Technology (www.envirosoc.org).

- Examine the several ways in which sociologists study environmental problems.
- Select one of the issues listed and explain how this specific topic can be studied sociologically.

Access the live/updated links at http://www.paradigmpublishers.com/resources/goldbergmedia.aspx

Sociological Association Section on Environment and Technology: Section Visitors 2012)

Our task in this chapter is to connect the scientific concerns regarding the environmental crisis to our social framework. Later in the chapter we will apply specific sociological concepts to problems of the environment.

As with the other topics in this book, it is impossible to cover the vast amount of information on the full range of environmental concerns. For the purposes of our exploration, we focus on two of the most important problems that underlie the environmental crisis and that are vividly demonstrated by dramatic oil spills in recent years: the availability and use of fossil fuels, especially oil, and global climate change. These interrelated issues represent the most challenging aspects of environmental degradation because they are so potentially dangerous and they impact many other environmental processes. Although the focus on these issues has an important scientific component, it must be remembered that people make choices about energy, transportation, and consumption that are social in nature. Thus, how the environmental crisis is addressed combines both an understanding of the science and an understanding of the role of human activity in the crisis. The catastrophe of the oil spill

in the Gulf of Mexico in 2010 graphically exemplifies the dual nature of the environmental crisis. Not only did the spill hurt the natural environment, it has the potential to alter a way of life where the fishing industry dominates the economy and defines the local culture. We will keep this in mind as we focus on the scientific and social aspects of the crisis.

This chapter first reviews the basic problems associated with fossil fuels and climate change. It then applies sociological concepts and theories to the social dynamics involved in these environmental problems. We will explore the cultural and structural underpinnings of society to show the connections between the environmental crisis and social experience. Finally, we consider future challenges and connect the environment to the other crises discussed in later chapters.

Our discussion of the environmental crisis starts with the documentary *An Inconvenient Truth*. Although some criticize it as one-sided, it did much to bring concerns about the environment to the attention of ordinary people. The film makes a strong argument for the role of human activity as the cause of global warming and it presses for political leaders and economists to address the problems of climate change. This film is a jumping-off point to address the environmental issues in this chapter.

Movie Picks 3.1
An Inconvenient Truth

An Inconvenient Truth (2006) is possibly one of the best-known documentary films on the environmental crisis. It is perceived by many to provide an excellent introduction to the issue of global warming, and it placed climate change on the political map. In this film, former US Vice President Al Gore presents what he sees as the incontrovertible evidence of climate change and asks us to consider the outcome of inaction. He suggests how we must move to reduce carbon emissions and argues that action needs to be taken on both global and personal scales. The film argues for the use of scientific evidence to make informed policy decisions before it is too late to stop global warming, and yet it has been the subject of much controversy among some politicians, teachers, and others who are skeptical about the facts presented in the film and about whether or not global warming exists and is truly a problem.

Mixed-Media Extra

View clips from the film and recent updates on the film's companion website (http://www .takepart.com/an-inconvenient-truth).

Thinking Sociologically

- What are the nature and scope of the global crisis depicted in the film?
- Do you have any evidence from your personal experience that you feel connects to the larger global crisis portrayed in the movie?
- Explore how environmentalism became a social movement.
- Is there evidence to refute Gore's claims about climate change?

Access the live/updated links at http://www.paradigmpublishers.com/resources/goldbergmedia.aspx

Focus: Fossil Fuels and Climate Change

Since the Industrial Revolution, there has been tremendous growth in the use of fossil fuels—specifically coal, oil, and natural gas—to develop and sustain industrial production, transportation, and electrical power, the most common forms of fossil-fuel consumption. As Figure 3.1 demonstrates, more than 80 percent of energy consumption in the United States comes from these fossil fuels, with about 40 percent being petroleum (oil). As the graph demonstrates, 71 percent of the petroleum resources are used in transportation and most of the rest (23 percent) are used in industry. In transportation, 93 percent of energy demand is met by petroleum. Approximately 17 percent of our energy consumption uses the remaining sources: renewable energy and nuclear energy. Transportation and industry combined account for about half of the energy consumption. The breadth of dependence on fossil fuels raises questions about their availability in the future and the effects that their extraction and use have on the environment, particularly climate change. Since oil represents over 35 percent of all energy sources, we focus on oil in this chapter.

Two essential issues are related to fossil fuels: one is their impact on global climate change and the other is access to and consumption of these resources. We first examine the relationship of fossil fuels to global climate change, or global warming.

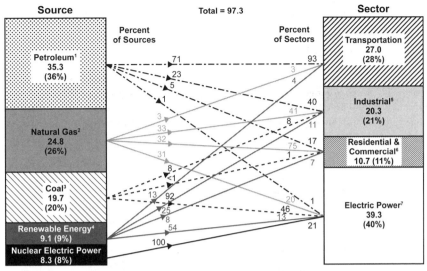

Figure 3.1 Primary energy consumption by source and sector (2011).
Source: US Energy Information Administration, http://www.eia.gov/totalenergy/data/annual
/pecss_diagram.cfm

What Is Global Climate Change?

As fossil fuels are consumed, carbon dioxide (CO_2) is emitted into the earth's atmosphere. Increasing amounts of these emissions cause a buildup of carbon dioxide and other gases known as greenhouse gases, so called because, as part of the earth's atmospheric layers, they trap heat from the sun, much like the glass panes of a gardener's greenhouse also trap warmth from the sun. These gases cannot easily escape, and as a result they create warmer temperatures around the planet. This process is especially evident in the resulting melting of glaciers and the polar icecaps, which, it is generally agreed, are melting at an increasingly rapid

pace. With smaller portions of the earth's surface covered by white, reflective expanses of ice and snow, less of the sun's energy is reflected by the planet, and more solar energy is absorbed, which further hastens the melting of ice and snow. Global warming thus advances relentlessly.

How much has the temperature of the earth increased? According to The Nature Conservancy (2011a),

the five hottest years on record have all occurred since 1997 and the 10 hottest since 1990, including the warmest years on record—2005 and 2010.... During the 20th century, the Earth's average temperature rose one degree Fahrenheit to its highest

Web Exercise 3.2
Evidence That the Globe Is Warming

Look at the evidence of the diminishing ice covering in the Arctic Ocean in the video "Global Warming 101" (http://video.nationalgeographic.com/video/environment/global-warming -environment/global-warming-101/). Also see NASA's website, "Global Climate Change: Evidence" (http://climate.nasa.gov/evidence). Consider its importance to the environment, both physically and socially.

- What is the evidence of global warming?
- What are the likely results of higher global temperatures?
- Who should be responsible for controlling the greenhouse effect?
- What simple activities can you do to help reduce the greenhouse effect?
- Are some social groups more likely than others to address issues of climate change?

Access the live/updated links at http://www.paradigmpublishers.com/resources/goldbergmedia.aspx

level in the past four centuries—believed to be the fastest rise in a thousand years.... Scientists project that if emissions of heat-trapping carbon emissions aren't reduced, average surface temperatures could increase by 3 to 10 degrees Fahrenheit by the end of the century.

Global warming may also slow or shut down ocean currents that maintain water temperatures, which would dramatically alter marine life as well as raise sea levels, change the distribution of fresh water (including both flooding and droughts), and create more dangerous storms. There is fear that changes in the sea temperatures in the Great Ocean Conveyor Belt discussed below might fuel such changes.

Effects of Climate Change

Scientists speculate that different regions of the world will be impacted differently. For example, they predict that communities in flooded coastal areas may have to move inland, rising sea temperatures will change the habitat in the sea, and we will see the loss of species that are important to ecological balance. Populations dependent on fishing may no longer be able to rely on their traditional source of income. Resulting displacements of populations will have important economic and social ramifications for families and communities. With rising sea levels, widespread human migration is likely to put economic and political pressure on regions receiving populations of new immigrants displaced by rising oceans.

In addition to increases in storms and rises in sea levels, drought brought on by higher temperatures will alter population densities and impact migration patterns of people as well as other living organisms. The Environmental Defense Fund predicts that by 2080 it is possible that 200 million people will be displaced "by more intense droughts, sea level rise and flooding" (2007). Scientists have shown how, in many ways, the ecological fabric of the earth will be dramatically affected even with relatively minor changes in temperature. A study by the US Global Change Research Program (2009) provides a detailed discussion of these effects on virtually all aspects of environmental significance: weather (including increased

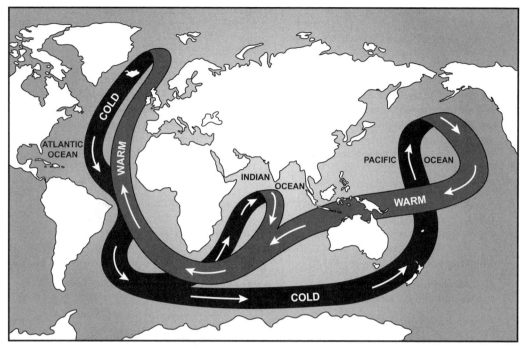

Figure 3.2 Great ocean conveyor belt: a global ocean circulation between deep, colder water and warmer, surface water strongly influences regional climates around the world.
Source: Argonne National Laboratory (Barry 2004) `http://science1.nasa.gov` `/science-news/science-at-nasa/2004/05mar_arctic/`

rainfall and heat waves), the seas (fish, coral reefs, and coastal communities), water and energy supplies, forests, and agriculture. In all these areas change has already occurred and is expected to be significant in the future if not addressed soon. It is important to begin to consider how social, economic, and political landscapes will change as we attempt to or fail to forestall these dramatic changes.

In summary, the development of fossil fuels for human consumption creates problems of global warming. The extent to which human populations can adapt to the effects of

Information 3.1
Risks of Melting Sea Ice

Freshwater will increase in the oceans, impacting sea currents.*
Precipitation—both rain and snow—will increase.*
Ocean-current patterns will be altered.*
Land areas will be lost, potentially including coastal areas of the United States.**
Populations may be displaced throughout the world.**

Sources: *Barry (2004); ** Nature Conservancy (2011b)

Movie Picks 3.2
The Day After Tomorrow

Possibly the most visually entertaining fiction film on global warming and its effects on the weather is *The Day After Tomorrow* (2004), which combines scientific facts and fantasy, ignorant and self-serving politicians, and heroic climatologists determined to save the world. Yet, beneath the entertainment value of the film are important undercurrents that hint at larger issues of concern including both physical and social effects of climate change. Students should investigate some of the basic premises of the movie and consider its value sociologically.

Mixed-Media Extra

View the video clip and read the article "The Science and Fiction of 'Day After Tomorrow'" (http://www.msnbc.msn.com/id/5058474/) to investigate whether there is a scientific basis for the film's premise regarding global warming and its possible impact on weather.

Thinking Sociologically

Consider both the legitimacy of the claims the movie makes about climate change and the social implications of that change.

- How realistic is the breakup of the ice shelf in Antarctica?
- Can global warming cause falling temperatures in some parts of the world?
- Was Hurricane Sandy in 2012 related to climate change?
- How do people make decisions in the face of calamity, and how does leadership emerge?
- What is the significance of gender, race, and class portrayed in the film?
- How are inequalities of power (science *vs.* politics) made apparent in the film?
- Will immigration be a serious concern if climate change occurs?

Access the live/updated links at http://www.paradigmpublishers.com/resources/goldbergmedia.aspx

---

climate change appears to be limited unless action is taken to reduce consumption of fossil fuels and the resulting global warming. The use of fossil fuels as a resource and the resulting environmental impact can be summarized as in the box "Fossil-Fuel Use and Global Warming."

How Much Oil?
Where Is It and Who Is Impacted?

An important concern in using fossil fuels is that they are finite resources requiring technologically sophisticated, environmentally damaging methods for extraction. Though there is some question about how much oil and other fossil fuels remain in the earth, there is no doubt that they are increasingly difficult to access and that extraction leaves an indelible impact on the health and well-being of those who work in these industries and live nearby.

As noted in Figure 3.1, oil consumption represents 36 percent of all fuel usage in the United States. The discovery of oil in the United States in the nineteenth century inspired widespread speculation, quick wealth, new technologies, and cheap prices. The dependence on oil today can be traced to the early days of oil exploration when many believed it to be an infinite source of energy for driving industrialization and transportation. Abundant and cheap oil supported the

Information 3.2
Fossil-Fuel Use and Global Warming

FOSSIL FUEL EXTRACTION ➡ CONSUMPTION FOR INDUSTRY AND PERSONAL USE ➡ CO_2 EMISSIONS ➡ GREENHOUSE GASES ➡ GLOBAL WARMING ➡ PROFOUND CHANGES IN ECOLOGICAL BALANCE ➡ HUMAN (SOCIAL) RESPONSE ➡ ADAPTATION/CHANGE

development of the automobile industry and the related patterns of modern highways and housing that would not be possible without popular use of oil-based transportation. As we see later in this chapter, such developments have had a tremendous impact on the culture of contemporary America.

In tracing the historical patterns of extracting oil from the earth, it becomes apparent that this resource is becoming more difficult to access while, at the same time, its extraction causes greater environmental damage to local communities. The industrialized nations, including the United States, have been using fossil fuels at an increasingly rapid rate since the beginning of industrialization (some argue since the rise of agriculture). Today, newly industrializing nations, particularly India and China, have begun to increase their use of fossil fuels, and the growth of oil consumption in developing countries creates large-scale problems that

Movie Picks 3.3
There Will Be Blood

There Will Be Blood (2007) is historical fiction and a character study of an early oil baron. The film shows how people responded to the discovery of oil and the greed that followed with the drive to become rich and powerful at all costs. While a work of fiction, this film portrays the early days of oil discovery in the United States.

Thinking Sociologically

Sociologically the film is of value largely because it shows how people develop a sense of entitlement over natural resources and over those who have less power and wealth. The American values of individualism, ambition, and hard work, as well as material greed, are vividly portrayed. See the section on culture and the environment later in this chapter for further discussion.

- Is individualism still valued when comparing the experiences of the early oil producers presented in this film to present-day companies that drill for oil deep in the seas offshore?
- What is the difference in how people responded to the early growth of the oil industry and the impact of the oil spill in the Gulf of Mexico in 2010?

Access the live/updated links at http://www.paradigmpublishers.com/resources/goldbergmedia.aspx

Fast Facts 3.1
Oil Consumption

Top Five Oil-Consuming Countries in Barrels per Day (2011 est.)

United States:	18,630,000
European Union:	13,250,000
China:	9,790,000
Japan:	4,464,000
Russia:	3,341,000
World Consumption:	87,630,000

The United States imports the most crude oil: 9,013,000 barrels per day (2009 est.).
US crude-oil production: 9,023,000 barrels per day (2011 est.).
Proven US oil reserves: 20,680,000,000 barrels (2012 est.).

Source: Central Intelligence Agency (2013).

can only be solved through action with both local and global initiatives.

With such rapidly increasing use of and dependence on oil, a central question is, Will we run out of this fuel? This question refers to the finite nature of natural resources, but also to the technological ability to access those resources that are becoming harder to find over time. The fact of large oil reserves shown in the box "Fast Facts: Oil Consumption" does not mean the oil is easily extracted. The oil-spill disaster in the Gulf of Mexico in 2010 is a case in point. The necessity of drilling in mile-deep waters to a depth of 35,000 feet in order to access oil deep under the sea bottom entails great risks. It also makes it enormously difficult to control the leaks and minimize the resulting environmental damage should problems arise.

Peak Oil

The concept of **peak oil** was first developed in the 1950s by M. King Hubbert. According to his analysis, we have already reached a point globally at which the rate of oil extraction begins to decline as new oil fields become harder to find and existing fields yield further oil with increasing difficulty. New extraction technologies can temporarily extend the lives of oil fields, but access to this finite resource has essentially peaked. According to the Global Education Project (n.d.), oil discoveries actually peaked in the 1960s. By the 1980s, consumption of oil outstripped discovery. The amount of exploratory drilling declined through the 1960s, picked up in the 1970s, peaked in the early 1980s, then dropped dramatically in the 1990s. During the 1980s, even though exploratory drilling was the highest in thirty years, consumption was greater than discovery. Today, consumption of oil is much greater than discovery of oil deposits.

Oil as a Source of Conflict

As the availability of oil becomes more limited and more expensive, the distribution of oil becomes ever more significant politically and economically. While the West continues its high level of consumption, developing

Web Exercise 3.3
Where to Drill?

Visit the website of the Association for the Study of Peak Oil and Gas for more information on peak oil (http://www.peakoil.net/about-peak-oil). Then watch the National Geographic video clip, "Explorer: Extreme Oil Drilling" (http://www.youtube.com/watch?v=QP2GejkLdwA).

- How hard is it to find oil today?
- Is there greater risk in drilling if oil gets harder to find?
- What are the political, economic, and social ramifications of the difficulty in finding oil?
- Research the impact of the oil spill in the Gulf of Mexico on local cultures in Louisiana. How has the spill affected jobs? family life? faith? community?

Access the live/updated links at http://www.paradigmpublishers.com/resources/goldbergmedia.aspx

nations are dramatically increasing consumption. The effects of the increased demand for oil and the increasing difficulty of access suggest the potential for conflict of a global nature as competition for the resource grows. The political turmoil that began in the Middle East in 2010 in Tunisia and carried over into 2011 in many oil-producing states demonstrates the importance of political dynamics in the ongoing drive for oil. These events have directly affected the price of oil in consuming nations, clearly demonstrating that volatile political events impact dependency on oil and draw a significant global response. As long as oil remains such a major source of energy and demands a high price, we can expect conflicts large and small over oil to significantly impact economic and political processes throughout the world.

In addition to concerns about the availability of oil, communities in the developing world that are rich in natural resources (including oil) but limited in political or economic power face environmental and health problems potentially beyond their ability to cope. Later in this chapter we discuss the ramifications of extracting fossil fuels for the people who work in the fields or live nearby. The complex relationship between oil-producing and oil-consuming nations,

the rise of new patterns of consumption while availability declines, and the changing climate all contribute to the environmental crisis. We now turn to sociology to provide a context for exploring these issues in more depth.

Sociology of the Environment

Perhaps the best place to start a sociological inquiry into the environmental crisis is a discussion of the connections between the physical and social worlds. In their assessment report on climate change for the Intergovernmental Panel on Climate Change (IPCC), Rajendra K. Pachuari and Andy Reisinger (2007) demonstrate the interwoven relationship between these worlds. Calling the two worlds *Earth Systems* and *Human Systems*, they show how changes in one area create dramatic and ongoing changes in the other. For example, economic patterns of production and consumption both create environmental problems and are changed by them. Pachuari and Reisinger effectively show the cyclical connection between the physical and social worlds and the delicate balance and response to imbalance necessary to maintain a livable earth. This is the heart

Movie Picks 3.4
Crude Impact

Crude Impact (2006) examines the role of oil in modern life, the realities of extracting fossil fuels, including the environmental, economic, and political impact of oil drilling and processing on communities and nations, and the concept of peak oil. This documentary connects the relationship of the global dependence on oil to the contradictions of life in oil-rich regions.

Mixed-Media Extra

Visit the film's website for information about the film and related resources (http://crudeimpact.com/). View clips from the film on Link TV (http://www.linktv.org/search/r/programs/q/crude%20impact).

Thinking Sociologically

The film explicitly shows the importance of oil as a source of power in creating and sustaining inequality between nations and in the relationship between those who live in communities where oil is extracted and those who benefit most from this resource. The health of people living in these communities and the political organization that emerges from the imbalance of power demonstrates how conflict results from basic inequalities. These topics are discussed later in this chapter in more detail.

- In what ways are communities impacted by the extraction of oil in nearby areas?
- If we have reached peak oil, how will that affect our social fabric in twenty years?

Access the live/updated links at http://www.paradigmpublishers.com/resources/goldbergmedia.aspx

of environmental sociology. The relationship of fossil-fuel use and global warming to social institutions can readily be traced in a detailed graph in their climate change study (see Web Exercise 3.4). Pachuari and Reisinger demonstrate how patterns in production, consumption, and technology drive the rise of greenhouse gases, resulting in climate change that then creates specific vulnerabilities for people. The study shows how increased vulnerability in the areas of food and water resources is connected to the related concerns of health and even where people are able to live. Once the problems are recognized, the study suggests that it may be possible to adapt to and mitigate the damaging environmental impact. How Human Systems both help create and respond to changes in Earth Systems is represented in the full range of social institutions including government action, technology, literacy, education, and economic analysis and change.

There are important links between the environmental crisis and human activity. Applying sociological analysis to this complex dynamic will help us see the interaction between the environment and society and better understand the role humans play in perpetuating the problem and perhaps alleviating it in the future.

The Sociological Imagination and the Environmental Crisis

We begin our analysis of the social components of the environmental crisis with the

Web Exercise 3.4
Climate Change, Flooding, and Society

Read "With Climate Change Comes Floods" (http://www.npr.org/templates/story/story .php?storyId=18022014). Connect environmental changes to the impact on people and their communities. Also study the Pachuari and Reisinger "Earth Systems/Human Systems" graph in their report, "Climate Change 2007" (http://www.ipcc.ch/publications_and_data/ar4/syr /en/mainssyr-introduction.html).

- Describe the specific threats of flooding as a result of climate change.
- Who is most vulnerable to floods from climate change?
- How are they vulnerable?
- What are some suggestions to mitigate the problem of flooding?

Access the live/updated links at http://www.paradigmpublishers.com/resources/goldbergmedia.aspx

sociological imagination to demonstrate the connection between our individual "troubles" and the wider social "milieu," to use Mills's terminology, as it relates to the environment.

Individuals are affected by environmental issues in a number of ways depending on their social location. Where one lives in the world, the personal resources to which one has access, even the amount of energy consumed, varies from region to region and, within regions, among people of different social ranks. These social, economic, and political manifestations are found across the globe, yet they also affect communities, households, and the individual choices people make. As a university student in the United States, you likely consume much more energy than a person your age in Sub-Saharan Africa or Southeast Asia. If you have a car, use a computer, or live in a home where you have your own bedroom, you consume

Reading Room 3.1
The Sociological Imagination

Mills's book *The Sociological Imagination* is one of the most widely read explanations of the value of sociology. You read an excerpt titled "The Promise" in Chapter 1 of this book. Review the excerpt (https://socialsciences.nsula.edu/assets/Site-Files/The-Promise.pdf) with the environmental crisis in mind.

- What does Mills mean when he says "our private lives are a series of traps"?
- Are we trapped by environmental issues?
- Why is it important to understand historical change when considering the environmental crisis?

Access the live/updated links at http://www.paradigmpublishers.com/resources/goldbergmedia.aspx

more energy than most people in the world and more than a poor person in your own country. You also probably have the luxury of not living near a toxic waste dump (at least as far as you know), and probably do not have family members working in coal mines or oil fields. You expect your water to be drinkable and your food uncontaminated. These assumptions, though, pertain mostly to a select group of people: the middle class and above. Inequalities, even on a college campus, make some people more vulnerable to environmental hazards than others. Awareness of individual connections to the environment can only be understood in the larger social context of greater or lesser access to and use of resources.

Consider how individual "troubles" might be connected to the environment. Safe water and healthy food are not guaranteed. There are many recent examples of contaminants in our water and food, including outbreaks of salmonella in a variety of food products. Drinking water must be monitored for contaminants, including chemicals such as pesticides found in runoffs from cities as well as industrial and agricultural waste. An unprecedented heat wave in the United States in 2011, although by itself not necessarily connected to patterns of climate change, portends individual suffering and significant social problems if the trend in global warming persists. Relatively new diseases like swine flu, West Nile virus, or Lyme disease have become more widespread as the environment changes. There are fears that global warming creates optimal conditions for the spread of such diseases that would normally be limited by colder temperatures that used to kill them off in the winter. Yet for most people, these fears seem remote. Consider these macro questions and how they impact individuals:

- What are realistic transportation options: public transportation? a bike? a car?

- Do oil prices impact personal decisions about where to live and work?
- On a community level, should funds be spent building roads or enhancing public transportation?
- How are resources distributed when disasters like Hurricane Katrina or Hurricane Sandy strike, or when oil spills contaminate food, water, and other resources?
- Are funds available for alternative, renewable sources of energy?
- Should there be stricter laws limiting carbon dioxide emissions?
- If less oil is used, how does that impact the international oil industry and the relationship of oil-consuming countries to countries that supply oil?
- Who is most vulnerable to the effects of climate change?

If we fire up our sociological imagination we see that individual "troubles" in choosing transportation, for example, are directly connected to the larger social dynamics of access to fossil fuels, the economic and political relationships among nations, the design and production of fuel-efficient cars, and the availability of public transportation. The sociological imagination helps demonstrate that global warming and availability of oil are directly connected to both individual decisions and structural components of modern transportation systems. There are other important environmental concerns that are not addressed in this chapter, but the application of sociology to global warming and oil provides a useful tool for addressing other relevant environmental problems.

Culture and the Environment

When sociologists study culture we examine what makes up the worldview shared by the people in a particular culture. How do people live their lives every day? What

Web Exercise 3.5
What Is Your Carbon Footprint?

Think about your impact on the environment. It may seem that one person doesn't have much of an effect on the environment, but consider what might happen if millions of individuals make the decision to recycle or to choose public transportation over cars. Trace your personal carbon footprint at the Nature Conservancy Carbon Footprint Calculator (http://www.nature.org /greenliving/carboncalculator/).

- What is your contribution to reducing global warming?
- Use your sociological imagination to examine how your personal experiences tie into the environmental crisis.

Access the live/updated links at http://www.paradigmpublishers.com/resources/goldbergmedia.aspx

tools and technology do they use? What do they value? How does language reflect experiences and express a worldview? In this chapter, we specifically ask: What behaviors regarding the environment can be expected from people who share a culture? As we learned in Chapter 1, material culture refers to the tangible things found in society while non-material culture is represented by language, values, norms, and the understanding of one's place in the world. Examining material and non-material culture is useful in understanding how environmental problems are perceived. In this section we focus on the deeply ingrained American values of material consumption, personal independence, and individualism and how they impact the environment.

Materialism and Conspicuous Consumption

Materialism is the desire and drive to own things, along with the meaning that people derive from that ownership. Americans like to buy things and replace old things with new ones. Many people believe that material possessions—clothes, houses, cars, cell phones, computers, and so forth—are a reflection of who they are as individuals and therefore are a source of well-being.

People often expect that owning these items will provide a sense of fulfillment and make them happy. Shopping and accumulating "stuff" has been a significant American cultural activity for a long time, especially since the 1950s. As a cultural touchstone, materialism is connected to **conspicuous consumption**, a reflection of one's status by displaying to others what is purchased, and thus demonstrating what is believed to be a person's well-being to his or her social network. On a larger scale, materialism is linked to the nation's economy, where consumer spending is vital to economic health in a far-reaching global capitalist economy. As such, the drive for material objects impacts the environment in important ways from production to consumption to waste products.

Automobile Culture

Closely connected to material consumption is the value of personal independence, and the American relationship to automobiles is a perfect example of a material item that is both useful in daily life and highly valued for its ability to enable individual independence. Note that in Figure 3.1 we saw that transportation makes up nearly 30 percent

Web Exercise 3.6
Your Stuff

Watch the video *The Story of Stuff with Annie Leonard* (www.storyofstuff.org/) for a global view of material consumption and the effects on the environment. As Americans, we seem to have a lot of "stuff."

- Select an item you own and trace its path from production to consumption to disposal to see what impact that item has on the environment.
- How is "stuff" part of our material culture and non-material culture?
- What values do we hold that reflect our ties to "stuff?"
- Do we have a responsibility as a society to reduce the amount of "stuff" we own?

Access the live/updated links at http://www.paradigmpublishers.com/resources/goldbergmedia.aspx

of energy consumption. Within that sector, oil provides 93 percent of the energy used in transportation, so it is useful to look at how the American automobile culture, both material and non-material, impacts the environment. According to the Environmental Defense Fund, "automobiles are America's biggest reason for oil dependence and therefore represent the single biggest piece of our global warming problem.... If American cars and light trucks were a nation, they would be the world's fifth-largest carbon emitter" (Environmental Defense Fund 2002). The Environmental Defense Fund provides further graphic evidence of the impact of automobiles on global warming: "In 2004, U.S. cars and light trucks emitted 314 million metric tons of carbon-equivalent (MMTc). That equals the amount of carbon in a coal train 50,000 miles long—enough to stretch 17 times between New York and San Francisco" (DeCicco and Fung 2006, iv).

Despite the contribution to global warming and concerns about oil depletion, new roads continue to be built, encouraging even greater use of cars. The environmental impact on local streams, wildlife, and nearby neighborhoods is especially significant in densely populated communities. For example, the Intercounty Connector, a new

toll road in suburban Maryland, is eighteen miles long and cost more than $2.5 billion to construct. After much resistance from environmental groups and communities impacted by the road, it was completed in 2012 (Intercounty Connector 2011).

Individualism

We like cars for their design and practicality, which we sometimes believe represent an extension of ourselves, but we mostly like them because they allow us to independently determine where and when we travel. This is a reflection of one of the most cherished of American values related to independence and **individualism**. Beyond their practical use, cars have become an important symbol of that individualism. Transportation needs can be satisfied in a number of ways, but the preference for automobiles and the power of the automobile industry has driven the building of highways and consumption of oil to satisfy the desire for independence and as an outlet for the expression of personal identity. Many Americans do not think of public transportation as a preferred mode of transportation, because it requires dependence on community rather than individual decisions about transportation. Individualism is central

Intercounty Connector.
Source: Daniel Lee

the culture of individualism for those who value technology that enhances the environment.

Beyond meeting individual transportation preferences, it is important to consider local, state, and federal support for roads and public transportation, as well as decisions to drill for oil in environmentally fragile environments. In 2011, a goal for new fuel standards of 54.5 mpg by 2025 was introduced by President Barack Obama and the automobile industry in an effort to reduce oil dependency. Internationally, access to oil reserves, the price of oil, and the relationships between oil-rich and oil-dependent nations have tremendous impacts on everything from foreign policy to our personal relationships with our cars. Globally, the economic and political relationships between oil-rich nations and major consumer nations are central to international policy, including decisions to go to war.

When we become aware of the threat to the oil supply (or gas prices go uncomfortably high) we may consider alternative forms of transportation, but this is a slow and difficult process that requires us to adjust our values. As a society at this moment in the twenty-first century, however, we have not yet accepted that the combustion engine must become a relic, even knowing as we do that oil is a finite resource. Indeed, according to the US Department of Transportation (2013), there are 255,917,664 registered vehicles in the United States. A cultural shift will occur when we understand that global

to American values, and investing in material items helps maintain individual identity and independence. Yet independence is a myth because we are highly dependent on oil companies and government policy to create ways to ensure that our cars will run. There is a complex web of interdependence with social institutions, especially economic and political institutions, which enable those who can afford cars to exercise their individuality. We are thus dependent on our incomes as well as the health of the automobile industry to provide affordable cars. The economic recession of the first decade of the twenty-first century has demonstrated the complexity of this interdependence. The "Cash for Clunkers" program of 2009 is a perfect example of a government attempt at reducing CO_2 emissions while also stimulating the auto industry and helping people purchase new cars. Along with other industries, automobile companies have recently begun developing hybrid and electric cars to meet a relatively new cultural awareness of all things "green." Aside from the positive effects of reduced use of oil and CO_2 emissions, this is a new addition to

Reading Room 3.2
What Does Oil Have to Do with War?

Read "A Crude Case for War?" by Steven Mufson in the *Washington Post* (http://articles
.washingtonpost.com/2008-03-16/business/36886089_1_oil-revenues-oil-fields
-cheap-oil).

- Is there a link between the dependence on oil and the war in Iraq?
- What alternatives are there to the dependence on foreign oil?

Access the live/updated links at http://www.paradigmpublishers.com/resources/goldbergmedia.aspx

warming is a direct result of our relationship to automobiles and the social values they represent.

Changes in Norms

How have our norms regarding transportation changed in recent years? Norms are the expected behaviors that derive from cultural values. The growth of public transportation systems, especially in cities, allows us to take the bus or subway as a normative activity to get from place to place. While we may prefer cars, public transportation has become both more practical and more affordable than automobiles for many people to get to work and school. While car ownership is still a highly valued expression of independence and status, we often frown on excess—too many cars, especially gas guzzlers, are increasingly seen as a form of selfishness and disregard for the environment rather than as a positive representation of individualism. Some "eco-radicals" use tactics such as physically attacking large SUVs like Hummers, which have been singled out as symbols of excess, to call attention to the environmental impact of such vehicles (Tamaki et al. 2003).

Reducing dependence on automobiles by choosing to take public transportation or buying small hybrid or electric cars reflects changes in values and norms and in our relationship to the material culture. However, this example of the role of the automobile in our society is only a piece of the environmental puzzle. Beyond automobiles there are multiple uses for oil in the material world and concomitant values associated with the extraction of fossil fuels. As seen earlier, more than 20 percent of energy is consumed by industry, most of which is supplied by fossil fuels. Corporate energy consumption requires more than individual decisions to find alternative sources of energy. As sociologists we can study what might drive businesses to defend the use of fossil fuels or to seek alternative forms of energy to reduce environmental damage. We can explore potential policy changes to reduce dependency on oil and address climate change.

Energy, Climate Change, and Inequality

In order to better understand the environmental crisis sociologically, we need to examine inequalities in the patterns of energy consumption, extraction of fossil fuels, and climate change. As we saw in Chapter 2, when examining global social structures, sociologists find it useful to categorize societies based on their relative degrees of development to understand vary-ing economic, political, and social trends regarding resources, income, sources of wealth, and so forth. In general, North America and Europe are considered the most developed and wealthy regions, whereas Asia, South America, and Africa are the least developed and poorest. The effects of regional inequalities are examined in more depth in Chapter 4. These categories are especially useful in examining the distribu-tion of energy resources. These categories also help us understand the unequal effects of climate change. We will first look at con-sumption patterns.

Unequal Energy Consumption

The United States uses a great deal more energy than countries with much greater populations, even those with high energy use. For example, the US per capita con-sumption of energy is about twenty times that of India, whose population is four times that of the United States. Similarly, the US per capita energy use is six times greater than in China (World Population Balance n.d.). These varying levels of energy consumption reflect in part the unequal use of fossil fuels for industrial and personal use, with the highest levels among the wealthiest nations and the lowest among the poorest.

The uneven distribution of energy con-sumption is beginning to change. Consider that, as recently as 2001, Asia consumed relatively little fossil fuel per capita, but today China and India are among the fastest-growing users of these forms of energy. These countries are developing their indus-trial infrastructures quickly and in the pro-cess are increasing the use of fossil fuels, with the expected effects of greater CO_2 emissions and the anticipation of a significant impact on global warming. Even if the West reduces its energy consumption, that positive step is expected to be offset by increased consump-tion in Asia. We must consider that efforts to curb the use of fossil fuels in the developed world may not reduce the overall effects of greenhouse gases, and global warming will continue to rise. In fact, one of the most vig-orous international debates about reducing greenhouse gases stems from the criticism by less-wealthy nations that wealthier nations are not working hard enough to curb CO_2 emissions while these developing nations increase their consumption as their econo-mies grow. According to UN-sponsored negotiations in 2009, "talks have been dead-locked for months over demands by poor countries that a block of wealthy nations commit to deep cuts in emissions of heat-trapping gases by 2020 while rich countries demand that every nation share the burden" (Max 2009). Debate at the UN Climate Change Conference held in Copenhagen in December 2009 indicated that the issue remains a serious impediment to movement forward to reduce CO_2 emissions.

Inequality and the Sources of Fuel

Consumption patterns are only one compo-nent of inequality regarding energy. Where are fossil fuels found today? Ironically, the regions richest in natural resources consumed by the developed world are themselves often the poorest and least developed regions. We learned earlier in this chapter that peak oil was reached in the United States in the middle of the twentieth century, so to con-tinue to have access to this product it became necessary to access oil drilled in other places where it continues to be available—that is, primarily in developing nations. In these developing nations, the wealth created by oil drilling does not filter down to the average citizen. Internal politics and external control over resources reflect a neocolonial relation-ship that enables the extraction of oil and the support of corrupt leadership in these nations to benefit large, powerful oil companies based in the wealthier, developed nations. These relationships impact the affordability of oil in the developed world but also have a direct effect on the communities from which oil is extracted. While we may be contemplating our transportation choices, a child in Ecuador or Nigeria may be drinking water contaminated by runoff from oil drilling. This possibility is quite real, as illustrated by a case in Ecuador in which oil production over forty years has created significant health issues for local communities. As explained on the ChevronToxico: The Campaign for Justice in Ecuador website concerning the Oriente, a region of eastern Ecuador:

> The oil infrastructure developed and operated by Texaco had utterly inadequate environmental controls, and consequently Texaco dumped 18 billion gallons of toxic wastewater directly into the region's rivers. The contamination of water essential for the daily activities of thousands of people has resulted in an epidemic of cancer, miscarriages, birth defects, and other ailments.... Those who bathe in contaminated rivers report skin rashes. Those who drink the water report diarrhea. In this way, oil contamination has become a constant,

oppressive, inescapable fact of life for thousands of residents of the *Oriente*.

Thus we see significant inequality in the access to and distribution of resources and a great deal of environmental degradation in the process of accessing and refining them, particularly in the health problems for people living in those areas.

Inequality and Climate Change

Inequalities do not stop with the production and consumption of resources; we also must consider climate change caused by this production and consumption. As we know, climate change affects the entire globe, but does it affect some groups more than others? Poverty especially is an important contributor to the unequal impact of climate change. With large numbers of people in poverty, and thus with limited resources, the impact of climate change will be dramatic. Poor people will suffer more from natural disasters, as exemplified in the earthquake that devastated so much of Haiti in 2010. Floods and droughts resulting from climate change

---

 Web Exercise 3.7
Who Is Responsible?

For information on the problems of drilling in Ecuador and the related lawsuit, check these two websites, which present alternative points of view: ChevronToxico: The Campaign for Justice in Ecuador (http://chevrontoxico.com/) and Ecuador Lawsuit: Facts About Chevron and Texaco in Ecuador (http://www.chevron.com/ecuador/). Also, view the photo exhibit entitled "Crude Reflections" on the ChevronToxico website. (http://chevrontoxico.com/news-and-multimedia/2005/0424-crude-reflections).

- What are the different positions presented on each website?
- Who is responsible for the environment and health impact of oil drilling?

The documentary *Crude: The Real Price of Oil* (2009) covers the effects of Chevron/Texaco oil drilling in Ecuador and the lawsuit filed on behalf of Ecuadorians who have suffered from the toxic effects of oil in their communities.

Access the live/updated links at http://www.paradigmpublishers.com/resources/goldbergmedia.aspx

will dramatically affect agriculture, the main livelihood of many of the poor. With limited resources, it is much harder for the poor to cope and recover than for people with more resources. While the poorest nations are the least responsible for creating the problems of climate change, they are likely to suffer the most.

A study by a group of international organizations entitled *Poverty and Climate Change* addressed the linkages of climate change to poverty. Their study of various regions concludes that the populations of the least developed countries will be least able to sustain themselves in the face of droughts, storms, flooding, and other effects of climate change. Developing countries are impacted more than developed countries,

due to the economic importance of climate-sensitive sectors (for example, agriculture and fisheries) for these countries, and to their limited human, institutional, and financial capacity to anticipate and respond to the direct and indirect effects of climate change. In general, the vulnerability is

highest for least developed countries (LDCs) in the tropical and subtropical areas. Hence, the countries with the fewest social and economic resources are likely to bear the greatest burden of climate change in terms of loss of life and relative effect on investment and the economy. (Sperling n.d., 5)

Even in the developed world, the uneven distribution of wealth and resources can have a devastating impact. As Americans, we do not have to look beyond our shores to see how inequality is experienced when environmental disaster strikes. Hurricane Sandy in 2012 was especially devastating for the poor in New York City, where loss of power made daily living in public housing challenging, and loss of wages put many on the brink of financial disaster. The heat wave in the summer of 2011 had a similarly disproportionate effect on the poor, who often struggled to access air-conditioned living space as record temperatures soared above one hundred degrees through July and August in the Midwest and South. When the oil rig in the Gulf of Mexico exploded in

---

 Reading Room 3.3
The Millennium Ecosystem Assessment

This World Resources Institute report includes a section by Daniel Prager and Valerie Thompson entitled "Box 2.1 Findings of the Millennium Ecosystem Assessment: How Do the Poor Fare?" (http://multimedia.wri.org/wr2005/box2-1.htm), which examines the relationship between poverty and climate change. Consider how social inequality is manifest in the problems associated with climate change.

- According to the report, what is the relationship of the problems of the world's ecosystem to poverty?
- Which parts of the world are most likely to suffer the greatest impact from climate change? Why?
- What are some specific examples of the problems the poor will suffer as climate change increases?
- Does it matter who controls resources?
- Do you think these inequalities will be experienced in the United States?

Access the live/updated links at http://www.paradigmpublishers.com/resources/goldbergmedia.aspx

2010 and spilled millions of gallons of oil into the Gulf, the fishing and tourist industries were decimated, taking away the livelihoods of many workers for the foreseeable future. In 2005 Hurricane Katrina devastated the Gulf Coast, especially New Orleans. The poorest residents of New Orleans had the greatest losses. For those without cars, depending on public transportation meant they were unable to leave the city before the extreme flooding occurred in their neighborhoods. The loss of lives, homes, and livelihoods was greatest for the poor. If, as predicted, climate change has the effect of larger and more frequent storms, and more droughts and floods, we can expect the poor to continue to bear the greatest burden of ill effects.

As we have seen, structural inequality, whether global, regional, or local, is manifest in environmental problems much as it is in other areas of society. Where individuals or communities have limited life chances, the effects of environmental degradation exacerbate inequality through a greater impact on the resources needed to sustain life. The irony that an abundance of natural resources in developing regions might have negative impacts on the health and well-being of local populations is an important example of how the unequal distribution of wealth and power maintains the status quo both locally and globally.

Applying Sociological Theory

For a macro understanding of the environmental crisis we can apply the two major structural theories in modern sociology: functionalism and conflict theory. They differ from each other in their approaches to analyzing environmental problems. Both theories examine the groups and institutions that contribute to the shape of society and the distribution of resources and interaction among social entities. As we saw in Chapter 1, functional theory examines how society is structured and how the major social institutions function. It argues that social stability is created by balancing various contending forces such as social institutions and interest groups. According to functional theory, social change occurs when social equilibrium fails due to dysfunction in the social system that requires society to correct the imbalance in order to maintain social continuity.

Conflict theory, on the other hand, presumes that social equilibrium does not exist, and in fact, that societies are constantly changing. The sources of change are found in social inequalities between groups. This theory contends that inequality by its very nature leads to conflict between unequal parties. The resolution of the conflict brings about social change. We now briefly apply each structural theory to the environmental crisis.

Web Exercise 3.8
Inequality and Hurricane Katrina

Read the summary by Susan Cutter (2006) on inequality and Hurricane Katrina in "The Geography of Social Vulnerability: Race, Class, and Catastrophe" (http://wasis.ou.edu/docs /Cutte_2005.pdf).

- What are the effects of Hurricane Katrina on different groups of people?
- How have race and class changed within the population of New Orleans in the aftermath of the hurricane?

Access the live/updated links at http://www.paradigmpublishers.com/resources/goldbergmedia.aspx

The Environmental Crisis: Functional or Dysfunctional?

What functions are served by the use of fossil fuels? There is no doubt that fossil fuels have played an important role in expanding industry and leading us into the modern age. There are clear benefits today in technology, transportation, and lifestyle, such as longer life spans, improved nutrition, and a comfortable material life for many. Because today's industrial infrastructure is dependent on fossil fuels to function, most activities in modern society tie into that infrastructure in significant and complex ways, making it difficult to consider alternative sources of energy. Some functionalists may argue that the environmental crisis serves a function by creating jobs to clean up toxic sites and developing opportunities for research and planning for cleaner energy.

Alternatively, functionalists may argue that the current environmental crisis with depleting resources and global warming is dysfunctional to society. Reestablishing social equilibrium would require rethinking energy consumption, which then challenges our individualistic values and requires a radically different approach that considers changes in every social institution. Retooling for clean industry and dramatically reducing dependency on fossil fuels requires immense changes in engineering and infrastructure that are costly and time consuming. Halting climate change would require that all the major social institutions adapt new ways to function in order to limit their environmental impact. There are already signs of changes in our values, even among large corporations that promote their "green" image. Other examples that may be seen as a social response to a dysfunctional environment include recycling (both personal and industrial), new laws requiring reduction in CO_2 emissions in cars and factories, and buy-local movements, among others.

Conflict Theory: Power and Politics of the Environment

Conflict theorists argue that inequalities in the extraction and use of fossil fuels provide for the well-being of the wealthiest and most powerful segments of society who are least likely to be harmed by that extraction and consumption—at least in the immediate future. Such consumers typically reside in the developed world. Those benefiting the most would be the individuals and corporations who are connected to fossil-fuel industries: oil companies and various other related industries, especially transportation. For example, the five wealthiest global oil companies earned almost $1 trillion in profit since 2000 (House Committee on Natural Resources 2011). At the same time, gas prices rose steeply for consumers.

When scientists argue that access to oil has peaked, the powerful oil and automobile lobbies invest a great deal of money and effort to sustain business as usual, benefiting them economically and politically. They may argue that peak oil is a myth, or that drilling doesn't harm the environment. They may deny the scientific evidence of climate change by presenting alternative data on temperature fluctuation over time. For example, according to Josh Harkinson (2009), "ExxonMobil gives millions of dollars to think tanks, researchers, and media figures to produce and promote phony science purporting to debunk global warming." The politics of oil can be found in election campaigns, public policy, and Congressional hearings. The slogan "drill baby drill" was echoed repeatedly by the Republican candidates during the 2008 presidential election and today one of the most contentious debates between political parties in the United States is about the existence of global warming. Touchstone issues like the 2010 oil-rig explosion and spill in the Gulf of Mexico and the Keystone XL oil-pipeline plans draw responses across the political spectrum. In the case of the Keystone project, extracting oil from oil sands in Canada and transporting them into the United States poses many questions about efficacy, cost, and environmental safety. It has generated debate across the political spectrum.

Those hurt most by the dominance of oil companies are those closest to the sources of oil and other natural resources that are extracted for the benefit of the large companies and rich nations that consume them the most. In order to understand environmental problems from the conflict perspective, we need to understand the dynamics between the powerful energy industries, consumers, and the citizens in oil-rich regions who have few political or economic resources. As we saw in the case of Ecuador earlier in this chapter, the health of people living in oil-rich regions is directly impacted by toxic wastes. For developing nations like China and India, which are increasing their use of fossil fuels, challenging the right of wealthy nations to continue to create large amounts of CO_2 emissions is a reflection of the unequal distribution of power and wealth. From a conflict perspective, the inequalities found in the process of extracting and consuming fossil fuels will continue to create global conflict and increase the likelihood of global warming until these inequalities are addressed.

Symbolic Interaction Theory: Communicating "Green"

Whereas macro theories help us understand the structural issues underlying the environmental crisis, micro sociology is useful in examining how people communicate and interpret the problem. The growth of new "green" vocabulary and new symbolic representations of environmentally friendly companies have become part of our social landscape. Many oil companies today work hard to demonstrate their concern about the environment through various marketing tools. British Petroleum (BP) developed an extensive marketing campaign after the 2010 Gulf oil spill in various media, describing their dedication to cleaning up the spill. From April 2010, the month of the oil spill, through July 2010, BP reported that it spent $93 million on advertising (Daly 2010). How useful was the ad campaign for improving BP's image? Daly reports that according to an AP poll, in June 15 percent of respondents approved of the company's handling of the oil spill, but by August the approval rate had risen to 33 percent. Even before the spill, the BP logo was a bright green and yellow sunburst showing their eco-friendly intent. Many new cars, especially hybrids, use "green" symbols in their marketing and even in the cars themselves to represent their commitment to reduce oil consumption. The all-electric Nissan Leaf is a perfect example of using a symbol of nature to represent a positive environmental image. Clearly oil and automobile companies as well as other industries understand the value of well-placed symbols and intensive advertising to influence the public. A quick search on the Internet in May 2013 for "green industries" resulted in 90,800,000 hits and more than 230 million for "green businesses," indicating its prevalence as an acceptable, even desirable business symbol. Symbolic interaction theory contributes to our understanding of how we communicate and interpret these symbols that have become so recently significant.

Social Construction Theory: Constructing Awareness

The growing awareness of the importance of the environment demonstrates the value of social construction theory. With some exceptions, realizing the importance of treating the environment as a fragile system in need of repair is expressed throughout the culture. Purchasing, marketing, recycling programs, tax breaks, energy-saving appliances, and media attention all recognize that human activities have damaged the environment. The social construction of an understanding of environmental responsibility has begun to permeate our society and is likely to gain more ground with demand for eco-friendly technology and acceptance of new norms that call for social responsibility regarding the environment. Many people consider the environment to be in crisis, so this is a new socially constructed reality that is likely to solidify in the future.

Looking to the Future: Thinking Sociologically about Environmental Issues

It is clear that when it comes to environmental issues—particularly those that are intertwined with oil consumption and global warming—we have much to think about. Most predictions about our environmental future hinge on whether action is swift enough and comprehensive enough to prevent irreversible damage, especially regarding global warming. Each sector of society—from private individuals to international policy makers—has offered solutions.

As sociologists, we have a useful framework through which to view these problems and a vital role to play in the global conversation about environmental issues. There will always be disagreements about environmental crises, but with a comprehensive and critical examination of the issues and an understanding of what is at stake, we will be in a better position to respond effectively.

In this chapter we have examined the structural underpinnings of the environmental crisis. We can see new efforts to improve the environment at every level of society. Communities encourage activities to reduce fossil-fuel usage and CO_2 emissions through increasing public transportation and recycling programs. Corporate and government investment into renewable energy sources like wind and solar power or hybrid cars is growing. For more than a decade the United Nations has sponsored meetings to create viable international policy on climate change. There remain significant challenges; for example, development of policy to cut CO_2 emissions comes up against the reality of unequal consumption patterns and the

---

Web Exercise 3.9
Is It Real?

Despite overwhelming scientific evidence, there is reluctance among some people to believe that we are facing a dire environmental crisis. They argue that climate change is not significant and that the discovery of new reserves of fossil fuels can ameliorate perceived shortages. Many of these people have a vested interest in maintaining our current use of fossil fuels. Whether they are connected to oil or coal companies or the automobile industry, or are politicians whose constituents depend on these resources for jobs, there are powerful people who resist the evidence of the looming environmental crisis. This reluctance is also experienced by ordinary citizens who may not have direct experience with environmental problems because they are not readily obvious to them personally. Watch *How It All Ends* (http://www.youtube.com/watch?v=mF_anaVcCXg) to see suggestions for how to understand the issue at a basic level.

- How can you decide who is right?
- Who has a stake in the position that oil will continue to be available for the foreseeable future?
- Who has a stake in denying global warming?

Access the live/updated links at http://www.paradigmpublishers.com/resources/goldbergmedia.aspx

industrialization of India and China, as discussed earlier in this chapter. Recently, the prospect of clean nuclear energy has been placed in jeopardy as a result of the damage done to the nuclear-power plants during the 2011 earthquake and tsunami in Japan. There are many organizations, including advocacy groups, private corporations, government agencies, and international groups working to keep the planet livable as we know it. One of the newest advocacy groups—350.org—is especially interesting in that it is a grassroots effort organized by scientists with a relatively clear and simple goal of reducing CO_2. It makes the following point about global warming:

> 350 parts per million is what many scientists, climate experts, and progressive national governments are now saying is the safe upper limit for CO_2 in our atmosphere. Accelerating arctic warming and other early climate impacts have led scientists to conclude that we are already above the safe zone at our current 400 ppm, and that unless we are able to rapidly return to 350 ppm this century, we risk reaching tipping points and irreversible impacts such as the melting of the Greenland ice sheet and major methane releases from increased permafrost melt. (350 Science n.d.)

Understanding the environmental crisis requires us to keep up with the science, with organized efforts at local, national, and international levels, and with our own choices. We will soon know if the damage to the environment can be reversed and what role we all play in that effort.

Looking Forward

There are important relationships between the discussion of the environment and other chapters in this book. The next chapter examines problems in the developing world. Having already learned of the inequalities associated with fossil fuels as a resource in the developing world, we will look more closely at the ramifications of neocolonialism, particularly the social fragmenting of communities resulting from unstable governments, poverty, and armed conflict. Environmental problems are exacerbated in regions with weak economies and unstable governments. Later chapters also connect to environmental problems. Regarding health

Web Exercise 3.10
Are You an Advocate?

Many sociologists believe it is important to go beyond analyzing a social problem and choose to advocate for change. Most universities have developed programs to address environmental issues on their campuses. Whether you want to advocate for change or not, consider the following:

- Find out about the recycling program at your university.
- Explore the types of transportation available on your campus and off.
- Is there a student environmental organization on your campus?
- Describe the kinds of programs you think students, faculty, or administrators would implement to improve environmental conditions on your campus.

Access the live/updated links at http://www.paradigmpublishers.com/resources/goldbergmedia.aspx

(Chapter 5), for example, as we saw earlier in this chapter, populations living near sources of fossil fuels run risks of suffering health problems associated with extraction of these resources. It is predicted that some diseases will spread because of global warming, leaving larger numbers of people vulnerable to diseases that are not today typical of the regions in which they live. In the area of technology (Chapter 7), our ever-increasing consumption and discarding of electronics, from computers to cell phones to high-definition televisions, creates an enormous amount of e-waste. Much of this waste is toxic and ends up in dumps in least developed nations, contaminating water and land, but also directly harming people. It is picked over and valuable metals are recycled, leaving behind a compromised environment. Gaining an understanding of the importance of the environmental crisis and its social consequences is imperative as we move through the twenty-first century.

Web Watch

Energy and climate change issues are covered extensively on the Internet today. Scientific reportage is easily found online on a regular basis. Debates about the reality of climate change and oil depletion abound. National and international organizations use the Internet to present compelling scientific evidence of the seriousness of environmental problems. In addition to scientific analysis, there are numerous educational and advocacy websites. Political websites keep the public abreast of the policy proposals and changes in laws regarding these issues. Some of the most comprehensive websites are found on the companion website for this textbook along with a selection of online videos. Here are a few useful websites:

Environmental Defense Fund: http://www.edf.org/

The National Geographic (Environment): http://environment.nationalgeographic.com/environment/

The Nature Conservancy: http://www.nature.org/

United Nations: https://www.un.org/ Search global warming or climate change on the UN website.

US Environmental Protection Agency: http://www.epa.gov/

CHAPTER 4

Crisis in a Fragile World

Child Soldiers, Human Trafficking, and Genocide

The Port-au-Prince, Haiti, earthquake survivor camp.
Source: Fred W. Baker III

January 2010: Yet another natural disaster has struck. This time it is an earthquake in Haiti, the poorest country in the Western Hemisphere. Approximately 250,000 people died and many more were horribly injured. About 245,000 buildings were destroyed or damaged beyond repair along with severe disruptions to livelihoods, communities, and most of the government. The quake registered 7.0 on the Richter scale, classifying it as a "major" earthquake. Other earthquakes have been as strong but not as destructive. Why? Unfortunately for the Haitian people, this catastrophe is a perfect example of the confluence of nature, politics, economics, and media. The physical destruction was compounded by deep poverty, lack of infrastructure, and absence of internal political leadership. Outside assistance was hampered by impassable roads and the lack of medicines or shelter. Wall-to-wall media coverage gave us gripping pictures and accounts of death, destruction, and survival against the odds, helping us see the visible disaster but not always helping us understand the social implications. Even long after the quake itself, there is little rebuilding in Haiti, cultural touchstones such as its world-famous art have suffered, and women experience brutal sexual violence in insecure shelters. How to make sense of this disaster? How does such a poor country exist in the midst of affluence? What can we learn about the developing world to help us understand the fault line that is Haiti? And how does Haiti inform us about the crises in the rest of the developing world?

What does the earthquake in Haiti have to do with global problems of development? And what can sociology offer to help explain the dynamics of inequality that contributed to the dire conditions in Haiti after the earthquake? This chapter examines some of the many problems facing the least developed nations that create crises for governments, economic systems, and people, and that have significant impacts beyond their borders. These crises have important global effects that affect the developed world in direct and indirect ways. In Chapter 2 we learned how the global inequalities that we see today emerged out of historical colonialism and empire building by European nations several centuries ago. The political independence gained by most former colonies by the twentieth century did little to encourage equality in the global economy. Indeed, neocolonial relationships solidified the modern equivalent of colonialism, creating politically unstable regimes, weak economic infrastructures, and disruptions to traditional cultures and communities. Ironically, Haiti, whose most recent crisis is described above, achieved its independence long before most former colonies, yet it remains one of the least developed countries in the world. The impact of the earthquake in Haiti provides a graphic example of the failures created by instability in social institutions that undermine the ability to respond effectively to a crisis. The earthquake demonstrated that although acts of nature are unavoidable, how people prepare for them and respond

to them vary dramatically based on specific social circumstances, especially the physical, economic, and political infrastructures. The earthquake in Haiti was significant by any measure, but the outcome for the people was a great disaster. To understand it we need to look at the global experience of inequality.

In Chapter 3 we applied a sociological analysis to environmental problems, showing the complex connections between nature and society. In this chapter we use sociology to examine other types of large-scale global problems, some of which have their origins in environmental concerns, and all of which are based in unequal social dynamics. We also look at the intersection of major social institutions, culture, and inequality to examine the local and global impact of these problems.

Social Problems in the Developing World: An Overview

Fragile and Failed States

Multiple interrelated crises face the least developed nations. A quick review of the conditions of these nations by such groups as the World Bank, the Global Policy Forum, and the United Nations demonstrates the complexity of applying universal categories to represent what these societies experience. Terms such as *fragile state* and *failed state* represent the relative position of these nations economically and politically in relationship

Information 4.1
Fragile States and Failed States Defined

Fragile states "is the term used for countries facing particularly severe development challenges: weak institutional capacity, poor governance, and political instability. Often these countries experience ongoing violence as the residue of past severe conflict. Ongoing armed conflicts affect three out of four fragile states" (World Bank 2009).

    Failed states "can no longer perform basic functions such as education, security, or governance, usually due to fractious violence or extreme poverty. Within this power vacuum, people fall victim to competing factions and crime, and sometimes the United Nations or neighboring states intervene to prevent a humanitarian disaster. However, states fail not only because of internal factors. Foreign governments can also knowingly destabilize a state by fueling ethnic warfare or supporting rebel forces, causing it to collapse" (Global Policy Forum n.d.).

to other nations and globalization as a whole.

Not only do these countries face daunting structural problems, their vulnerability in the face of natural disasters and environmental problems is made worse by their inability to respond effectively to such disasters to meet the needs of their people. These problems lead to political and economic competition over resources that spill over into traditional conflicts, often along the lines of ethnic and religious rivalries. That instability impacts the rest of the world in numerous ways.

The Developing World and Environmental Problems

Access to natural resources, both for survival and economic gain, constitutes one of the most significant and enduring problems faced by these nations. Indeed, many of the crises in the least developed nations are directly related to the environmental problems we examined in the previous chapter. There we saw how oil is both a necessity for modern life and an increasingly difficult and dangerous resource to access.

Extraction of oil by large corporations from environmentally and socially fragile regions such as the Niger Delta in Nigeria is a case in point. In the Niger Delta the effects of the oil industry on the environment, local economy, and culture have led to increased inequality, instability, and conflict. In 2011 a study by the United Nations determined that it would take twenty-five to thirty years to clean up the oil contamination at an initial cost of $1 billion (UN News Service 2011).

There are many other examples of conflicts that have arisen out of competition for resources that are profoundly impacted by environmental change. Although uneven access to resources is central to the potential for conflict, most situations are more complex than they appear on the surface. Traditional ethnic or religious rivalries—divisions that commonly are remnants of colonial rule and uneven development—have helped highlight the inequalities leading to conflict. Having learned about the likelihood of climate change in Chapter 3, we know that there will be a need to adapt as the earth's temperature increases, and a region's access to essential resources can easily lead to

Web Exercise 4.1
Oil in a Fragile State

Read "Curse of the Black Gold" by Tom O'Neill (http://ngm.nationalgeographic.com/2007 /02/nigerian-oil/oneill-text), and watch the additional video clips on the website on the impact of oil production in Nigeria. This valuable resource creates enormous wealth for oil companies and the government of Nigeria. Overall, though, the impact has been devastating for local communities.

- How has oil production in the Niger Delta impacted local communities economically and culturally?
- What inequalities are exacerbated by the way oil is developed and extracted?
- What are the conflicts between the government, protesters, and rebel groups?
- What connections can be made between these problems and the demand for oil in the West?

Access the live/updated links at http://www.paradigmpublishers.com/resources/goldbergmedia.aspx

internal or cross-national rivalries. Water is a case in point. Scientists predict that global warming will result in floods and droughts throughout the world, and the areas most severely affected will be those that cannot secure adequate water for their populations. Among the most dangerous regions is Kashmir, a region straddling the border between India and Pakistan. There, the Indus River is a major source of water for each country, and access to its water already contains the seeds of conflict. A treaty currently providing for the distribution of water has been honored by both nations for many years, but it is important to consider what might happen if global warming causes water shortages among these densely populated antagonistic nations, both armed with nuclear weapons. A preview of the devastation that might occur in the future was the catastrophic flooding in Pakistan in 2010. Large portions of the country were affected, and many lives and livelihoods were lost. There is fear that economic and political destabilization would contribute to an already fragile infrastructure and government and create opportunities for terrorist organizations to gain greater traction.

Globalization and Social Crises

We now shift from the problems associated with natural resources and the environment to man-made problems, remembering that the global relationships between resources, political systems, and communities are inexorably tied together. In the remainder of this chapter, we examine three specific problems that demonstrate the ways globalization has contributed to the inequalities that have destabilized the most fragile states: child soldiers, human trafficking, and genocide.

These crises are among the most dynamic and widespread problems faced by people throughout these societies as they clearly relate to the unequal distribution of resources and power, and are often exacerbated by natural disasters or environmental changes. They have a profound impact on the people directly experiencing them as well as having global significance. While there are many other important problems, these three serve as examples of the connections between local, regional, and global crises that impact us all. The sociological imagination, concepts such as culture and inequality, and the

Web Exercise 4.2
Water Wars of the Future

Read "The Last Straw" by Stephan Faris (http://www.foreignpolicy.com/articles/2009/06
/22/failed_states_index_the_last_straw) and "The Green Zones" at the *Foreign Policy*
website (http://www.foreignpolicy.com/articles/2009/06/22/2009_failed_states_index
_the_green_zones). The ongoing conflict between Pakistan and India, already quite volatile,
has the potential to be catastrophic if global warming diminishes availability of water from the
snowmelt of the Himalayas, as is expected later this century. Another related, valuable reading
is found in Al Jazeera, "Kashmir and the Politics of Water" (http://www.aljazeera.com
/indepth/spotlight/kashmirtheforgottenconflict/2011/07/20117812154478992.html).

- What is the worst-case scenario if there are critical, long-term water shortages?
- How does the relative economic and political stability in each of the countries impact the
  ability to solve this problem?
- What is the connection between the environmental crisis and the potential for war over
  resources? Immigration?
- From a sociological perspective, what might the impact be on the cultures of each of
  these nations if their conflicts increase over water?

For a broader view of the future of the freshwater supply globally, watch the documentary *Flow:
For the Love of Water.*

Access the live/updated links at http://www.paradigmpublishers.com/resources/goldbergmedia.aspx

application of sociological theory later in the chapter will also illuminate our understanding of these complex issues.

Consider these questions:

- In the case of child soldiers, why does this phenomenon exist? What problems are faced by children who are armed, who may be orphans, and who ultimately might become refugees? How are children reintegrated into society once hostilities end?
- Human trafficking is an international activity that by its nature crosses borders and in which vulnerable people, mostly women and girls, are used in the sex trade and as slave labor. How does the mix of gender and poverty increase vulnerability and encourage trafficking? How might traditional culture be used to further gender

oppression and sexual exploitation of women and girls?
- Examining genocide in its historic context can help us see how groups of people are singled out for destruction within systems of inequality and power struggles. What constitutes genocide and related forms of human destruction?

It is important to keep some things in mind as we explore these crises. First, as sociologists we see that the concept of inequality is central to understanding these issues because of the potential for inequalities to evolve into conflicts. Second, the ease of attaining information on global crises brings the world closer together, with more direct political, economic, and cultural impacts among all nations. Last, as with all the chapters, there are significant connections between the different topics presented in this book. As with the discussion of oil fields in Nigeria, climate change and conflict over water in Kashmir, or the earthquake in Haiti, it is of great value to keep in mind the relationships between this chapter and the others. It is important to recognize how limited resources and unstable social and political institutions increase the chances of disastrous outcomes for people in the least developed parts of the world. The vulnerability of children as participants in war, the experience of human trafficking, and the potential for genocide increase with the destabilizing effects of natural disasters and social upheaval. We will next provide an overview of each of these three crises and then apply sociological concepts and theories to better understand them.

Child Soldiers

In this section we explore the nature of warfare that uses children as soldiers, the breadth of the problem, and the reasons for its widespread practice. Historically, children have played roles in warfare throughout the world, though rarely as major combatants. The widespread use of children starting in late twentieth-century conflicts is unique in the history of warfare, and it persists today despite objections from international bodies like the United Nations and many child-advocacy groups. It is generally agreed among most nations and international organizations that **child soldiers** are those individuals under the age of eighteen who participate in combat or as support for combat. It can be seen as a somewhat arbitrary and socially constructed notion, but across cultures and political entities, there is agreement that the age of eighteen is an appropriate cutoff under which children should not serve as soldiers.

Where Are the Child Soldiers?

Child soldiers are found throughout the world acting in many capacities, both combat and non-combat roles, to support government or non-government armed forces. While their presence is widespread, they are unlikely to be found in stable democratic states. Firm statistics are hard to come by either because governments are unwilling to

 Fast Facts 4.1
Child Soldiers

- Child soldiers participate in about thirty conflicts throughout the world in both state-sponsored and non-state warfare.*
- Up to 300,000 children are child soldiers.*
- Although most child soldiers are teens, some are as young as six.**
- Although both boys and girls have combat roles, girls are more likely to experience sexual violence and rape, and consequently pregnancy.**
- Attempts at rehabilitation after a war ends have limited success.**
- Numerous international organizations work to challenge the use of child soldiers; the lead response is the UN Convention on the Rights of the Child, especially the Optional Protocols.***

Sources: *UNICEF (n.d.); **Singer (2006); ***UNICEF (2005).

Web Exercise 4.3
Case Study of Child Soldiers

Read "Facts and Figures on Child Soldiers" on the Child Soldiers Global Report 2008 website (http://www.child-soldiers.org/global_report_reader.php?id=97). In order to get a fuller picture of the importance of child soldiers, select one country to explore in depth. Consider the following:

- What are the circumstances of warfare in this country?
- What are the basic statistics on the participation of children in warfare in this country?
- How are they recruited?
- What do you think are the long-term consequences for child soldiers in that country?

Access the live/updated links at http://www.paradigmpublishers.com/resources/goldbergmedia.aspx

share that information or because information, especially from rebel groups, is unreliable. Regionally, child soldiers are mostly found in Africa and Southeast Asia but also in Colombia, the Middle East, the Philippines, and Indonesia. Singer (2006, 29–30) found that 68 percent of armed groups that are still in combat or were in recently ended wars used child soldiers, including many children under fifteen years old. Additionally, 18 percent used children twelve years old and younger. While child soldiers are found in both government and non-government groups, they are more prevalent among rebel and political opposition groups and groups involved in ethnic fighting.

Why Child Soldiers Today?

By the mid-twentieth century there were significant changes in the conduct of war. Singer (2006) argues that a traditional code of ethics outlining conduct during war eroded, allowing civilians to be targeted and children to be recruited as combatants. Accompanying these changes we also find increased likelihood of ethnic cleansing and the rise of modern genocide, to be discussed later in this chapter. While children

historically have participated in limited ways during warfare, their smaller size and limited strength, along with requirements for long-term military training, precluded them from having combat roles for the most part.

Today, many of the restrictions regarding strength and training have been eliminated by advances in technology. The majority of weapons used today are lightweight small arms, requiring little maintenance or training, and they are relatively cheap to buy. At the same time their firepower is enormous: "a handful of children now can have the equivalent fire power of an entire regiment of Napoleonic infantry" (Singer 2006, 47). Further, children are easily manipulated and mostly powerless to resist recruitment and participation. Some have been orphaned by war, disease, or natural disasters. Many are never paid for their work. This combination of access to weapons and control over the children by warring adults helps create the vacuum within which the ethics regarding child soldiers are easily ignored.

There are broader considerations regarding the use of child soldiers. Singer (2006) argues that globalization itself encourages the use of child soldiers. The influx of economic domination from outside a fragile nation's borders destabilizes economies and erodes

Movie Picks 4.1
No Childhood at All: A Story of Burma's Child Soldiers

This documentary provides an overview of the complex issues that face Burma (Myanmar) regarding child soldiers, ethnic conflict, and civil war. The film covers aspects of Burmese history and culture to help us understand how war and the use of children in combat have impacted the culture.

Thinking Sociologically

- How has the ongoing war in Burma undermined traditional culture, especially regarding the place of children in society?
- How are the experiences of boy and girl soldiers similar and different?
- What role does ethnicity play in this conflict?
- What options do children have if their communities or ethnic groups are attacked?

Access the live/updated links at http://www.paradigmpublishers.com/resources/goldbergmedia.aspx

traditional cultures and norms. The loss of access to water and impact of other environmental effects increases the likelihood of conflict as groups compete for limited resources. Children also become more vulnerable when natural disasters strike. Diseases such as AIDS compound the instability of economies and cultures. Many of the least developed countries have large numbers of youth with few economic prospects, some orphaned by war or disease, leaving them vulnerable to recruiters from rebel groups or state armies. Additionally, much of today's warfare among least developed nations has less to do with political and ideological differences and more to do with attempts at economic dominance. For example, conflicts over valued natural resources such as conflict diamonds in Sierra Leone (discussed in Chapter 2) and oil reserves in Nigeria are chiefly motivated by hopes for private or state profit.

Not all vulnerable children become soldiers. Some are able to flee their villages and

Reading Room 4.1
Seeing Child Soldiers in a Global Context

Read "Child Soldiers a National and Global Security Issue, Expert Says, April 8, 2008" by Jane Morse (http://iipdigital.usembassy.gov/st/english/article/2008/04/20080408151429j esrom0.5473444.html#axzz2gjIFa9ou). Interviewed for that article, P. W. Singer argues that more attention must be paid to the role of child soldiers in conflict. After reading the article, consider both the larger context of how children can be exploited and the more direct impact on children.

- How is the recruitment of children into warfare similar to recruitment into gangs?

Access the live/updated links at http://www.paradigmpublishers.com/resources/goldbergmedia.aspx

war zones and travel to safer areas, though this does not guarantee their safety or necessarily improve their life chances. Most of these children are separated from their families, have no personal resources, and may be responsible for younger siblings. Some walk long distances to towns or into refugee camps across national borders. Perhaps most significantly, they are abandoned and, as the most powerless members of society, ignored and invisible. The prospect of becoming child soldiers shapes the limited options available to these children, who must make life-and-death decisions in the context of chaos and deprivation.

For children who serve as soldiers, if they escape, or once the conflict is over, they face serious problems of potential rejection from family and community, psychological struggles, and for girls, pregnancies and sexually transmitted disease. There are programs that are more or less successful in helping children reintegrate into their former lives. According to a report by the Child Soldiers International (2008), such programs have helped thousands of children demobilize and reintegrate into society, but many children have not been reached through these programs. Further, even where reintegration programs exist they do not have much political or financial support for ongoing work with children, especially community programs that otherwise would appear to be highly effective. Most programs provide more assistance for boys than girls. In fact, the report points out that because girls may be victims of sexual assaults, they may experience stigma and rejection differently from former boy soldiers, so reintegration programs must take gender into account

---

 Movie Picks 4.2
Invisible Children

Watch the documentary *Invisible Children* about children trying to escape abduction into the war in Uganda (http://topdocumentaryfilms.com/invisible-children/). These children appear to be lucky compared to child soldiers—without homes, even without parental supervision, they find shelter away from their potential captors—but at what price? Consider the disruption of basic social institutions with which these children must contend.

Mixed-Media Extra

Updates on these children and more information about children caught in conflict can be found on the Invisible Children website (http://invisiblechildren.com/).

Thinking Sociologically

Consider how these children try to create structure in their lives despite their desperate circumstances.

- How do the children organize their disrupted lives?
- What social institutions do they try to replicate despite their circumstances?
- Why are they mostly boys?
- Is there a role for American college students in the lives of these children?
- Compare the life chances of these Ugandan children to those of children in your community.

Access the live/updated links at http://www.paradigmpublishers.com/resources/goldbergmedia.aspx

Movie Picks 4.3
Lord's Children

The film *Lord's Children* from PBS *Wide Angle* (http://video.pbs.org/video/1168586547/) examines the experiences of former child soldiers as they go through rehabilitation and reconciliation. It effectively shows the traumatic impact of committing acts of war on children and their families.

Mixed-Media Extra

Explore the resources on the accompanying website (http://www.pbs.org/wnet/wideangle /episodes/lords-children/introduction/1769/).

Thinking Sociologically

- How does being child soldiers impact the other parts of the children's lives when they return to their communities?
- What is the responsibility of family, community, and government toward these children?
- Is there any international responsibility toward these children?

Access the live/updated links at http://www.paradigmpublishers.com/resources/goldbergmedia.aspx

in helping children reintegrate into their communities.

Some children do not return home. Many remain refugees who live for long periods in refugee camps or seek asylum in other countries. Although they may be safer than if they stay home, they still experience deprivation and myriad social problems made more difficult if they are orphaned or removed from their families. The lack of sufficient resources or support makes them vulnerable to stigma and exploitation. When they cross borders they must learn to adapt to different cultures, which we explore later in this chapter. Another area of concern is their vulnerability to trafficking, which may include forced prostitution, domestic and factory work, or other forms of exploitation.

Human Trafficking

Human trafficking, also called trafficking in persons or trafficking in human beings, is one of the richest examples of the effects of globalization. It is clear from our discussion of child soldiers that many children without resources or family support are especially vulnerable to people who would exploit them. But the problem of human trafficking is far wider and encompasses virtually all corners of the world. In this section we define human trafficking, examine trafficking as a factor in globalization, and describe the victims.

Defining Human Trafficking

According to the United Nations, **human trafficking**

> shall mean the recruitment, transportation, transfer, harbouring or receipt of persons, by means of the threat or use of force or other forms of coercion, of abduction, of fraud, of deception, of the abuse of power or of a position of vulnerability or of the giving or receiving of payments or benefits to achieve the consent of a person having

Working child Brickaville, Madagascar,
carrying wood for the family.
Source: Harald Kreutzer, Madagaskar Vision

control over another person, for the purpose of exploitation. Exploitation shall include, at a minimum, the exploitation of the prostitution of others or other forms of sexual exploitation, forced labour or services, or slavery or practices similar to slavery, servitude or the removal of organs. (Omelaniuk 2005, 7)

Human Trafficking and Inequality

The disturbing facts about human trafficking point to specific kinds of inequality in the context of globalization. The patterns of trafficking include moving the most vulnerable people from the most unstable, fragile nations to more affluent parts of the world for the purposes of profit for the traffickers. Thus, the patterns of trafficking associated with globalization are not unlike the removal of natural resources from the least developed nations for the benefit of private corporations and the most developed nations. It is then no surprise that the United States is a major destination for traffickers from around the world. Americans are not immune from trafficking themselves, however. It is estimated that about 300,000 American children risk being trafficked into the sex trade (US Department of Justice 2011). Trafficking for sexual exploitation is a common form of trafficking, thus making women and girls, already the poorest of the poor, especially vulnerable. But even

 Reading Room
Reading 4.2 What Is Trafficking in Persons?

Explore the "Trafficking in Persons Report 2013" from the Office to Monitor and Combat Trafficking in Persons of the U.S. State Department (http://www.state.gov/j/tip/rls/tiprpt /2013/). There is much information on this website including definitions, country rankings, and statistics. Be sure to read the section "Victim's Stories" for personal accounts of the experience. After examining sections of this report, consider the impact trafficking has on individuals, communities, and nations. As a college student, do you feel vulnerable to trafficking? Why or why not?

Access the live/updated links at http://www.paradigmpublishers.com/resources/goldbergmedia.aspx

Fast Facts 4.2
Human Trafficking

- More than 12 million people were trafficked worldwide in 2010.**
- Estimated annual revenue from trafficking: $5 to $9 billion.*
- Trafficking ranks second in the world in generating illegal profits, close to other organized crimes trafficking in drugs and weapons.*
- Women and girls comprise between 56 percent** and 80 percent* of trafficked persons.
- 20,000–50,000 women are trafficked to the United States each year, making it the second-highest destination in the world.*

Sources: *United Methodist Women's Action Network (2008); **US Department of Justice (2011).

more people are trafficked for forced labor, including domestic work, agricultural and factory labor, and other menial unpaid labor amounting to servitude or slavery.

In areas of the world suffering from poverty or conflict, trafficking flourishes. Vulnerable people are recruited in a number of ways. In desperation, family members may sell a child to a trafficker. In other cases, an unsuspecting person may be abducted. However,

in most cases, the potential trafficking victim is already seeking a chance to migrate when she is approached by an acquaintance or lured through an advertisement. Some are tricked into believing they are being recruited for legitimate employment or marriage abroad. Others know they are being recruited into the sex industry and even that they will be obliged to work in order to pay back large recruitment and transportation fees but are deceived about their conditions of work. (World Conference Against Racism, Racial Discrimination, Xenophobia and Related Intolerance 2001)

With the large number of trafficked persons being women, gender inequality is central to understanding the position in which these women find themselves, even if they are aware they are being trafficked. In addition to gender, the relative powerlessness that comes with poverty as well as discrimination against racial and ethnic minorities are also components of trafficking. A close examination of recruitment patterns suggests that "when attention is paid to which women are most at risk of being trafficked, the link of this risk to their racial and social marginalization becomes clear. Moreover, race and racial discrimination may not only constitute a risk factor for trafficking, it may also determine the treatment that woman experiences in countries of destination" (World Conference Against Racism, Racial Discrimination, Xenophobia and Related Intolerance 2001).

Responses to Human Trafficking

Illegal status, lack of language skills, lack of outside support, and intimidation keep the trafficked person dependent on the trafficker. In addition, traffickers benefit from the low risks involved, given the typically lax laws in many countries and the ability

Movie Picks 4.4
The Day My God Died

This film documents the trafficking of girls from Nepal to India as part of the sex slave trade. Many of the girls were abducted with the use of drugs, suffered from multiple abortions, and were infected with AIDS in this highly lucrative business. Several organizations work to rescue the girls and help them try to create a normal life.

Thinking Sociologically

Consider the factors that make these girls vulnerable to trafficking—their personal circumstances, the significance of gender, and the girls' position in the global marketplace.

- Describe the living and working conditions in which the girls must function.
- Is the primary factor in their vulnerability their gender? their age? their poverty?
- How successful are the attempts at saving and rehabilitating these girls?
- Using your sociological imagination, what connections can you as a college student make to the lives of these girls?

Access the live/updated links at http://www.paradigmpublishers.com/resources/goldbergmedia.aspx

to easily move people across international borders. Even where laws exist, penalties for trafficking are light and difficult to enforce. According to the US State Department (2010), the criminalization of trafficking became a reality in 2000, both in the United States with the Trafficking Victims Protection Act (TVPA) and internationally with the UN Protocol to Prevent, Suppress, and Punish Trafficking in Persons, Especially Women and Children, known as the Palermo Protocol. In addition to criminalization of trafficking, governments are encouraged to incorporate the "3P" paradigm: *prevention*, criminal *prosecution*, and victim *protection* (US State Department 2010). However, the lure of cheap or unpaid labor can make governments complicit in trafficking. In 2009,

the world imported and exported billions of dollars in products tainted by forced labor in manufacturing and raw materials procurement, according to the International Labour Organization (ILO). Governments

knowingly and unknowingly deported trafficking victims and failed to provide victims shelter and reintegration services, which led to undercutting investigations and delaying the rehabilitation of victims. They continued to struggle with poorly constructed immigration laws that increased the vulnerability of migrant populations to trafficking. (US State Department 2010)

Although human trafficking is not new, the modern experience of it is fueled by globalization, inequality within and between nations, ease of travel, and limited legal constraints. Those most vulnerable—the poor, women and girls, and citizens of fragile states—are not able to advocate for themselves, while the traffickers can make enormous profits and governments look the other way. This is a crisis for those trafficked, but it also shapes the larger crises that impact the least developed nations, and thus all of us as globalization encourages economic and political interdependence across international boundaries.

Reading Room 4.3
"A World Enslaved"

E. Benjamin Skinner's article "A World Enslaved" (http://www.foreignpolicy.com/articles /2008/02/19/a_world_enslaved) describes the ease with which one can buy another human being today and the prevalence of modern slavery. He addresses the complexity of enslavement as well as the difficulty of ending human trafficking.

- How is the modern experience of slavery different from our understanding of the historical experience of slavery in the United States?
- Why does Skinner say it is problematic if more attention is paid to prostitution than to other forms of slavery?
- What are some of the social and psychological factors that make ending slavery difficult?

Access the live/updated links at http://www.paradigmpublishers.com/resources/goldbergmedia.aspx

Genocide

The term *genocide* is often used to describe killing on a large scale, particularly of a specific group of people, but it is more complex and its historical context helps us understand its relevance today. Genocide is often associated with ethnic cleansing, but they are not the same. **Ethnic cleansing** singles out specific ethnic groups and may include killing, but it generally involves taking over ethnic neighborhoods or regions and forcibly removing members of ethnic groups to "cleanse" an area of that group. In this section we first define genocide and look briefly at its historical origins and then apply it to recent conflicts.

Defining Genocide

The origins of the term *genocide* emerged out of the systematic and nearly successful attempt at exterminating Jews by Nazi Germany in World War II, known as the Holocaust. In an effort to comprehend the destruction perpetrated by the Nazis, the term was created "by combining *geno-*, from the Greek word for race or tribe, with *-cide* from the Latin word for killing" (United

States Holocaust Memorial Museum 2010). As the term gained wider acceptance, the United Nations provided a legal definition of genocide as a crime (see Information box 4.2 on the "UN Definition of Genocide"). Thus, the first use of the term applied to the Holocaust, and all consequent killings on a mass scale have been compared to that historical moment. In this section we will see how modern genocide is tied to issues of development, resources, and ethnic conflicts.

It is important to distinguish between the many mass murders that occur during wars, or conquests, and genocides. Although millions of people have been murdered during conflicts, and often by their own governments, whether these are considered to be genocide depends on whether the definition used is legal or general. Rummel (2002) points out that in addition to the Holocaust, which killed around 6 million Jews, genocide also occurred most recently in Rwanda and Yugoslavia during internal conflicts in the 1990s, as determined by the United Nations. Rummel argues that if we accept a more general definition of genocide, there have been many more examples through the twentieth century and into the twenty-first century. There are ongoing discussions about the use of

Information 4.2
UN Definition of Genocide

In the wake of the Holocaust, the United Nations Convention on the Prevention and Punishment of the Crime of Genocide in 1948 defined **genocide** as "any of the following acts committed with the intent to destroy, in whole or in part, a national, ethnical, racial or religious group, as such:

(a) Killing members of the group;
(b) Causing serious bodily or mental harm to members of the group;
(c) Deliberately inflicting on the group conditions of life calculated to bring about its physical destruction in whole or in part;
(d) Imposing measures intended to prevent births within the group;
(e) Forcibly transferring children of the group to another group.

Source: United Nations (1948, 2000).

the term *genocide* and related terms such as *crimes against humanity*, which do not fit exactly the definition of genocide but which are nevertheless important acts of mass destruction and killing. Rummel suggests that the conditions that make genocide more likely include totalitarian and authoritarian governments, involvement in wars, and the belief that a particular group threatens those in power. These factors may be combined with ethnic and religious animosity, envy, the belief that the society would be more "pure" without the presence of particular minority groups, large-scale "ideological transformation of society," and economic growth (Rummel 2002).

One of the best ways to understand genocide is to examine briefly two recent well-documented cases: Rwanda and Darfur. This helps us understand the particular

 Reading Room 4.4
Defining Genocide

In "Genocide" Rummel provides a detailed discussion of the legal definition, historical roots, and application of sociology to the concept of genocide (http://www.hawaii.edu/powerkills/genocide.ency.htm) Consider the connections between the historical origins of the term and its application today.

• How is it determined if genocide has occurred?
• How is genocide distinguishable from other types of mass murder?
• In what ways are ethnicity, religion, and culture connected to genocide?
• What are the differences between legal, sociological, and general concepts of genocide?

The Genocide Watch website also has many articles and news items about genocide (http://www.genocidewatch.org/).

Access the live/updated links at http://www.paradigmpublishers.com/resources/goldbergmedia.aspx

experience of genocide while also placing it in a global context.

The Rwandan Genocide: Colonial History Fueling Ethnic Hatred

Rwanda is a small nation in Central Africa. It was once a colony of Belgium and the colonial legacy is an important key to understanding what led to the genocide of 1994. Belgium controlled the economy and politics of Rwanda, including creating the formal classification of the major ethnic groups, the Tutsis and the Hutus. Prior to independence, Tutsis were better educated and had greater economic and political power, though the Hutus were larger in number. A complex power struggle ensued after independence,

and in 1994 Hutus massacred 800,000 Tutsis and moderate Hutus in 100 days in an escalation of the ongoing conflict. Lack of international interest in controlling the violence emboldened the Hutu attackers. This was considered an act of genocide because it was perpetrated on a group of people targeted because of their ethnic identity, with the intention of wiping out that group.

Darfur: Sudan in Crisis

Like Rwanda, Sudan was a colony prior to its independence, though its history is a complicated mix of Ottoman and British rule. After independence in 1956, conflict arose between the Muslim-dominated government in the north and the smaller population

---

 Movie Picks 4.5
Hotel Rwanda

This fictional account of the real events that took place during the genocide in Rwanda portrays fear, heroism, and frustration as thousands of citizens were killed because of their ethnicity in the midst of political chaos.

Mixed-Media Extra

Watch *Confronting Evil: Genocide in Rwanda (featuring Alison DeForges)* on the Human Rights Watch website (http://www.hrw.org/video/2009/02/13/confronting-evil-genocide -rwanda-featuring-alison-des-forges). This short video discusses the origin of the genocide in Rwanda and lack of international response. Detailed excerpts from *Ghosts of Rwanda*, a *Frontline* video, can also be viewed online (http://www.pbs.org/wgbh/pages /frontline/shows/ghosts/). It explores the international response as well as the events and aftermath of the genocide.

Thinking Sociologically

Consider how history and ethnic division fueled the genocide in Rwanda.

- How did the history of colonialism in Rwanda encourage the genocide?
- How has the conflict reflected ethnic differences?
- In what ways are these ethnic groups social constructions?
- Why was the international response so tepid?
- Is the conflict in Rwanda considered to be genocide in the United Nations' definition of the term?

Access the live/updated links at http://www.paradigmpublishers.com/resources/goldbergmedia.aspx

of Christian and animist practitioners in the south. Several other factors influenced the economic and political complexity of Sudan, including the discovery of oil in the South and Osama bin Laden's residency in Sudan in the early 1990s. Both of these drew the attention of the West. The interest of the United States in particular was drawn to bin Laden after the bombings of the American embassies in Kenya and Tanzania in 1998 and the terrorist attacks of 9/11.

The recent conflict in Darfur, a western region of Sudan, began in 2003 and involved local rebel groups fighting the central government while contending that the "Arab" government was oppressing "African" citizens, thus framing the conflict in racial terms. Both groups are Muslim. Competition for resources and conflicts between farmers and herders helped distinguish the competing ethnic groups and exacerbated the conflict. The government used a mounted militia called the Janjaweed to suppress the opposition in the Darfur region, resulting in mass murder, destruction of villages, and the movement of thousands of refugees, mostly to Chad. The association of the concept of race with this conflict demonstrates the power of the social construction of race as a reality in Sudan.

The importance of genocide as a global crisis can be explored in many ways sociologically. First, the immediate impact on the people affected by the atrocities must be considered in itself. The suffering of civilians at the hands of armed militias because of their ethnicity is a prime example of genocide, but in order to fully understand it the historical context as well as the connections between nations is vital. The simple fact that Sudan housed bin Laden illustrates that the international connections between even the most local events to the larger global stage are significant. Understanding these events sociologically, along with our earlier discussion of child soldiers and human trafficking, is our next task.

Sociology and the Global Crises

We first briefly review how the two basic approaches to studying society introduced in Chapter 1, micro and macro sociology, are useful. Micro sociology, or **micro theory**, focuses on small groups and the interactions

---

Web Exercise 4.4
The Crisis in Darfur

The conflict in Darfur is compounded by issues of gender, race, and religion and an uneven international response. Read "Darfur Crisis" by the DARFUR Consortium (http://www.darfurconsortium.org/darfur_crisis/timeline.html) and watch the video *On Our Watch* from Refugees International (http://refugeesinternational.org/blog/video/our-watch). After learning more about Darfur, consider the following:

- Is it appropriate to refer to this crisis as genocide? Why or why not?
- How is gender a factor in the conflict?
- Does the distinction between "black" and "Arab" made by people in Darfur represent racial differences or some other division in society?
- Why do you think the international response has been so limited?

Access the live/updated links at http://www.paradigmpublishers.com/resources/goldbergmedia.aspx

among individuals, hence the experience of suffering the loss of life, family, village, and home is an important sociological phenomenon. Micro sociology, especially symbolic interaction theory, offers an analysis regarding how people communicate or fail to communicate across cultures through language and shared meaning, which is important in addressing global issues. Macro sociology, or **macro theory**, uses a "big picture" approach to examine social structures and the interfaces of societies globally. On a macro level the impact on societies of destabilization effects in the form of war, refugees, and international responses demonstrates the global importance of these events. As a structural orientation, it is useful to apply both functional theory and conflict theory, which we revisit later in this chapter.

Because macro sociology takes into account large social structures and the changes that occur within and between them, it can be seen as a global approach to the study of society. It is thus the main approach we take in this chapter. We must remember, however, that although people live within social structures and institutions, if we only understand the crises in this chapter in structural terms, we miss understanding the individuals who are directly impacted by the experiences of being child soldiers or victims of trafficking or genocide. Both micro and macro sociology are important components, then, of our analysis. To more fully understand the connections between individuals and society we start by applying the sociological imagination to global problems.

The Sociological Imagination in a Global Context

The sociological imagination requires us to place ourselves in relation to experiences and events that may seem unrelated to our lives. Keeping Mills's idea of connecting one's personal "troubles" to the larger historical and social context helps us see both the micro and macro applications of the sociological imagination. Consider where college-educated citizens of a stable, affluent society such as ours fit into the global picture. Do you know if the clothes you wear were made by slave labor? Are there domestic workers in your community who are unpaid or who cannot leave the premises in which they live? Would you consider purchasing a diamond without knowing its specific origin? You may have already met refugees from countries in conflict, people who escaped war, trafficking, or ethnic cleansing and genocide. They may be fellow students, neighbors, or members of your religious communities. Consider what you know about them and their experiences. How are your personal "troubles" similar to or different from theirs? Persons traumatized by their experiences who must cope with new surroundings may be hard to relate to unless you understand the historical and social contexts of their experiences. You also might consider your place in the wider global picture that helped generate the problems they face. Policies regarding military action, economic investment, or political support impact whether conflicts continue or end, refugees are supported or neglected, and women and girls are rescued from slavery or are forced to endure it. As more refugees and others from fragile states immigrate to the United States, consider how they impact your access to resources, education, and jobs. What is the effect of large numbers of immigrants on American culture? Applying the sociological imagination enables you to increase your awareness and the role you play in these crises.

The Cultural Context of Global Problems

In Chapter 3 we explored culture in the context of the environmental crisis, and in that

Web Exercise 4.5
Understanding Refugees

The United Nations High Commissioner for Refugees (UNHCR, The UN Refugee Agency) aids refugees around the world. In 2011 there were 15.2 million refugees. Explore the agency's publication, *A Year of Crises: UNHCR Global Trends 2011*, on the UNHCR website (http://www.unhcr.org/4fd6f87f9.html). Consider how the sociological imagination can be used to comprehend the magnitude of the refugee experience.

- Describe the demographic characteristics of the refugees: sex, age, race, or ethnic origins.
- Why are they refugees?
- Where are they seeking to resettle?
- What kinds of support do refugees receive once they find a place to live?
- How can applying both macro and micro sociology add to your understanding of refugees?
- Use your sociological imagination to see in what ways you are connected to the refugee experience.

Access the live/updated links at http://www.paradigmpublishers.com/resources/goldbergmedia.aspx

case we looked internally to the enduring American values of independence and individualism and to how social norms reflect those values. In this chapter, applying the concept of culture to global issues requires us to recognize the variety of cultures across societies. The term **cultural relativity** refers to an understanding that there is a great deal of variation of norms, beliefs, and values across cultures and that no one society can claim that its own culture represents universally correct values and norms. In other words, sociology requires us to step outside our own culture and try to be neutral in analyzing the cultures of groups unlike our own, even when we personally find those cultures mystifying.

Societies in the least developed parts of the world will likely have very different cultural touchstones than those in the developed world. The differences are compounded by the necessity of coping with extreme poverty, war, and intrusions from the outside world as well as the specific histories that

helped shape their cultures. Traditional practices and beliefs come up against increasing poverty and powerful economic and political influences, both internal and external. Their material cultures often lack the basic resources taken for granted in the developed world and their dependency on outside support increases when crises occur. Haiti is an example of a society whose already fragile material culture collapsed with the earthquake in 2010. Most poor nations have insufficient material wealth or technology to develop the resources necessary for recovery from a crisis, and so depend on outside technology and expertise to develop those resources. As we know, material culture impacts non-material culture. When new technology and knowledge enter a traditional society, they impact values and norms in unpredictable ways. Parts of society may embrace change while other parts reject it and become more insular. In any case, cultures inevitably change as societies adapt to new realities.

Reading Room 4.5
Human Trafficking in Haiti

Read Stephen Lendman's article "Child Slavery in Haiti" (http://sjlendman.blogspot.com /search?q=child+slavery+in+haiti). Also read Amanda Kloer's article, "Slavery Will Be the Next Disaster for Haiti's Children" (http://cjaye57.wordpress.com/2010/01/21/slavery -will-be-the-next-disaster-for-haitis-children/). After reviewing the history of child slavery in Haiti, consider how the earthquake has contributed to greater poverty and instability.

- In what ways are children even more vulnerable to trafficking today than before the earthquake?
- What are the material and non-material aspects of the culture that are most relevant in considering Haiti's problems with trafficking?
- Is there agreement across cultures that human trafficking is wrong?

Access the live/updated links at http://www.paradigmpublishers.com/resources/goldbergmedia.aspx

Cultural diffusion refers to the sharing of culture, both material and non-material, as contact is made across the globe. Cultural diffusion is embedded in human history. Introduction of ideas, technology, beliefs, and practices occurs every time people make social contact. Today, cultural diffusion is enhanced by rapid transportation and mass media, especially the Internet, across the entire globe. Whether cultures adapt to or reject aspects of other cultures depends on many factors. In the case of the crises discussed in this chapter, we may see the involuntary imposition of new practices or the disruption of traditional practices causing discomfort, resentment, or dramatic change in normative behaviors. When this happens rapidly, as is often the case today, it can be particularly disruptive to traditional culture and to an individual's sense of self and security. Lack of understanding of traditional culture by outsiders from more modern societies can breed misunderstandings, resentment, and resistance. **Culture shock** refers to the experience of being introduced to new cultures with limited or no familiarity with the new culture. This is likely to happen

with our rapidly changing global contacts, especially when people are forced to leave their own cultures and live in new ones. The situations in which victims of human trafficking and refugees find themselves are often those in which culture shock is likely to be greatest and the ability to adapt most difficult.

Contact across cultures resulting in cultural diffusion and culture shock is common among refugees and other immigrants who leave their countries abruptly to escape dangerous conditions, only to find themselves in a completely different world while also lacking basic personal resources to enable them to comfortably adapt. One of the best examples of this experience involves a group of refugees known as "the lost boys of Sudan." As children orphaned or abandoned during the conflict in their country, and fearing induction as child soldiers, they traveled great distances to refugee camps in Kenya and then immigrated to the United States. Their experiences have been documented in a wide variety of media.

As global issues become more prominent, understanding cultures different from yours becomes increasingly important. In

Movie Picks 4.6
The Lost Boys of Sudan

This documentary describes the journey of a group of young refugees from the war in Sudan. The film explores their experiences in the United States and the culture shock they experience as they try to adapt. Information on the film can be found on its website (http://www.pbs.org /pov/lostboysofsudan/).

Mixed-Media Extra

For an update, watch the *60 Minutes* episode "The Lost Boys of Sudan: 12 Years Later" (http:// www.cbsnews.com/video/watch/?id=50143932n). Also view articles online with updates such as "The Lost Boys of Sudan in Chicago" (http://www.lostboyschicago.com/). To explore gender issues, read the article "Lost Girls of Sudan" on the NPR website (http://www.npr.org /templates/transcript/transcript.php?storyId=12198369) or listen to the audio (http:// www.npr.org/templates/story/story.php?storyId=12198369).

Thinking Sociologically

Using the concepts of cultural relativity, cultural diffusion, and culture shock, think about the greatest cultural differences between the traditional lives of these boys and what they experience in the United States.

- What are the main challenges facing these young men when they first come to the United States?
- What new aspects of material culture and non-material culture are they exposed to?
- How do they adapt to social institutions such as work, education, and religion?
- Why are they all boys?
- How does race factor into their experiences?
- Can cultural diffusion go both ways? Which aspects of their culture impact Americans?
- If you were in charge of a similar refugee program, what would you do differently?

Access the live/updated links at http://www.paradigmpublishers.com/resources/goldbergmedia.aspx

acknowledging cultural relativity, we can expect many differences in both material and non-material cultures across the globe. Most pronounced will be differences between the most developed and least developed nations, not only because of large differences in access to resources, but also in knowledge and skills, and ultimately in values and beliefs. Without knowledge of a group's culture, we can neither understand their circumstances nor respect their values and belief systems. As organizations, governments, and corporations from developed nations invest in and otherwise impose themselves on these least developed nations, misunderstandings and conflict are likely to occur.

It can be challenging to retain a position of cultural relativism in the face of problems such as those introduced in this chapter. When do traditional practices become unacceptable in a universal sense? When is it appropriate to intervene? It can be a difficult task to balance respect for another culture, on the one hand, with intervening and preventing certain activities within that culture that may harm people, on the other hand. Although cultural diffusion is a neutral concept, if one group is more powerful and can impose its beliefs and practices on another, diffusion becomes skewed to the advantage of the more powerful group and thus it changes the social dynamics in important ways. Understanding inequality in the context of global issues is central to a sociological analysis of the issues presented in this chapter.

Inequality: The Global Context

Inequality is at the heart of the problems facing the least developed nations. Poverty is embedded in the relationships these countries have with the rest of the world. The intractable problems of inequality are encapsulated in the irony that removing resources needed by the developed world often impoverishes the local populations in these least developed societies, or endangers their health. In addition to the overarching economic and political inequalities that define these nations, there are specific areas of inequality that need examination: internal class inequality, gender inequality, and race and ethnic inequality. These contributions to inequality impact life chances in important ways and complicate the ability to fully comprehend the experience of inequality. Our task is to examine these inequalities in order to understand the limited life chances with which people in these societies live.

Class Inequality within Fragile Societies

When we think of the global problems presented in this chapter, we mostly consider the inequalities between societies exacerbated by the exploitation of natural resources and people by outside corporations and nations, but that is not the full picture. Inequality and conflict are displayed internally as well. Small groups of wealthy and powerful citizens within these fragile states control most of the internal wealth. They may have gained their positions from a mutually beneficial neocolonial relationship with the developed world, and they continue to thrive economically and politically by virtue of both that relationship and their own entrenched power within their borders. The rest of the population is often poor and powerless, leaving a small middle class and an enormous gap between those at the top and those at the bottom. Often the most powerful people are also the most corrupt and politically ruthless and they are able to maintain their positions in

---

   **Reading Room 4.6
"Why Are We Still Poor?"**

Read this 2009 article by Lord Aikins Adusei, which asks important questions about corruption and the collusion of developed nations and international banks and corporations in keeping most citizens of African countries poor while enhancing the wealth of political leaders (www .modernghana.com/news/218434/1/why-are-we-still-poor.html).

- How does corruption impact a nation's stability?
- What is it about the relationships between the developed world and the least developed nations that contribute to inequality?
- How does social class inequality in the United States differ from inequality in least developed nations?

Access the live/updated links at http://www.paradigmpublishers.com/resources/goldbergmedia.aspx

part from support from outside investors and other countries with an economic or political interest in the region. The gap between rich and poor, and the lack of democracy, create the potential for conflict, so regimes are often repressive. Indeed, it is the very lack of power, both political and economic, that makes so many people vulnerable to the problems we presented earlier in this chapter.

Conflicts resulting from such inequalities burst onto the international scene in 2010 and 2011 when demonstrations for jobs and democracy rocked the countries of Tunisia, Egypt, Yemen, and Libya, the outcomes of which remain to be seen. These conflicts, and especially the ongoing civil war in Syria, have engulfed the Middle East and drawn worldwide attention.

Gender Inequality

We have seen how gender is a factor in all three of the problems we have addressed in this chapter. In the case of child soldiers, girls' roles differ from those of boys in important ways. There are fewer girl soldiers and fewer still in combat. Girls' support roles reflect a distortion of traditional gender expectations that are forced on them, often involving rape and other sexual relations with older soldiers, sometimes resulting in pregnancy. Similarly in the case of trafficking, women and girls are abducted, sold, and enslaved for a variety of work, including the sex trade where their exploitation often leads to pregnancies, multiple abortions, and diseases such as HIV/AIDS. In these cases, gender plays a pivotal

---

 Movie Picks 4.7
Osama

This fiction film, based on the lives of real women and girls when the Taliban were in power in Afghanistan, depicts the humiliation and physical destruction suffered by women and girls in a toxic mix of traditional patriarchy and distorted interpretations of Islam under Taliban rule.

Mixed-Media Extra

Visit the website of The Revolutionary Association of the Women of Afghanistan (RAWA) and explore the news stories and historical events described on the website (http://www.rawa.org/index.php). See especially the section entitled "Afghan Women Under the Tyranny of the Brutal Fundamentalists" (http://www.rawa.org/women9.htm). Also watch *Sosan's Story: Domestic Violence in Afghanistan* to explore the limited options women victims have to get away from violent family members (http://www.cultureunplugged.com/documentary/watch-online/play/9622/Sosan-s-Story-Domestic-Violence-in-Afghanistan-).

Thinking Sociologically

- In *Sosan's Story* how does gender inequality impact the ability to meet basic physical and social needs?
- How are men affected by the extremes of gender inequality?
- Why did the Taliban resort to extreme treatment of women and girls?
- After reviewing the RAWA website and *Sosan's Story*, do you see changes in gender inequality after the Taliban rule ended?
- Is it okay for women to be exploited if the culture condones it?
- Does *Osama* experience a form of human trafficking similar to the girls in *The Day My God Died* presented earlier in the chapter?

Access the live/updated links at http://www.paradigmpublishers.com/resources/goldbergmedia.aspx

role in their experience, as women and girls are the most disadvantaged and vulnerable groups in traditionally based patriarchal societies.

Race and Ethnic Inequality

When examining race globally it becomes clear that there is no universally accepted criteria for determining a person's race. It is a social construct tied directly to the particular history and experience of a given society. Although ethnicity is associated with culture and language and thus is more readily understood, in real social experience there is often an overlap between the two concepts, as we saw in Chapter 2. As sociologists we must take into account the historical experiences that help define race in any given society and the importance of ethnicity in the lives of people. Inequality derived from or contributing to conflict associated with race or ethnicity has resulted in a variety of destructive outcomes. Politically or economically unstable countries are especially vulnerable to conflict of this sort. If limited resources and a fragile state make people insecure, and if inequality is pronounced, devastating conflicts can flare up. The most explicit and dramatic examples of race and ethnic inequalities are found in the experiences of ethnic cleansing and

genocide. As we have seen in the complex cases of Rwandan genocide and ongoing conflict in Sudan, ethnic differences fuel the distrust and hatred that make it easy for people to be manipulated into serving the interests of one or the other of the conflicting sides. There are many other experiences of ethnic cleansing and violence that do not meet the definition of genocide, but they are instructive and serve as examples in which ethnic conflict is applied in power struggles. In the summer of 2010, for example, attacks against ethnic Uzbeks in Kyrgyzstan resulted in killing or displacing many people.

As factors in global inequality, class, gender, race, and ethnicity present a complicated world. It is all the more difficult to understand this world across cultures and geographic, political, and economic boundaries, even despite the ability to access information about events quickly through the media. We next use what we have learned so far and examine our findings using sociological theory.

Applying Sociological Theory

Given the nature of global inequalities, conflict theory contributes significantly to our understanding of the crises in the developing

---

 Watch Online 4.1
Ethnic Violence in Kyrgyzstan

A Human Rights Watch video shows how members of ethnic groups are singled out and punished for their ethnicity. Watch *Ethnic Violence in Kyrgyzstan* (http://www.youtube.com /watch?v=942roKSoL1o). The fallout from these attacks includes food shortages, burned neighborhoods, and a mass exodus from affected areas. Consider the relationship between ethnic conflict and political instability. Find additional information on ethnic violence on the Human Rights Watch website (http://www.hrw.org/).

Access the live/updated links at http://www.paradigmpublishers.com/resources/goldbergmedia.aspx

world, but we can also learn a great deal by applying functional theory, especially as it pertains to social institutions in their attempts to provide stability and meet the needs of society. Using both theories provides a broader understanding of the problems described in this chapter. We look first at functionalism, then conflict theory. Later we use the micro theories of symbolic interaction and social construction theory to better understand the crises facing a fragile world.

Functionalism and Social Institutions

We know from previous discussions that functionalism emphasizes the importance of equilibrium, or balance, in providing stability to a society, and that at any given point in time we can examine the stabilizing forces at work in social institutions. There can be little stability in fragile or failed states, so functionalist theory would argue that these are dysfunctional societies that will of necessity eventually find a new equilibrium if they are to survive. Social change is a result of loss of equilibrium, so in the view of this theory, these societies face change on a large scale. Unlike conflict theory, it does not make clear the role that inequality or conflict specifically plays in causing change. The weakness of the theory becomes quite pronounced when we see how seriously unstable are the least developed nations as evidenced by our discussion of child soldiers, human trafficking, and genocide. Can societies become more stable while also confronting internal civil rebellions and outside influence? Further, it is not clear that understanding the instability of these societies as only dysfunctional helps move in the direction of greater stability. However, functional theory can provide much insight even in the most unstable societies by looking at the major social institutions. These institutions provide the social infrastructure of every society, so when they fail, the infrastructure is weakened, societies become fragile, and people suffer. We

next examine briefly the major institutions of family systems, economic institutions, politics, education, and religion.

Family systems are important in all societies but they are especially central in the least developed nations where traditional family and kin networks meet the essential needs of most members of society. In all societies, families serve as stabilizing forces not only for their members but for society as a whole. Their purpose is to provide for the legitimate reproduction of members of society, the protection and socialization of its members, basic economic functions, and the passing on of culture. Thus, the breakup of families through extreme poverty, war, or disease, or the necessity of immigration under difficult circumstances, serves to undermine the very aspects of family life that would normally provide stability. As we saw, child soldiers were left unprotected from recruiters precisely because their parents were dead or because they were separated from family members by the chaos of war. In the case of human trafficking, families typically cannot and sometimes will not protect members from being sold or enslaved, thus often permanently breaking family bonds. By its very nature, genocide destroys families in whole or in part and thus contributes to destabilization of society. Family disintegration is perhaps the most devastating experience for people in traditional societies because it has traditionally been the most stabilizing and enduring institution.

Economic institutions provide for the production and distribution of goods and services. When valuable natural resources are taken away and labor is exploited, many people struggle economically. As we have noted before, the unique circumstances in the developing world of having significant valuable resources from which the population does not benefit lead to large-scale poverty from which individuals and even nations cannot escape. These deeply poor people are most vulnerable to trafficking, especially if they are young and female, as these are the poorest and least powerful members of these societies.

We have seen how important colonialism and neocolonialism have been in shaping the politics of the least developed nations. Colonialism imposed outside political control, and following independence in many countries political inequality continued with despotic leaders who were beholden to outside investors or committed to creating their own vast wealth by exploiting citizens and controlling them through brutal dictatorships. As we saw in the examples of Rwanda and Sudan, the instability of political institutions with power struggles, civil unrest, and outside pressure contributes to maintaining instability rather than resolving it.

Education, both formal and informal, serves the function of preparing members of society to fill important social roles in each generation. When people are embroiled in conflict and are deeply poor, education takes a backseat. The upheavals of war may result in the closing of schools and even in the punishment of teachers and students. For example, the ongoing turmoil in Afghanistan is reflected in its literacy rates among youth fifteen to twenty-four years old. According to UNICEF (2010) the literacy rate in Afghanistan between 2003 and 2007 for male youth was only 40 percent and for female youth, 18 percent. In many of the least developed countries, education is limited for the poorest sectors of the population even in times of relative stability.

Religion provides a systematic way for people to express their beliefs in the sacred, their understanding of life and death, and their place in the universe. Religious beliefs and practices are deeply embedded in culture. Some conflicts in the developing world are about religion, but many are not. In fact, sometimes religious persecution is a stand-in for power struggles for which religion is a useful enticement to people to join a movement. The civil war that broke up Yugoslavia

in the 1990s is a prime example of a power struggle between religiously affiliated ethnic groups. The Serbian ethnic cleansing and genocide against Bosnian Muslims resulted in dramatic changes in the political landscape of that region. We can also see the role that religion takes in helping people cope with disaster. For example, after the 2010 earthquake in Haiti, many survivors relied on their religious beliefs and practices to cope.

Examining social institutions helps us understand the intricate experiences that bind a society. When problems arise in one institution, they are all affected. Conflicts that disrupt education also affect the ability of someone to make a living. The loss of a job impacts the fate of a family. War disrupts all institutions on which people rely. Religious and political conflicts often go hand in hand. While functional theory does not explain the relentless forces of change that cause social disruption, or those that transform society, it can help us see the importance of social institutions in meeting the needs of society. We now consider the applications of conflict theory with its analysis embedded in conflicts arising from inequalities.

Conflict Theory: Inequality Results in Conflict

As we have seen repeatedly in this chapter, significant conflicts abound in the areas of the globe that are least developed. Conflict theory argues that all social dynamics involve inequalities, large and small. In our discussion of inequality earlier, we saw how a person's social class, gender, race, or ethnicity often determines the type of inequality experienced and its severity. When inequalities interfere with the ability to meet social and political needs, serious conflict is likely. In the cases presented in this chapter of child soldiers, human trafficking, and genocide, we are looking at major systems of inequality that force people into intolerable, even fatal, situations. Where such inequality exists, people are driven to resolve those inequalities through conflict.

The most extreme examples today come in fragile and failed nations where civil unrest and power struggles are central. Conflicts in the least developed nations differ in important ways from conflicts in the developed nations. Most developed nations have relatively stable economies and political structures, enabling the conflicts to be resolved with little long-term damage to basic institutions or disastrous effects on people. In contrast, those living in the poorest, least stable states face significant life-altering challenges every day. Many of these challenges are imposed by drastically unequal economic circumstances, often related to struggles over control of natural resources. The experiences of becoming a child soldier and killing or being killed; of being trafficked for slave labor or sexual exploitation; or of murdering people because of their ethnicity or risking being murdered for yours, can best be understood as conflicts resulting from severe inequalities. As long as those sorts of inequalities persist, conflicts will continue to destroy the social fabric.

Social Construction Theory: Defining Social Context

This theory is especially valuable when looking at the variety of historical and cultural experiences across the globe. Social construction theory argues that what people know and experience is shaped by their different social locations over time. With the historical impact of the colonial experience on most of the developing world, we must understand how that experience shapes people's understanding of time, place, and even identity. Each former colony has a unique experience with its colonial past, as does each former colonizer. To understand the present circumstances of each area of turmoil, one has to understand the social construction of the past and its influence on the present. Additionally,

different material and non-material cultures shape one's understanding of the world, providing multiple perspectives.

Specific examples from this chapter demonstrate the value of social construction theory. In the case of child soldiers we learned that most nations and international bodies have determined that a child soldier is someone under eighteen years old who serves in a military capacity. Why that age? Why not seventeen or nineteen? There is a current agreement among most developed nations today that eighteen marks the age at which people can make informed decisions, but this has not always been so, nor is it true across the globe today. In the United States, one can join the military and vote at eighteen, evidence of our confidence in a person's ability to make adult decisions, but eighteen-year-olds may nonetheless be prevented by law from drinking alcohol. This irony is not lost on college students. Further, these age limits have varied over time. They are not based on scientific evidence but rather on socially determined criteria that have only recently become an international norm. Although pressure to limit participation in war has not ended child soldiering, it has brought the notion to light. International bodies may condemn it, but thousands of children still perform the duties of soldiers because it serves a purpose. Similarly, human trafficking can be seen as a social construction, especially regarding child labor, a widespread practice throughout the world. Some people see child labor as exploitative while others see it as the only way to support their families.

Another example of the importance of social construction theory lies in the social definitions of race and ethnicity as they apply to ethnic cleansing and genocide. As we saw in Chapter 2, there is no confirmed scientific definition of race nor is there universal agreement on the number of races in the world. Sociologists generally agree that only by seeing race and ethnicity as social constructions are we able to understand them.

In the United States we are accustomed to using biological markers such as skin color to organize our ideas about race, but they are meaningless without an understanding of our historic experience of slavery. In that sense, race is a useful concept because it is a social construction that places it in time and in a cultural context. Race is real because it is socially significant.

The experience of genocide provides a useful conduit by which we can analyze the creation of race as a social force. Since genocide is defined in clear terms by the United Nations, we then can determine whether genocide has been committed based on whether a group of people defined by their race or ethnicity has been targeted for persecution or even death. But who defines a group as a race or ethnic group? These terms mean different things in different societies based on historical and cultural experiences. In Rwanda, it was generally agreed that the slaughtering of the Tutsi ethnic group by the Hutu majority constituted genocide. Exploring the historical relationships of these two groups, the impact of colonialism, and their struggle for power after independence helps us understand the conflict as genocide. This is not as clear-cut in Sudan regarding the conflict in Darfur. It is hard for outsiders to understand the differences between the groups identified by the Sudanese as "blacks" and "Arabs" (especially since both groups are Muslim), but the differences clearly matter much to the Sudanese themselves. The sociological perspective is beneficial in that it appreciates the social context in which these concepts are constructed.

Symbolic Interaction Theory:
Communicating Difference

Most of this chapter has looked at the overarching structural issues regarding the crises facing the least developed nations, but we cannot forget that individuals suffer through these crises. Many of the films and web exercises showed the experiences of individuals. To fully appreciate the social dynamics involved, we must also see who is suffering and how they suffer and the role of social interaction in describing that suffering. Language is a person's main source of communication and so it gives us information necessary to be part of a group. Our earlier discussion of the definition of genocide points to the power of language to shape how we see the world around us. International efforts to agree on a definition are important to guide world bodies in addressing genocide as a global concern. For example, labeling—that is, what we call people—has profound social effects. When people are targeted for discrimination because of their identification with their ethnic group, the symbolic representation is powerful and effective. For example, the label "cockroach" was applied in the Rwandan genocide to dehumanize people and unleash great suffering because of ethnic identity. Labels, language, and other symbols all serve to represent conflicting sides in warfare, in human trafficking, and most clearly in genocide.

Conflict and Reconciliation: The Hope for Future Stability

There seems to be no end to global crises both because of limits to the efforts to control conflicts and because of the lack of commitment to resolve the extreme inequality that breeds deep poverty. Competition for resources, ethnic conflicts, and the effects of natural disasters all seem to work against improvement for the world's poorest people. It is very hard for the average person in more developed nations to understand the problems a poor woman in Afghanistan faces, or the people of the Niger Delta who have lost their livelihoods. Our understanding of the reasons for conflict in Rwanda or Sudan is limited by the news relegated to the back pages of newspapers unless we seek out the information to help us know why these and other conflicts persist. Without that understanding, the crises of child soldiers, human trafficking, and genocide remain mysteries to us. We need to apply the sociological imagination first to see our connection to these issues, for they seem so far away and foreign to us. But they are not really so far away. If we can't learn from the current crises, what can we expect in the future?

On the positive side, among the most promising recent activities are the attempts at reconciliation after conflicts have ended. Are these examples of peaceful resolution of conflict and reconciliation valued and useful actions? Do they serve to inform other societies in conflict?

Reconciliation efforts demonstrate that even in the aftermath of genocide, social institutions can stabilize and perform the functions necessary for social cohesion. There are many organizations and individuals who advocate on behalf of victims who have suffered in the global crises described

in this chapter. Exploring those efforts is an important piece of understanding the big picture.

Despite the efforts of advocacy groups and international organizations, the world continues to experience extremes of inequality, exploitation of the poorest and least powerful, power struggles, and extraction of valued resources for the benefit of the developed world. As the world gets smaller, all corners of the globe will continue to be affected by these dynamics. A sociological understanding of the problems as we move through the new century is vital to finding our place in the world as a society and as individuals.

Looking Backward/ Looking Forward

At the beginning of the chapter we read about two examples of problems experienced in the least developed nations. The effects of oil drilling in Nigeria and the potential

---

 Web Exercise 4.6
Reconciliation in Rwanda

After the genocide in 1994 Rwandans decided to actively seek reconciliation. Trials of the perpetrators of mass murder were conducted. As a result some were imprisoned while others returned to their communities. Watch these two videos: *Rwanda Today: Rising from the Ashes* (http://www.unmultimedia.org/tv/21stcentury/detail/1907143222001.html) and *From Child Soldier to International Prosecutor* (http://www.youtube.com/watch?v=fxjPMDS09q0). Further details about reconciliation in Rwanda can be found in the article "The Justice and Reconciliation Process in Rwanda" (http://www.un.org/en/preventgenocide/rwanda/pdf/bgjustice.pdf) and on the website, "National Unity and Reconciliation Commission of Rwanda (http://www.uri.org/cooperation_circles/detail/nurrwanda). Other nations have also gone through a reconciliation process.

- Do you think reconciliation is possible in every society?
- Which cultural characteristics best lend themselves to this process?
- Which sociological theory best explains the success of reconciliation? Why?
- Does reconciliation help eliminate the inequalities that fueled the conflicts?

Access the live/updated links at http://www.paradigmpublishers.com/resources/goldbergmedia.aspx

Web Exercise 4.7
What Can One Person Do to Help Resolve a Social Problem?

While the problems presented in this chapter may seem insurmountable, one person or an organization can make a difference. The International Criminal Court works to prosecute war crimes. Watch the POV documentary *The Reckoning: The Battle for the International Criminal Court* for an in-depth look at the history of the court and its impact on war crimes in various parts of the world.

Also watch the videos *Nepal: Women on the Move* (http://www.youtube.com/watch?v =pyvG2DhQb7Q) and *Rwanda: Lessons from a Hero* (http://www.youtube.com/watch?v =q2WFMtJUVz0). Although one story is about human trafficking and the other is about bravery in the face of genocide, they share a common thread of the importance of individual effort and commitment and how that can change people's lives.

- How can micro and macro sociology help us understand the experiences in these videos?
- Using your sociological imagination, explain how individual heroism can affect social outcomes.

Access the live/updated links at http://www.paradigmpublishers.com/resources/goldbergmedia.aspx

conflict over water in Kashmir are only two of the many crises facing fragile states that are tied to the environmental crisis. The crises described in Chapter 3—oil depletion and climate change—affect everyone, but not equally. In the case of oil resources in unstable nations, we find specific problems associated with the exploitation of local workers, the loss of local livelihoods, and the endangered health of local communities. Regarding access to water, a universal problem, the poorest nations may be the first to suffer the consequences of limited supply, and they may resort to conflict over this essential resource. We need to understand how the problems of the environment are tied to these fragile societies. When conflicts result in these situations, the risk of war, the use of child soldiers, human trafficking, and even genocide can be projected as real possibilities, for they are already realities in large portions of the least developed nations. Societies on the brink can easily decline into chaos when their already fragile states are harmed by environmental destruction.

As we look toward Chapter 5, which addresses health issues, we must keep in mind the vulnerability of people from fragile states. In general the greater the instability, the less likely health systems can work effectively. We will see that infectious diseases like HIV/AIDS have devastating effects on families, communities, and nations, for example. Even in the United States, the inequality of health-care delivery is significant. In later chapters we tackle the issues of terrorism and technology, which have global implications in a number of respects. If you keep this chapter in mind as we go forward, you will gain a greater understanding of the scope of the crises we face both globally and domestically.

Web Watch

The Internet plays an instrumental role in providing information from all over the world so that people are now routinely exposed to ideas and experiences once reserved for only the most traveled and educated. There are especially great benefits in accessing the resources on these pages to broaden our understanding of the crises of the developing world about which we might otherwise have little knowledge. The crises discussed in the chapter are especially likely to change rapidly as conflicts expand or are resolved, making the Internet especially useful. Following are online resources included in the chapter as well as additional resources that may be of interest.

Amnesty International USA: http://www .amnestyusa.org/

"The Day My God Died": http://www .pbs.org/independentlens /daymygoddied/

Genocide Watch: http://www .genocidewatch.org/

Global Policy Forum: http://www .globalpolicy.org/

Human Rights Watch: http://www.hrw .org/

IRIN: humanitarian news and analysis, a project of the UN Office for the Coordination of Humanitarian Affairs: http://www.irinnews.org/

International Labour Organization: http://www.ilo.org/global/lang-en /index.htm

United Nations: http://un.org/

United Nations 21st Century Television Series: http://www.un.org/av/ unfamily/21stcentury.html

World Bank: http://www.worldbank.org/

CHAPTER 5

The Crisis in Health and Health Care

Obesity, HIV/AIDS, and Health-Care Reform

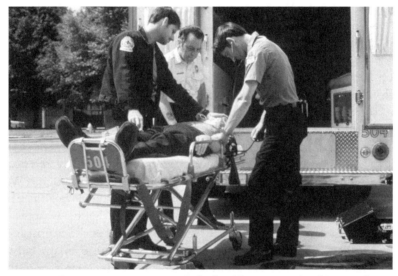

Every society creates ways to meet the health-care needs of its members,
but not every need is met equally.
Source: Centers for Disease Control and Prevention

*Imagine an overcrowded health clinic with people patiently waiting hours, some-
times days, to see the overwhelmed doctors, nurses, and dentists who perform
examinations and procedures in temporary structures. Haiti? Sub-Saharan Africa?
Southeast Asia? Actually, it's a medical expedition in America. The volunteers for
Remote Area Medical serve all over the world, but today 60 percent of their work
is done in the United States. They provide medical, dental, and eye care for thousands of the working poor—under- or uninsured Americans. Residents of Virginia,
Tennessee, Kentucky, California, even Washington, DC, have received free health
care from this volunteer organization. Who are the people receiving help? Why
does this need exist? When does a personal health crisis become a social crisis?*

Every society has ways to provide for the health and well-being of its members. Whether with folk remedies or sophisticated technology, traditional herbs or modern pharmaceuticals, health-care specialists perform the healing arts in all human societies. Health care is especially significant in modern society, given the strides made in improving overall health, its great expense, the number of people engaged in the health-care industry, the economics and politics of health care, and relative access to effective treatment. In fact, many sociologists consider health care a social institution in itself because of its central role in so many areas of life today. In sociology the analysis of health and health care focuses on the social experience of health and illness, the patterns of diseases in various populations, the significance of the social factors associated with illness, and the inequality of access to care based on factors such as class, gender, race, and ethnicity. Fields such as medical sociology and sociology of the body explore various aspects of health and well-being to provide the social context for the health crises people face.

As we have seen in the opening vignette, even in a technologically advanced and wealthy country, access to care is uneven. Regardless of one's station in life, serious health problems constitute a crisis for the individual. For those without adequate access to health services, that crisis may become a catastrophe that profoundly affects a person's life chances, indeed the chance to survive at all, and this crisis expands to family members, communities, and the society as a whole. Thus, when examining how society addresses problems of health and health care, we can see a social crisis of importance beyond the individual. The need for basic services, the astronomical costs of care, and the spread of new diseases and health problems make for a crisis throughout society that can potentially affect the social order.

This chapter begins with a brief overview of health and health care. We then focus on three areas of the crisis: the obesity epidemic, HIV/AIDS as a domestic and international crisis, and the status of health-care reform.

Obesity and HIV/AIDS have been widely described as crises both in the United States and globally. They have potentially terrible consequences for people who experience these health problems. Both have profound effects on the life chances of those afflicted and their families, but they also can overwhelm health-care providers and raise the cost of care to amounts that can potentially destabilize health-care systems. The cost to society is also significant in terms of providing treatment and in loss of production due to the inability to work while ill. We will examine the trends in obesity and HIV/AIDS and look at both the causes and the consequences of these problems. These areas are only two of the serious health problems we face, but studying them will give us an opportunity to utilize sociological tools to understand how health issues are social in nature, and not simply physical problems requiring medical solutions. We will then explore the issue of health reform in the United States. Finally, we apply sociological concepts and theories as in earlier chapters and consider the overlaps between health crises and other crises presented in this book.

A sociological study of the crisis of health and health care focuses on the social contexts in which health problems are experienced, taking into account both physical and social conditions that enable us to see health and disease trends. Sociologists trace the course of illness, treatment, the individual, and social responses, and even political and economic manifestations. Although the experience of being sick is a social and personal one, understanding disease takes into account many factors that determine potential outcomes for those who are ill, their families, and even society at large. Trends in diseases are often important indicators of a variety of environmental and social factors that must be part of our understanding of health. For example, people with the same medical diagnosis who receive treatment from a private doctor will experience their disease differently from those who must seek public care as seen in the vignette above. The field of **epidemiology** focuses on the connections between illnesses as medical concerns and the social factors that contribute to the patterns diseases take in various populations. As in the case of HIV/AIDS, the impact of the disease goes much further than the physical nature of the virus would indicate. The same is true of the issue of obesity, in which physical and social elements are intertwined in important ways.

By seeing disease as a social phenomenon, we acknowledge it as a social construct that we need to keep in mind as we explore obesity and HIV/AIDS. Because health and illness are usually defined in medical terms, we rarely question the definition upon which a diagnosis is based. However, we will see later in the chapter the importance of social construction, even in the medical definitions of these conditions. The social construction of disease matters because how we address the concern—whether and how it is treated—and the potential for stigmatization contribute to the social context of disease, which is ever-changing. The same is true of most diseases once we understand the social lens through which we understand health and illness.

Brief Overview of Health and Health Care

Before we examine health trends, it is worth taking a few minutes to consider your place in the overall picture of health and health care. As a college student, you may have experienced serious health issues, but more likely you take your health for granted and see yourself as a low health risk, as do many young adults. Are you a healthy weight? Are your meals nutritionally sound? Do you experience a high level of stress? Do you participate in risk behaviors in sexual relationships? How does the health of family members affect you? What does your health-insurance policy cover? Reading this chapter provides a good opportunity to take stock of your health in relation to larger social issues to see where you fit in the health spectrum.

 Web Exercise 5.1
How Healthy Am I?

Read "College Health and Safety" on the Centers for Disease Control (CDC) website (http://www.cdc.gov/family/college/). As a college student you may feel you have other priorities than your health. Consider the ten tips discussed on this website.

- Which areas are the most important to you personally?
- About which issues are you the most informed? least informed?
- Does the college environment help or hinder your ability to be healthy?
- From a sociological perspective, why do you think there are health issues of special importance to college students?

Access the live/updated links at http://www.paradigmpublishers.com/resources/goldbergmedia.aspx

Status of Health in the United States

We start with some basic statistics to help us understand the state of health in the United States, beginning with data on the trends regarding life expectancy, infant mortality, and diseases that inform us of the important factors facing our health future. There are numerous online sources of this information, including the Centers for Disease Control (CDC) and the Kaiser Family Foundation—one a government site and the other a private site—on which we will rely for our domestic data. We also find useful international data on health through the World Health Organization and UNAIDS—both of them arms of the United Nations—among others.

Global Health

To better understand the state of health in the United States, it is useful to see it in a global context, thus we next examine some basic indicators of health in various regions in the world. In previous chapters we have examined the importance of levels of development in determining life chances, and there is no more clear measure of life chances than life expectancy and infant mortality. The figures below represent the relative access to healthful living across varied levels of wealth and poverty as well as health-care infrastructures.

According to the World Health Organization (2013b), life expectancy varies considerably by region. For people born in 2011, life expectancy ranges from the lowest in the African region, at age fifty-six, to the highest in the Americas, Western Pacific, and Europe, at age seventy-six. Infant-mortality rates (that is, the probability of dying by one year of age out of 1,000 live births) in 2011 are similarly varied: Africa: 68.1; Americas: 13.1; Europe: 10.9; and Western Pacific: 13.4 (World Health Organization 2013d). These disparities are important in understanding the state of health globally. In part, the differences in life expectancy rates are a reflection of the impact of AIDS. We will see later how HIV/AIDS has had a more devastating effect on the lives of people in poor regions in the world than in the more developed regions. It is especially useful to compare

---

 Fast Facts 5.1
United States Health

- Life expectancy at birth: 78.7 years.*
- Leading causes of death: heart disease, cancer, lower respiratory disease, stroke.*
- Infant mortality rate 2011: 6.05 deaths out of every 1,000 births.*
- Percent eighteen to sixty-four years old with no health insurance 2011: 21.3 percent.*
- Percent eighteen to sixty-four years old with private health insurance: 64.2 percent.*
- Percent eighteen to sixty-four years old with public health coverage: 15.9 percent.*
- Prescription drug expenditures in 2008: $234.1 billion.**

Sources: *Centers for Disease Control (2011, 2012, 2013 multiple links); **Lundy (2010).

Note: Throughout this chapter you may see slight differences in the data representing specific health statuses. These differences are mostly due to the years the data represent.

the United States to similarly developed countries. Table 5.1 shows some of the most interesting differences between the United States and European nations.

Table 5.1 indicates that even though we have essentially the same life expectancy as other developed countries, there is significant variation in how much is spent on health care and the sources of that spending. As the table shows, the percentage of the US GDP (gross domestic product) spent on health care is much greater than comparable nations. We also see that the distribution between public and private spending is vastly different, raising the question of the value of

the expenditures and the distribution of the burden of the expense. These comparisons relate directly to the debate about health-care reform that we address later in the chapter.

Health Crises: Obesity and HIV/AIDS

Examining basic health data gives us a snapshot of the state of health domestically and globally, and is a good starting point for a discussion of health crises. We could choose to study any number of health issues, including those that take the most lives in the United

Table 5.1
Mortality and Health Expenditures Comparison of the United States
and Selected Other Developed Countries

Country	Life Expectancy 2008	Total Expenditures as % of GDP	Government Expenditures	Private Expenditures
United States	78	15.7	45.5	54.5
Canada	79	4.9	70.0	30.0
Germany	77	10.4	76.9	32.1
France	78	11.0	79.0	21.0
Japan	79	8.0	81.3	18.7

Source: World Health Organization (2010b): "Mortality and burden of disease" (Table 1) and "Health expenditures" (Table 7)

Reading Room 5.1
Health at a Glance

Review "Health at a Glance 2011" by the Organization for Economic Cooperation and Development (OECD), and especially examine the PowerPoint slides in the "Statistics" section (http://www.oecd.org/els/health-systems/49084488.pdf). You will see comparisons for a range of health issues including life expectancy, the distribution of disease, and health-care coverage across a range of relatively wealthy nations. Pay close attention to areas in which the United States stands out to help you see the position this country holds in a global context. The entire report can be downloaded if interested.

Note: US data are not represented on every slide.

Access the live/updated links at http://www.paradigmpublishers.com/resources/goldbergmedia.aspx

States—heart disease and cancer—which could be considered crises in themselves. Instead we concentrate here on two health concerns of epidemic proportion that have recently received much attention and that are likely to continue taxing our health for the foreseeable future: obesity and HIV/AIDS. A study of these provides a unique window into some of the overarching problems of health and health care that we face as part of our social fabric. They are important components of the health-care crisis not only because they are a great cost to individuals and society, but also because they raise important questions about the people and social trends involved in these problems and, more generally, the social meaning of health. Despite the fact that they are entirely avoidable, they are among the central health issues of the twenty-first century that continue to grow in importance and for now remain unsolvable.

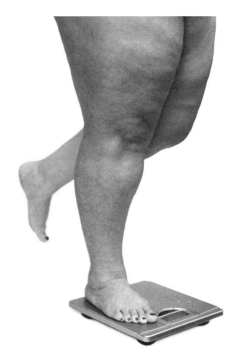

Stepping on a scale is one way to measure obesity.
Source: ThinkStockPhoto.com

The Epidemic of Obesity

Defining Obesity

To understand **obesity**, we first must define it. That would seem an easy task, but it is really rather complicated. In fact, being "obese" is actually a condition found on a continuum that includes being "overweight." According to the CDC, "overweight and obesity are both labels for ranges of weight that are greater than what is generally considered healthy for a given height. The terms also identify ranges of weight that have been shown to increase the likelihood of certain diseases and other health problems" (Centers for Disease Control and Prevention, 2010a). The CDC provides specific definitions based on an adult body-mass index, derived from a person's weight and height, with alternative definitions for children and adolescents. A number of other physical considerations also contribute to the definition. It becomes clear that some of the distinctions between being

overweight and being obese are ranges rather than absolute characterizations, thus we can understand obesity as a social construction. Nonetheless, it is important to have a reliable measure of some sort for this problem that health experts agree is a serious medical condition with significant consequences for individuals and society. Consider some basic information in the box "Fast Facts: Being Overweight or Obese."

Why the Increase in Obesity?

According to the CDC (2010c) the causes of obesity are social in nature. "American society has become 'obesogenic' ["obesity producing"] characterized by environments that promote increased food intake, non-healthful foods, and physical inactivity." The World Health Organization agrees. It cites a worldwide combination of changes in diet with "an increased intake of energy-dense

Fast Facts 5.2
Being Overweight or Obese

United States 2009–2010*

- Obesity rates increased dramatically since the 1960s from 13.4 percent to 35.7 percent.
- 68.8 percent of adults in the United States are overweight or obese (64 percent women; 74 percent men).
- 35.7 percent of adults in the United States are obese (approximately equal between men and women).
- There is a higher rate of obesity among blacks and Hispanics than among whites.
- Child obesity rates: 12.1 percent, ages 2–5; 18 percent, ages 6–11; and 18.4 percent, ages 12–19.

*Source: Weight Control Information Network (2013).

World**

- 2008: about 1.4 billion adults are overweight and 500 million are obese.
- 2011: at least 40 million children under five years old are overweight.
- 2008: More than 10 percent of the world's population is obese.
- Obesity is found even in the least developed countries, especially in cities.

**Source: World Health Organization (2013c).

foods that are high in fat" and "an increase in physical inactivity due to the increasingly sedentary nature of many forms of work, changing modes of transportation, and increasing urbanization" (2013c). Put more simply, we eat more and exercise less.

It is worth examining some of our modern lifestyle issues in more depth to better understand the problems we face as an increasingly obese society. We will look at the prevalence of unhealthy eating patterns first. According to the Center for Science in the Public Interest (2004), comparisons of daily calorie intake for men and women in the United States between 1971 and 2000 show an increase of 168 calories for men and 335 for women. Children are especially likely to drink sugar-laden soft drinks that add more calories to their daily intake. Data on teens' consumption patterns show a large increase in soda while also decreasing the consumption of milk. The ease with which we consume fast food is an important contributor to the increase in calorie intake. The rise of the fast-food industry is linked to the pace of work and school life, modern family structure, and the desire for relatively cheap, predictable food. Children today consume five times the amount of fast food that they did in 1970. Child consumers of fast food ingested 187 more calories a day than children who did not eat fast food (CBS News 2009). Our eating patterns also include increased portion size and food choices that increase caloric intake.

As for exercise, despite the popularity of the fitness movement, as a nation we do not burn enough calories. Our transportation of choice is the car, which, as we saw in Chapter 3, is both deeply embedded in our culture and an environmental danger. We do less physical labor than in the past, and we have

Movie Picks 5.1
Supersize Me

The documentary film *Supersize Me* shows the health effects of a pure fast-food diet. We follow the filmmaker in his quest to eat only from a fast-food menu for a month and observe the consequences.

Mixed-Media Extra

Read "Fast Food Facts from the *Supersize Me* Web Site" (http://www.vivavegie.org/101book /text/nolink/social/supersizeme.htm). Also view the map of the distribution of McDonald's and Starbucks around the world at International Networks Archive/Map of the Month (http:// www.princeton.edu/~ina/infographics/starbucks.html).

Thinking Sociologically

- Link the events in the movie to the data presented on the website and this chapter.
- What is the attraction of fast-food restaurants in terms of the food, ambience, efficiency, and predictability?
- How does mass media encourage fast-food consumption?
- What lifestyle/cultural patterns encourage the consumption of fast food?
- Do you expect Americans to consume more or less fast food in the future? Explain.
- Has the distribution of fast-food franchises around the world impacted traditional eating habits and contributed to obesity?
- College dining: Are the offerings in your dining service healthful? What fast-food outlets are on or near your campus?

Access the live/updated links at http://www.paradigmpublishers.com/resources/goldbergmedia.aspx

many sedentary options when it comes to entertainment, especially with the expansion of cable television, game systems, and social networking. Physical exercise is at least in part a determinant of whether a person will be overweight or obese, so it is no surprise that as our eating has increased, physical exercise has remained about the same over time. In 2010 over 30 percent of Americans did not participate in any "leisure-time physical activity" (HealthyPeople.gov 2013). Men and women differ in physical activity levels by about five percentage points. Race differences in leisure-time physical exercise are significant. Among whites 27.9 percent are inactive whereas 42.7 percent of blacks and 44.6 percent of Hispanics are inactive. Since these figures represent leisure activity, they do not take into account work-related

physical labor, which may impact total physical activity. We will explore the implications for these differences in our discussion of inequality, as factors such as education levels and affluence have significant impacts on the amount of money and time people have to indulge in leisure activities.

Why Do We Care about Obesity?

The health costs to individuals who are obese are quite specific: increased chances for Type 2 diabetes, heart conditions, some kinds of cancer, and early death. Obese patients pay considerably more for care than non-obese patients. The individual medical and non-medical costs, such as lost wages due to absenteeism, are $4,879 per year for an obese woman and $2,646 for an obese man (Dor et al. 2010, 1).

The costs are not to individuals alone, as they have important implications for employers and the society at large. According to Hammond and Levine (2010), the costs to the US economy due to obesity are substantial. Both direct medical and indirect productivity costs run in the billions of dollars. Their study suggests that the total economic cost to society runs about $215 billion a year. In addition to medical costs, this includes costs to productivity, transportation, and human capital, such as loss of education. For example, people of larger size may commonly require larger, more expensive cars, and airlines pay more for fuel to transport oversize passengers. In terms of education, Hammond and Levine refer to research that finds that obese women achieve less education than non-obese women; on average, lower levels of education, combined with lower incomes and fewer marriages, mean that obese women tend to be poorer than non-obese women.

These costs are problematic for individuals and for society as a whole. In fact, a recent report by retired military leaders emphasized the impact obesity has had on recruitment. (See Web Exercise 5.2: "Too Fat to Fight.")

The Role of Stigma in Obesity

In addition to direct health and economic costs, stigma is very strong against obese people and sometimes results in discrimination. Whether in the work place, a school setting, or even in getting medical care, obese people are subject to prejudices that impact their life chances. In each of these settings obese people are often regarded as lazy, lacking self-control, ugly, and having less potential for success (Obesity Action Coalition 2010; Obesity Society 2010). Regarding work, research into hiring, promotion, earnings, and firing indicates that discrimination against obese employees exists. In school, both peers and teachers discriminate, starting as early as preschool. Overweight children report being teased by peers, with a greater percentage of girls reporting teasing than boys. There is evidence that obese youth are less likely to be admitted to college and more likely to leave before degree completion.

Health-care experiences are no different. Between 12 and 31 percent of nurses expressed negative attitudes toward obese patients. Doctors and psychologists also reported biased attitudes toward obese patients. Obese people are also less likely

Web Exercise 5.2
Too Fat to Fight

Read the report "Too Fat to Fight" (http://cdn.missionreadiness.org/MR_Too_Fat_to _Fight-1.pdf) to better understand the problems of being overweight or obese among young Americans and the problems with military recruiting of out-of-shape young people. The report goes further than just complaining about the physical condition of our youth.

- Why should we be concerned that obesity impacts the military's ability to recruit?
- What does the report ask the government to do?
- What connections are made between the military and other social institutions that are implicated in the obesity epidemic?
- Would you consider this problem a social crisis? Why or why not?

Access the live/updated links at http://www.paradigmpublishers.com/resources/goldbergmedia.aspx

to get regular medical exams and screening tests, and they cancel appointments more often and spend less time with doctors than non-obese patients (Obesity Action Coalition 2010). It is not surprising that when faced with stigma, obese people internalize the stereotypes, thus creating their own limitations of lower self-esteem and greater depression (Obesity Society 2010).

Obesity will remain a significant social problem with consequences for individuals and society as a whole into the foreseeable future. Programs to reduce obesity among school children, increased awareness of the causes of obesity, and various medical programs to reduce obesity will help address the problem. However, the trend toward greater obesity has much to do with our lifestyle and cultural dynamics. The crisis of obesity will follow us well into the future.

The Crisis of HIV/AIDS

The HIV/AIDS crisis has had a substantial global impact. There is probably no better example of the impact disease can have on society than the case of HIV/AIDS. With its rapid rise and lack of a cure it holds a special place in the study of the dynamics of disease. It is an unrelenting crisis for individuals, families, and societies affecting all major social institutions. We will briefly describe the virus, cover the historical rise of HIV/AIDS, examine current statistics on its distribution, and consider the social manifestations that have so profoundly affected people worldwide and in our communities.

Defining HIV/AIDS

Unknown as a specific disease in medical terms until the latter part of the twentieth century, HIV (human immunodeficiency virus) is a retrovirus that is spread by specific kinds of contact, especially involving blood and semen. It is typically spread by unprotected sexual contact or sharing of intravenous needles, and can be transmitted as well during birth or through maternal nursing. HIV is not the same as AIDS. AIDS (acquired immunodeficiency syndrome) is diagnosed when the HIV virus has multiplied to the point that the body can no longer resist "opportunistic infections" that cause serious deterioration in the body's ability to survive. A person can have the HIV virus in her or his body for a number of years without becoming sick, though the virus can be passed to someone else in that time. Thus, HIV by itself is not a fatal disease but the virus's ability to replicate reduces the effectiveness of the immune system to a level that increases the likelihood of dying, at which point a person is determined to have AIDS. Without recently developed antiviral drugs, the likelihood of survival is slim.

Historically, HIV first arose in Africa. It then spread throughout the world. The patterns it took in different regions of the world reflect the development of medical knowledge about the disease, cultural patterns in sexual activity and drug use, and the relative willingness to address AIDS in the general population. Today anti-retroviral drugs can keep the virus under control, thus enabling the extension of life for many people. In such cases, AIDS can be considered as chronic rather than as always fatal. Yet AIDS still kills in large numbers. When we examine the trends in the disease we will more fully understand how important social dynamics are in determining the course of HIV/AIDS. (See the box "Fast Facts: HIV/AIDS.")

Global Patterns in HIV/AIDS

As mentioned earlier, HIV/AIDS was first found to exist in Africa. There is some debate about its origin, but there is widespread agreement that Africa remains the source

Fast Facts 5.3
HIV/AIDS

Global (2011):

- 34 million people worldwide were living with HIV/AIDS.
- 2.5 million people were newly infected.
- 1.7 million people died of AIDS.

Source: World Health Organization (2013a).

United States

- More than 1.1 million people were living with HIV/AIDS in 2009.
- About 50,000 people are infected each year.
- Infection rates vary by class, sex, and ethnicity.
- About 636,000 people have died of AIDS through 2010.

and it is also the region that has suffered most from its spread. In Sub-Saharan Africa 23.5 million people live with HIV and 1.8 million were infected in 2011 alone. More than one million died in 2011. No other region comes close to those figures, though other parts of the world are also significantly affected: 3.4 million people live with HIV in South and Southeast Asia. In Latin America and North America each, 1.4 million live with HIV. Eastern Europe has 1.4 million people living with HIV. The infection and death rates have decreased in the first decade of the twenty-first century (UNAIDS 2012).

Sub-Saharan Africa has been especially hard-hit by the AIDS epidemic so it is worth a closer look. Not only did HIV have a head start there, allowing the infection to spread

 Web Exercise 5.3
Exploring the Global AIDS Epidemic

View the facts and figures and explore the interactive maps and materials on the UNAIDS website, *AIDSinfo: Epidemiological Status* (http://www.unaids.org/en/dataanalysis/datatools /aidsinfo/). Compare the rates of HIV/AIDS across the globe as well as the availability of treatment. Select one region in which you can learn about AIDS in depth.

- What do the "epidemiological data" reveal about that region?
- What "regional dynamics" demonstrate the importance of social factors in the trends in HIV/AIDS in that region?
- How might a sociologist use that information to analyze the role HIV/AIDS plays in that region?

Access the live/updated links at http://www.paradigmpublishers.com/resources/goldbergmedia.aspx

long before the virus was identified or tests and treatments were developed, but the likelihood of infection is increased by sporadic health care, patterns of work, gender dynamics, and the lack of resources for drugs and other care. According to Avert.org (2010) AIDS has not only impacted life expectancy, but many people dying of AIDS are in their childbearing years and are major contributors to family income. Losing breadwinners and caretakers of young children places a devastating personal and economic burden on families. Some children are orphaned and some of those children are also infected with HIV. Other social institutions are also dramatically affected. Health-care systems are overburdened, and productivity is reduced by the loss of workers, thus impeding economic progress. In Africa the major form of transmission is through heterosexual sex. Cultural patterns of marriage, out-of-marriage relationships, separation from spouses because of employment, and rejection of condom use

are among the factors that impact the trends in HIV/AIDS infection. Some of these patterns make it especially likely that women will be infected, so the gender dynamics in African communities plays a role in the spread of HIV/AIDS as it does in other parts of the world.

It should be noted that there are many different countries in Africa with different approaches to addressing HIV/AIDS. Although some countries have embraced education and condom distribution, others have rejected those basic steps in limiting the spread of HIV. In some countries antiretroviral drugs are more accessible than in other countries. As a result, even though on the whole Africans suffer the most from HIV/AIDS compared to other regions, there are important differences from country to country both in cultural practices and in response to the epidemic.

As for other parts of the world, like in Africa, cultural patterns affect the trends in

 Movie Picks 5.2
Yesterday

The movie *Yesterday* is a fictional account of the experience of a young African woman infected with HIV. She must help her husband, who infected her, and raise her child, while contending with limited access to medical care and the community's response to her situation.

Mixed-Media Extra

Read "Women: The Face of AIDS in Africa" by Michael Fleshman for an examination of how AIDS affects African women (http://medilinkz.org/old/Features/Articles/Oct2004/women_aids04.asp).

Thinking Sociologically

- What are the life chances of women like Yesterday?
- What roles do gender and poverty play in the situation of African women with HIV?
- Does the family as a social institution help or hurt women with HIV?
- Using your sociological imagination, how are your circumstances similar to or different from the conditions in which Yesterday finds herself?

Access the live/updated links at http://www.paradigmpublishers.com/resources/goldbergmedia.aspx

HIV/AIDS, and understanding the course of the infection means understanding each country's particular experiences with HIV. In Thailand, for example, which has the highest rate of AIDS in Southeast Asia (1.3 percent of the population), the HIV infection rate fell from its peak of 143,000 cases in 1991 to 19,000 cases in 2003. At the end of 2009, 530,000 people were living with HIV/AIDS. Sex work in Thailand is commonplace, and the reduction in HIV infections is tied to fewer men participating in sex for hire as well as increased condom use (Avert.org 2013). In Eastern Europe, injection drug use and sex work comprise the major forms of transmission of HIV (World Health Organization 2010a). In Western Europe, with the exception of people who have come from regions with high HIV rates, transmission is typically among men having sex with men, and among a small number of IV (intravenous) drug users. Overall, the HIV rate in Western Europe is small (Avert. org. n.d.).

The AIDS Crisis in the United States

HIV/AIDS has had a unique history in the United States and the infection trends demonstrate how this disease impacts different segments of the population and social institutions in important ways. HIV first entered the United States population by mostly infecting men who were having sex with men. The US medical establishment was among the first in the world to recognize the infection we now call HIV/AIDS, but only after a long and deadly path that AIDS took through the gay community. In the late twentieth century, when a large number of young and normally healthy men began getting very sick and soon died of unusual illnesses, the belief was that a "gay cancer" was traveling through that population.

Because this virus appeared to target gay men, most Americans were unconcerned, believing that the disease was outside their own exposure and therefore not of importance to them. Intolerance of homosexuality played an important role in enabling people to turn a blind eye to the devastating infection, much to the dismay of men who were losing friends in large numbers. These attitudes, along with a reluctance to talk about sexual practices that exposed people to the virus, played an instrumental role in delaying serious research into the disease, thus laying the foundation for the infection to travel into the general population. It took several years to determine an accurate test for HIV and even more years to develop treatments that reduced the death rate. When it was determined that the most common modes of transmission in those early days in the United States were men having sex with men and the sharing of needles among IV drug users, it reinforced the stigma against some of the most marginalized members of society—gay men and drug users.

The issue became highly politicized through the 1980s as gay-rights organizations argued for greater funding for AIDS research, which was very scarce at the time. For IV drug users, there were widespread debates about the ethics of needle-distribution programs aimed at controlling the sharing of needles by supplying drug users with new, clean needles. This debate continues today. In time, it was discovered that HIV had entered the medical blood supply, and this affected people who were neither gay nor IV drug users, including people who received blood, especially during surgery or as treatment for hemophilia. In these cases, HIV was often unknowingly passed along to the partners of those infected, both male and female. By the time the virus was eliminated from the blood supply, there was a growing recognition and dread that HIV had entered the non-drug-using heterosexual population.

Mothers gave birth to HIV-infected babies and/or infected them unknowingly through nursing. Men and women unaware of their HIV status had unprotected sex, thus infecting their partners. Despite the transmittal of HIV to the wider population, people continued to associate the disease with IV drug use and taboo sexual practices between men, and they therefore remained suspicious and fearful of those who were infected. It is instructive to view these statistics graphically. Today we see more than half of the transmissions include men having sex with men (61.8 percent), but we also see a significant number of cases transmitted sexually between men and women (27.6 percent). The two graphs shown in Figures 5.1 and 5.2 represent new infections of HIV by transmission category in 2011 (Centers for Disease Control and Prevention 2013a).

Although early transmission in the United States occurred among predominantly white gay men, there have been some important race and ethnic changes in the transmissions by 2011. Of those infected in 2011, 42 percent were black men and 23 percent were Hispanic men infected by having sex with men, as seen in Figure 5.2. For women, 63 percent of those infected were black and 17 percent were Hispanic.

As Table 5.2 indicates, although "male-to-male sexual contact" was still by far the most common mode of transmission, 13,801 cases of HIV were from heterosexual transmission in 2011 (Centers for Disease Control and Prevention 2013a).

The statistics presented above tell us much about the transmission of HIV today. We will explore the implications for gender and race as well as class later in the chapter when we look at inequality in health.

The Role of Stigma in HIV/AIDS

It is important now to understand that as Figures 5.1 and 5.2, as well as Table 5.2, indicate, even as recently as 2011 over 50,000 people were infected that year in the United States. Because this is an entirely preventable disease

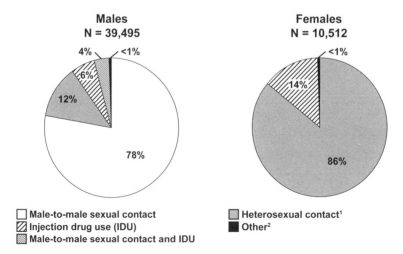

Note: Data include persons with a diagnosis of HIV infection regardless of stage of disease at diagnosis. All displayed data have been automatically adjusted to account for reporting delays, but not for incomplete reporting.
[1]Heterosexual contact with a person known to be at high risk for HIV infection.
[2]Includes hemophelia, blood transfusion, prenatal exposure, and risk factor not reported or not identified.

Figure 5.1 Diagnosis of HIV infection among adults and adolescents by sex and transmission category.

Source: http://www.cdc.gov/hiv/pdf/statistics_surveillance_Epi-HIV-infection.pdf

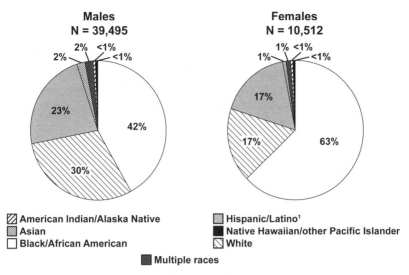

Males
N = 39,495

Females
N = 10,512

American Indian/Alaska Native
Asian
Black/African American
Hispanic/Latino[1]
Native Hawaiian/other Pacific Islander
White
Multiple races

Note: Data include persons with a diagnosis of HIV infection regardless of stage of disease at diagnosis. All displayed data have been automatically adjusted to account for reporting delays, but not for incomplete reporting.
[1]Hispanic/Latino can be of any race.

Figure 5.2 Diagnosis of HIV infection among adults and adolescents by sex and race/ethnicity.

Source: http://www.cdc.gov/hiv/pdf/statistics_surveillance_Epi-HIV-infection.pdf

Table 5.2
Diagnoses of HIV Infection among Adults and Adolescents,
by Transmission Category, 2011—United States and 6 Dependent Areas

Transmission Category	No.	%
Male-to-male sexual contact	30,896	61.8
Injection drug use (IDU)	3,836	7.7
Male-to-male sexual contact and IDU	1,423	2.9
Heterosexual contact[a]	13,801	27.6
Other[b]	51	0.1
Total	**50,007**	**100.0**

Note: Data include persons with a diagnosis of HIV infection regardless of stage of disease at diagnosis. All displayed data have been statistically adjusted to account for reporting delays and missing transmission category, but not for incomplete reporting.
[a] Heterosexual contact with a person known to have, or to be at high risk for, HIV infection.
[b] Includes hemophilia, blood transfusion, perinatal exposure, and risk factor not reported or not identified.
Source: Centers for Disease Control and Prevention 2013a

when people take precautions such as wearing condoms during sex, not sharing needles when injecting drugs, and regular testing, we have to wonder why HIV infection has not been eliminated. For that we turn to the concept of stigma. Many diseases, especially fatal and infectious diseases, carry stigma. People are often fearful of others who are ill. They are confused about their relationships to sick people and are afraid of "catching" whatever disease may be harbored in someone's body. In the case of AIDS, not only is it infectious and deadly, but there is no known cure, and only recently have treatments been developed.

Risk behaviors involving sex and drug use also carry a stigma. From the beginning of the epidemic in the late twentieth century, HIV has been associated with homosexuality in the United States, and as such has had tremendous stigma attached to it. Prior to the rise if HIV, gay men and lesbians were routinely discriminated against in employment, housing, the military, and even in their own families and among friends. This stigma has made it very difficult to have honest and open discussions about prevention and care for those infected. Education programs in the United States are scant by comparison to other countries. By relegating people with HIV/AIDS to an undesirable category, an aura of ignorance and fear developed about the disease rather than a scientifically based approach to controlling or eliminating it.

The HIV/AIDS crisis is worth an in-depth examination not only because it is an important health problem, but also because it so clearly demonstrates the importance of understanding the social dimensions regarding transmission, social costs, disease trends, and stigma. By examining HIV/AIDS globally and in the United States we can see how it is experienced differently in different regions and among different populations. The differences are not coincidental. The experience of HIV/AIDS is very much tied to social, cultural, economic, and political developments nationally and internationally. Without understanding the crisis as a social phenomenon, we miss being able to fully understand it and control it. As you can see by the statistics in this chapter, we have a long way to go before HIV/AIDS is controlled, and it will remain a health crisis for a long time to come.

Studying obesity and HIV/AIDS is valuable in demonstrating the distribution of

---

 Movie Picks 5.3
Philadelphia

The movie *Philadelphia* dramatically demonstrates the problems faced by an otherwise mainstream gay man who acquires HIV and has to face discrimination, illness, and death while also trying to deflect the stigma that hurt so many people in the early days of the epidemic.

Mixed-Media Extra

Read stories about coping with HIV/AIDS and watch interviews with HIV-positive people at "Inspiring Stories of People Affected by HIV/AIDS" at The Body website (http://www.thebody .com/index/inspire.html).

Thinking Sociologically

- How important is stigma in determining how people address health problems in general and HIV in particular?
- Is stigma regarding AIDS and homosexuality as strong today as it was twenty years ago?
- How is stigma regarding AIDS similar to or different from stigma regarding obesity?
- Are you aware of anyone in your family or social circle who is infected with HIV?
- Would you treat a person differently if you learned of their diagnosis with HIV?
- Would you consider dating or marrying someone with HIV?

Access the live/updated links at http://www.paradigmpublishers.com/resources/goldbergmedia.aspx

Movie Picks 5.4
The Age of AIDS

The four-part PBS *Frontline* documentary *The Age of AIDS* covers the rise of AIDS throughout the world and in the United States (http://www.pbs.org/wgbh/pages/frontline/aids/view/). The film covers the origins and history of AIDS, the development of treatments, and the political ramifications of the disease in a detailed and thorough examination of medical, social, and political factors affecting its spread and impact on society.

- Use your sociological imagination to place yourself in the context of AIDS. Where do you fit?
- How were your prior ideas about AIDS changed by the film?
- How is AIDS experienced in different parts of the world?
- What social factors in each region contributed to the trajectory of AIDS?
- How do social institutions respond to the AIDS epidemic?

Access the live/updated links at http://www.paradigmpublishers.com/resources/goldbergmedia.aspx

disease within and across societies. They are only two of the considerable health challenges faced by society today. Heart disease and cancer, for instance, are also tremendously important contributors to the health crisis. Although this chapter does not address these and other health problems directly, the way in which social factors play into defining and treating any disease can be examined sociologically. It is now time to turn more broadly to access to health care and the role health insurance plays in determining how the health crisis is dealt with by individuals and society.

Getting Care: The Crisis of Access

The vignette at the beginning of the chapter provides a snapshot of the problems the poor face in getting care. It should come as no surprise that the less money you have, the less you are able to meet your health needs, whether it means staying in good health, accessing care, or affording prescription drugs. The combination of increased likelihood of disease, few resources, and lack of

health insurance adds to the misery of many Americans.

Although health reform in the form of the Affordable Care Act was passed by Congress and signed by the president in 2010, it is too soon to know what effect it will have on access to care, so for now we need to look at the burden of the costs of care on people in the first decade of the twenty-first century. As noted above, lack of good, reliable, affordable health care puts the poor in a constant state of crisis. Any illness can be a setback that can permanently change the course of their lives. But the poor are not alone in having trouble getting their health-care needs met. Many Americans struggle to pay for care even if they are insured.

Health Insurance

We now turn to the issue of health insurance to see how it impacts access to care and how well it protects the welfare of people who are ill. With the enactment of health-care reform in 2010, significant changes are expected to take place, but the

Web Exercise 5.4
"Hidden Hurt"

Read "Hidden Hurt: Desperate for medical care, the uninsured flock by the hundreds to a remote corner of Virginia for the chance to see a doctor" by Mary Otto (2008) in the *Washington Post* (http://www.washingtonpost.com/wp-dyn/content/article/2008/10/31 /AR2008103101756.html). Explore the related videos and photos by clicking on "View all items in this story." It includes scenes of help provided by the Remote Area Medical organization described at the beginning of this chapter. Consider the health problems of the people in the story.

- What factors make it so hard to get medical care?
- Why are these people sicker than the rest of society?
- Whose responsibility is it to provide care for poor people?
- Connect the information from the story to the data on life expectancy and social class.

Access the live/updated links at http://www.paradigmpublishers.com/resources/goldbergmedia.aspx

types of health-care coverage are not likely to change much in the near future. There is a dizzying array of health-insurance plans from which people must choose. The 65 percent of Americans with private health-care insurance mostly enroll through their workplace, where the employer and employee each pay a portion. On average, employer-sponsored insurance premiums for family plans cost approximately $15,745 in

Movie Picks 5.5
Sicko

Michael Moore's movie *Sicko*, a critique of the American health-care system, focuses on people who are underinsured. He meets people who have suffered both physically and economically, and sometimes tragically, because they could not afford care despite having insurance. He also compares our pre-health-care-reform system to other systems of health care.

Mixed-Media Extra

View the factual backups for *Sicko* at the Michael Moore website (http://www.michaelmoore .com/books-films/facts/sicko and http://sickothemovie.com/checkup/).

Thinking Sociologically

- In your view what are the responsibilities of individuals and of society in providing health care for citizens?
- What social and cultural factors account for the differences between the health-care system in the United States and in the other countries covered in the film?
- How would you describe the social-class positions of the people portrayed in the film?
- What do you know about your own health-care coverage?

Access the live/updated links at http://www.paradigmpublishers.com/resources/goldbergmedia.aspx

2012, with increases in premiums of 4 percent over the previous year (Altman 2012). Between 2002 and 2012, insurance premiums nearly doubled though (an increase of 97 percent), and the contribution toward premiums made by employees increased 102 percent (Henry J. Kaiser Family Foundation 2012). Government programs including Medicare (for those of age sixty-five or over) and Medicaid (for those of low income) provide insurance to about 13 percent of Americans. In 2011, 18.2 percent of Americans (48.2 million) were uninsured (Centers for Disease Control 2012). A sizable number of people with insurance are considered underinsured; that is, their coverage is too limited to adequately meet their health needs. These are often employed, middle-class people who risk losing their life savings in order to pay for costly medical care when facing serious health issues. It is estimated that 29 million Americans were underinsured in 2010, an increase of 80 percent since 2003 (Schoen et al. 2011).

Prescription Drugs

In addition to the cost of doctor's visits, hospital stays, and procedures, the cost of prescription drugs has risen a great deal over time. According to research by the Kaiser Family Foundation, prescription-drug expenditures in the United States in 2008 amounted to $234.1 billion, compared to $40.3 billion in 1990 (Lundy 2010). What has caused this increase? The research points to several important factors that contribute to the enormous cost of prescription drugs:

- Growth in the number of prescriptions—increasing 39 percent between 1999 and 2009.
- The price of retail prescriptions nearly doubled between 1998 and 2008.
- An increase in new drugs, which may cost more than older drugs.

- Increased advertising expenditures by drug companies—$6.6 billion in 2009.
- Increased sales and profit.

The skyrocketing cost of health care pervades society at all levels. Most Americans agree that health care needs to be reformed, but there are intense debates about how that should be done and the outcomes will have profound effects not only on health care but on politics and the economy for years to come. We now turn to the current state of health-care reform.

Health-Care Reform

The battle over health-care reform has been, and still is, a contentious battle. Most people are unaware that attempts at health-care reform in the United States started in the early twentieth century. Then, health care was heavily influenced by the growing medicalization and institutionalization of care through doctors and hospitals. Various efforts were made throughout the century on the part of corporations, unions, insurance companies, and political parties to shape health reform. The most successful attempt at reform has taken place in the last few years and it has made an indelible impression on the current political dynamics of the United States.

Since the Affordable Care Act was signed into law in 2010, several provisions have taken effect and others will take effect over the next few years unless the law is successfully challenged. The status of the law depends on court challenges as well as ongoing attempts to repeal the law. It is likely to be a major political issue for the foreseeable future. For now, health-care reform is a work in progress that requires the attention of people on all sides of the debate. Special attention should be paid to the role of media, insurance companies, elected officials, medical institutions, and advocacy groups as they jockey for influence in shaping the future of health care.

Reading Room 5.2
Health-Care Reform Historical Timeline

View the historical timeline of health-care reform in "History of Health Reform Efforts in the US" at the Kaiser Family Foundation website (http://kaiserfamilyfoundation.files .wordpress.com/2011/03/5-02-13-history-of-health-reform.pdf). See also the interactive article in the *New York Times* by Elisabeth Goodridge and Sarah Arnquist, "A History of Overhauling Health Care" (http://www.nytimes.com/interactive/2009/07/19/us /politics/20090717_HEALTH_TIMELINE.html). Consider the different types of influence that shaped health reform in the past. How is reform in the past similar to and different from the experience of reform today?

Access the live/updated links at http://www.paradigmpublishers.com/resources/goldbergmedia.aspx

Global Comparisons

Compared to other countries in the developed world, Americans pay a great deal more for health care with little difference in outcomes. Universal health care drives the lower cost of care for citizens in Western European countries, Canada, Japan, and Australia, among others. Americans on the whole have roundly rejected the idea of universal care despite data that indicate care would be as good or better at lower cost for most of us.

Movie Picks 5.6
Big Bucks, Big Pharma: Marketing Disease & Pushing Drugs

Watch *Big Bucks, Big Pharma* and consider the relationship between the pharmaceutical industry, media, doctors, government, and you.

Mixed-Media Extra

Watch an hour of evening news on a major commercial network television station. Record the names of the drugs advertised, what they are for, and disclaimers. Describe the audiovisual presentation—what cultural message is promoted? How does it reflect the purpose of the drug advertised?

Thinking Sociologically

- What effect does mass-media advertising play in prescription-drug use?
- What aspects of American culture are tied to the use of drugs and health?
- How might changes in the definitions of disease impact our use of drugs?
- What is the relationship between expenditures for marketing and lobbying by the pharmaceutical industry and the cost of drugs?
- What do you know about the prescription and over-the-counter drugs you are using?
- Apply the sociological imagination to develop an understanding of patterns of drug development and use and your personal use of drugs.

Access the live/updated links at http://www.paradigmpublishers.com/resources/goldbergmedia.aspx

Reading Room 5.3
Health-Care Reform Updates—Are You an Advocate?

There are many websites that argue for and against health-care reform, and many that argue for alternative forms of care. To keep updated on the current state of reform as it exists in law, first view the website, HealthCare.gov. In the section titled "Learn" you will find detailed information on the provisions of the law, which reforms are currently in place, and which will be put in place in the future. Carefully read the limitations placed on insurers and what consumers can expect. To understand the political debate about health-care reform, search online for "pros and cons" regarding health reform. Read a few of these from different political perspectives to better understand the debate and help form your own ideas.

- After reading about health-care reform do you think it is important for citizens to advocate for the type of reform they prefer?
- How might you advocate for the reforms you want?

Access the live/updated links at http://www.paradigmpublishers.com/resources/goldbergmedia.aspx

Marketing, advertising, and support from interest groups play a large role in framing the debate about universal health care, with the greatest investment opposing universal care and supporting the status quo. Dislike of universal health care appeals to our value of individualism, a cultural trait less important in other developed countries, at least as far as health care is concerned.

There are significant differences in the experiences of health and illness among different sectors of society. To better understand these, we now turn to the application of sociological concepts and theories.

depend on one's social class, gender, race, and ethnicity. When we focus on obesity and HIV/AIDS, these differences become evidence of the relationship of social factors to disease and the ability to receive care. As sociologists, our job is to understand the social forces that contribute to the risk of disease and affect access to care for individuals and society as a whole. What makes for a healthy society? What determines who gets sick, the patterns of disease, and how care is distributed? Applying sociological concepts and theories will help us answer some of these questions.

Sociology of Health and Health Care

In this chapter we have seen that life chances for good health and access to care are tied to a number of social factors. By examining basic measures of health such as life expectancy and infant mortality globally, we saw differences that matter a great deal in understanding outcomes for individuals and societies. In the United States, differences in health and health care for different segments of society

The Sociological Imagination and Health

We all have health concerns, or to put in Mills's terms, "troubles," which must be addressed at various points in our lives. Health is among the most intimate of personal issues, raising important questions of life, quality of life, and death. As we have seen in our examples of obesity and HIV/AIDS, good health and even survival depend

Movie Picks 5.7
Sick Around the World

The *Frontline* video *Sick Around the World* examines health-care services in five different countries around the world: Great Britain, Japan, Germany, Taiwan, and Switzerland. It examines the type of care citizens get and the costs. Watch the video and consider the differences between care in the United States and in these other countries (http://video.pbs.org/video/1050712790/).

Mixed-Media Extra

Find more information and graphs on the *Sick Around the World* website comparing the countries in "Five Capitalist Democracies and How They Do It" (http://www.pbs.org/wgbh/pages /frontline/sickaroundtheworld/).

For detailed statistics comparing a variety of health data in a number of countries in the developed world, view the PowerPoint presentation at the chart set for "Health at a Glance 2011" found at the Organization for Economic Cooperation and Development website (http:// www.oecd.org/els/health-systems/49084488.pdf).

Thinking Sociologically

- How do different societies provide health care?
- What are the public/private relationships in these various care systems?
- Compared to the United States, why do you think these countries have better care at less cost?
- What cultural differences contribute to the differences in health-care systems in different countries?

Access the live/updated links at http://www.paradigmpublishers.com/resources/goldbergmedia.aspx

at least in part on an understanding of personal risk in relation to one's place in the larger society.

The sociological imagination is useful for understanding our health status as individuals and for making informed decisions about care as well as our consideration of health as part of the larger social structure. If you are unhealthy, you must address your health as an individual, but if large numbers of people in society have the same health problem, it becomes a structural issue worthy of sociological study. In the case of obesity, knowledge about nutrition and exercise coupled with ability and willingness to act on that knowledge helps engender health for individuals and encourage social practices regarding healthful eating and exercise.

Thus, obesity is both a personal problem and a social crisis. Its recent growth has taken a toll on the health of individuals and the status of health in society. Our examination of HIV/AIDS shows the direct connection between risk behaviors and risk of disease. A person's choice to have an HIV test, encourage others to do so, and practice safe sex are three of the most proactive steps individuals can take. For both obesity and HIV/AIDS, the degree to which people take steps to acknowledge a problem and protect their health can be understood on both an individual and social level. The decision to get an HIV test is an individual decision, but it is made in a social setting. Where are tests available? Is confidentiality completely assured? How is information about testing distributed? Similarly, a person addressing obesity makes an individual choice in a social context. The social effects of education, tolerance, stigma, and acceptance all impact the choices individuals make in facing health problems. For people experiencing disease, the sociological imagination enables them to see beyond their own personal troubles to the larger social and historical context, which in turn can help them cope and make decisions about their care.

The earlier discussion of the power of advertising pharmaceuticals is another example of how applying the sociological imagination can help people make informed decisions and see their troubles in a larger social context. Without an understanding of the role of advertising in meeting the profit goals of the drug industry, we can mistakenly make poor decisions about our health. Since even our doctors and elected officials are influenced by the powerful pharmaceutical lobby, it is crucial to understand how our health is tied to the larger social world. The ability to see a doctor, ask the right questions, and pay for care is not independent of one's place in society. Even the direction our country takes in terms of health-care reform is both structural and personal. All of these examples point directly to the value of using the sociological imagination to place people in a social context and provide knowledge from which people and whole societies can make decisions in the face of crisis.

Culture and Health

How do societies experience health and illness? American cultural values are expressed in the material culture of medicine, especially the technology that enables sophisticated tests, procedures, and surgery, often at great cost even in the case of impending death. Non-material culture, including knowledge, values, and beliefs, demonstrates that Americans value the practitioners of medicine and accord them high status and high salaries for their expertise. We also value youth, fitness, and long life—attitudes that inform our decisions about medical procedures, sometimes to the detriment of patients and their families. This cultural investment in life over death at almost any cost pervades much of our understanding of the role of health, medical practice, and the value of life itself. These values especially resonate when considering the advances in medical technology in which people sometimes can remain alive indefinitely with the help of machines. The **cultural lag** between technology and our social, legal, and economic responses to expensive life-saving equipment leaves us without clear guidelines about the ethics of medical intervention. There is also the unintended consequence of financial ruin for families who go into debt in the hopes of keeping loved ones alive.

Cultural practices regarding eating are reflected in our study of obesity. What we eat, when we eat, and our preference for large quantities of food are cultural factors that contribute to obesity. These are not just personal eating habits, but they reflect significant lifestyle trends, so addressing the problem of obesity requires an understanding of the contributions of culture. Similarly, the trends in HIV infections cannot be understood without examining cultural practices and attitudes about sex in various segments of our society. Educating people about risk behavior requires an understanding of the cultures and subcultures where HIV is most prevalent.

The cultural value of **individualism** plays an important role in the case of health reform. Many Americans equate reform with government interference in decision-making, thus challenging the cultural value of individualism that is held so dear. The importance of individualism in our culture becomes especially clear when comparing our health-care system to that of other, less-individualistic systems, such as those observed in the movie picks, *Sick Around the World* and *Sicko.* The dynamic between the rights of the individual and expectations regarding government's role in providing for the common good vary considerably from society to society. Understanding these differences helps us see how the non–material aspects of culture influence the experience of health care.

It is useful to apply the concept of ideal versus real society in considering cultural values and practices regarding health. For example, the earlier discussion of obesity points to some considerable contradictions between values and behavior. On the one hand we value physical fitness and youth as indicators of health. Millions of dollars are spent on gym memberships, diet programs, fashion, cosmetic surgery, and other attempts to retain health and appear young. The ideal culture presents youth as preferable over age, fitness over a sedentary lifestyle, and recently, healthful food over fast food. If these are indeed powerful cultural values, why are we still unfit and overweight as a society? We have easy access to unhealthy food, which also happens to taste good. We value large quantities of food (as in *Supersize Me*) over quality. Our lifestyles are more sedentary than in the past. This social reality makes it very hard to live up to the values of health and fitness, and may, for example, translate to driving our cars to the gym to exercise on sophisticated machines that measure our fitness status. Thus, relationships between dissimilar aspects of culture illustrate a paradox between the ideal society and the real society.

Stigma plays an important role in how health and disease are viewed as well. We are uncomfortable with all types of disease, but feel most strongly about conditions or diseases that are preventable, so there is a tendency to blame people for their poor state of health in these cases. As we learned earlier, stigma against obesity has much to do with the perception that obese people lack self-control and as a result people often act in discriminatory ways toward them. Similarly, patterns in the HIV/AIDS epidemic reflect social views about the disease. Fear, lack of information, and stigma related to sexual behaviors keep many people silent about their own infections and this silence is reinforced by criticism from religious organizations, among other institutions. Stigma has played a significant role in enabling the infection to move through wider and wider segments of the population that were not initially impacted by the infectious disease.

Inequality and the Health-Care Crisis

Inequality is an important component in developing a sociological understanding of health and health care. Indeed, there is nothing more directly connected to a person's life chances than health. In this section we briefly outline the basic inequalities regarding health in the United States and then explore the cases of obesity and HIV/AIDS. As expected, the most relevant areas of health inequality are class, gender, race, and ethnicity. We will see in this section how variations in these characteristics have important effects on the risk of ill health and the access to health care.

Inequalities in Life Expectancy and Infant Mortality

As we have seen in previous chapters, the major factors affecting inequality are deeply intertwined, so it is often difficult to separate class, gender, race, and ethnicity dimensions of inequality when it comes to examining health. Keeping this in mind, we will connect these factors to life chances starting with the most basic characteristics of health, life expectancy, and infant mortality. The statistics presented at the beginning of the chapter

Movie Picks 5.8
Unnatural Causes ... Is Inequality Making Us Sick?

This four-part series documents the relationship between health and social class, race, and ethnicity, focusing in on effects of inequality as manifested, for example, in the neighborhoods we live in, the diseases we face, and the stresses we live with. Clips can be found on the film's website (http://www.unnaturalcauses.org/).

Mixed-Media Extra

Explore the Unnatural Causes website where there is a great deal of information on health inequality. Be sure to take the Health Equity Quiz found under "Media and Documents."

Thinking Sociologically

- Use your sociological imagination to place yourself in the context of inequality and health. Does your class or race give you an advantage or disadvantage in living a healthy life? How does that inform your decisions about your health?
- Consider the community in which you live. How does it impact your health and that of your neighbors?
- Create a diagram showing the relationships between health and specific indicators of inequality as shown in the film.

Access the live/updated links at http://www.paradigmpublishers.com/resources/goldbergmedia.aspx

looked at these characteristics as a whole, but there are important differences when we look at class and race. It should come as no surprise that the higher one's social class position, the longer one's life expectancy, but one might expect that the gap between more and less affluence over time would remain about the same. A 2008 study found that when comparing the differences in the years 1980–1982 to 1998–2000, life expectancy for all groups has increased, but the life-expectancy gap had widened between people of greater and lesser affluence, as seen in Table 5.3. Measures of affluence included characteristics such as "education, income, poverty, housing and other factors" (Pear 2008).

The main reasons given for the socioeconomic differences that influence the growing gap in life expectancy are access to health care and health insurance, education, smoking patterns, and neighborhood safety (Pear 2008). Consistent with this research, a Congressional Budget Office (CBO) report (2008) pointed to heart disease and cancer as major contributors to the increased gap.

Table 5.3
Life Expectancy by Level of Affluence

| | Affluence Level | | |
	Low	High	Gap
1980–1982	73.0 years	75.8 years	2.8 years
1998–2000	74.7 years	79.2 years	4.5 years

Source: Pear (2008)

Another possible contributing factor is obesity, which is more common among people with less education than among people with higher levels of education. The widening gap between social classes and related health effects grows as the class gap expands. The CBO report also considers health problems themselves as not just *resulting* from lower socioeconomic status but also *contributing* to lower socioeconomic status. "Poor health itself has been shown to be a cause of lower income, either because it can inhibit educational attainment or because disabilities can limit work opportunities" (Congressional Budget Office 2008). A person suffering from physical or mental impairment struggles with the cost of care, the availability of treatment, holding a job, finding transportation, and the need for family support, among other issues. So health problems themselves become a source of inequality.

Race and ethnicity factor into the analysis of life expectancy largely because minority groups have a higher risk for poverty. Life expectancy for black men has risen over time, but still remains lower than for white men. As for gender, women have a longer life expectancy than men. Black women's life expectancy has risen at a faster rate than that of white women, though their life expectancy is still lower than that of white women (Congressional Budget Office 2008). Although women outlive men in each racial category, gender plays a role in the distribution of disease and in the resources available for research and treatment of diseases that are of particular relevance to women, especially

breast cancer. The racial differences in disease patterns and mortality are coupled with differential access to screening for disease and health insurance that are likely to impact treatment and survival. The CDC (2007) data from 2000 below show stark racial and ethnic differences in mortality:

- Deaths from heart disease were 29 percent higher for black adults than white adults.
- Minorities were at least twice as likely as whites to be diagnosed with diabetes.
- Black women die of breast cancer and cervical cancer at higher rates than white women.

Infant-mortality rates follow a similar pattern to that of life expectancy. The infant-mortality rate is measured by the number of deaths of infants under the age of one for every 1,000 live births. Overall, there has been a decline in infant mortality in the United States over time, but little to no decline so far in the early twenty-first century. In 2009 the infant-mortality rate was 6.9 deaths for every 1,000 births (Henry J. Kaiser Family Foundation 2009). There are few data available to connect higher rates of infant mortality among different social classes, but race and ethnic data provide some insight into differences related to poverty. Table 5.4 compares poverty rates and infant-mortality rates by race and ethnicity.

Table 5.4 shows an especially strong connection between poverty rates and infant-mortality rates when comparing whites and

Table 5.4
United States Poverty, Race, and Infant Mortality 2009

	White	Black	Hispanic
Poverty rate (%)	13.0	35.0	33.0
Infant mortality rate (deaths per 1,000 live births)	5.7	13.6	5.6

Sources: The Henry J. Kaiser Family Foundation (2009, 2011)

blacks. Although Hispanics have a much higher rate of poverty than whites, their infant-mortality rates are similar. Why is that so? Risk factors play a role in some cases: "preterm and low birthweight delivery, socioeconomic status, [and] access to medical care" (MacDorman and Mathews 2008) may explain some of the differences between Hispanic and black rates. A closer look at ethnic groups that share the experience of poverty but have different experiences during pregnancy and birth may help explain some of the differences in infant-mortality rates, though there needs to be more research.

Inequality and Obesity

The problem of obesity disproportionately affects different populations. Women and men have equal rates of obesity, though more women than men are "extremely obese." Blacks have the highest rate of obesity (49.5 percent), followed by Hispanics (39.1 percent) and whites (34.3 percent) (US Department of Health and Human Services 2013). Racial differences suggest that the poor are more likely to be obese than are members of more affluent groups. According to the Food Research and Action Center (2010), poverty and obesity are linked by a number of structural factors in poor communities. When people have limited funds they often turn to cheaper, less nutritious food, which is also likely to be high in calories. High-quality food is more expensive than low-quality food and it is often hard to find a variety of healthy food in poor neighborhoods where there is little access to supermarkets. Further aggravating the situation is that opportunities for exercise are limited in poor neighborhoods due to safety concerns, lack of open space, and few places to play. In many school systems, especially in poor communities, physical-education programs may have been eliminated or severely cut back. Lack of opportunities for exercise due to restricted leisure time contributes to the problem.

Limited access to health care and higher stress levels than are typically found in more affluent sectors also contribute to higher levels of obesity. Ironically, obesity can be associated with hunger among the poor, who may have to limit their food intake for periods of time. Mothers, especially, sometimes choose to eat less in order to feed their children. This may result in poor eating habits even when food is available, such as eating more than is needed when food is available. Further, fattening food is cheaper than nutritious food, thus contributing to increases in obesity while also increasing hunger.

Inequality and HIV/AIDS

Poverty, gender, racial, and ethnic differences stand out when examining trends in HIV/AIDS over time. A study by Denning and DiNenno (2010) found that in urban poverty areas in the United States the HIV/AIDS rate was 2.1 percent, about the same as the rates in countries such as Burundi, Ethiopia, and Haiti, which are considered among the least developed countries. In examining the rate of HIV/AIDS within the United States they found that the lower the income level, the higher the HIV rate. Households with incomes below $10,000 had a nearly 3 percent infection rate, whereas households earning over $50,000 had a less than 0.5 percent infection rate. As we saw earlier, men having sex with men are most at risk for infection. Men of color, especially black men, have an increasingly larger share of diagnoses. For black men the infection rate was seven times higher than the infection rate for white men in 2010, and for Hispanic men it was twice as high. The Centers for Disease Control and Prevention (2013b) reports that among the factors that play a role in this trend are the overarching effects of poverty, which African Americans experience at a higher rate than whites, and related factors such as less access to education about HIV/AIDS, and limited health-care options. Lack of awareness of one's HIV status is also significant. Stigma regarding homosexuality and AIDS among blacks and Hispanics runs very high, so information about HIV can be difficult to communicate, and people with HIV/AIDS in those groups may hide their status from others, including sexual partners.

Recent trends indicate that women comprise an increasing share of those infected. In 1984–1985, 12 percent of new diagnoses were among women, while by 2010 women comprised 20 percent of new diagnoses (Kates et al. 2013, 9). Women of color, especially black women, are increasingly vulnerable to infection. Sixty-four percent of new infections in women are among black women, 18 percent among white women, and 15 percent among Latinas. Black women also comprise 65 percent of deaths and 60 percent of women living with HIV (Kates et al. 2013, 10).

Measuring inequality by examining life expectancy, infant mortality, and the distribution of disease tells us a great deal about the importance of social stratification in understanding the world of health and health care. We now turn to the application of sociological theory to further understand the crisis of health and health care.

Applying Sociological Theory

As with earlier topics, it is beneficial to see how the application of sociological theory can help us understand the larger social context of the crisis of health and health care. Since functional theory likens society to an organic body with functioning organs, it is fitting to utilize it to further our understanding of the health crisis to see how social institutions contribute to the health of society. Conflict theory is best utilized to examine the toll inequality takes on society and the potential for conflict. Both of these macro theories help us see the structural dimensions of the health crisis. We will also apply social construction theory and symbolic interaction theory to show the impact of how we define health and communicate about our understanding of health.

Functionalism and Social Institutions

The ability of a society to survive and thrive depends on its institutions, according to functionalism. If those institutions can serve the needs of the members of society, then a society is considered to be in equilibrium, or functional. If institutions fail to meet the needs of society, then they become

Web Exercise 5.5
The Unequal Distribution of HIV/AIDS in the United States

View the two fact sheets, "The HIV/AIDS Epidemic in the United States" (http://kff.org/hivaids/fact-sheet/the-hivaids-epidemic-in-the-united-states/) and "Women and HIV in the United States (http://kff.org/hivaids/fact-sheet/women-and-hivaids-in-the-united-states/). Pay special attention to the information about gender and race.

- What trends do you see in the infection patterns over time?
- Why has the infection rate increased among women and people of color?
- A large portion of the funds for care comes from Medicaid. What does that tell you about poverty in relation to HIV/AIDS?

Access the live/updated links at http://www.paradigmpublishers.com/resources/goldbergmedia.aspx

dysfunctional and we can expect social change in order to reshape society—or, if not, the death of the society itself becomes possible. The interplay between the physical nature of health and social experience is the basis for examining the role of social institutions from a functionalist perspective. In considering obesity, for instance, we know it is a social trend that presents tremendous costs to individuals and society and it is projected to be even more widespread in the next generation. Will obesity become the norm? At what point does obesity become dysfunctional to society? What changes will society make to reduce or accommodate obesity? In the case of HIV/AIDS, society can become destabilized when large numbers of people are infected and die. The more fragile the society and its health-care system, the greater will be the impact of AIDS. We will now look briefly at major social institutions to see the role of each in dealing with these health concerns.

Families are the most directly affected by the health problems of their members. They are involved in care and support, both emotional and financial. The quality of care and the availability of health insurance are important factors in how families cope and in their ties to the larger society. If a parent becomes ill, insurance status, job loss, or loss of life play important roles in family dynamics. When dependents become sick, whether they are children or elderly relatives, families are often burdened with enormous financial and time constraints. In places where AIDS has devastated communities, for example, children may be orphaned and cared for by extended relatives or orphanages, dramatically changing family dynamics and upsetting the stability of the community. Family ties to other institutions are demonstrated as we sort out access to care, costs, health-care reform, and other large-scale economic and political considerations that will have direct impacts on families.

Education is an important contributor to understanding risks of disease, as we saw with obesity and HIV/AIDS, but also with health overall. What we learn about preventive measures for any disease is determined by access to information to keep us healthy. The lack of education about HIV/AIDS has led to a greater spread of the disease than might have happened with more effective educational programs. Religion, too, plays a role. In the case of HIV/AIDS, condemnation of people with AIDS was, and in some cases still is, led by some religious institutions strongly opposed to same-sex relationships and/or the use of condoms. How each of these institutions functions with regard to health and disease is useful in knowing how well society overall manages the health of its members. Political and economic institutions are also profoundly affected by these health problems. From the political ramifications of health-care reform to the economic cost to society of responding to obesity and HIV/AIDS, the strains on these social institutions are significant.

From what we have learned about health in this chapter, we have a long way to go. While we live longer, we are faced with diseases that impede our life chances, especially if we are poor. We are faced with conditions such as obesity that are intricately interwoven between individual behavior and social dynamics. We have no cure for HIV/AIDS. A functionalist might argue that health-care reform is an attempt to correct a dysfunctional system of care. From a functionalist perspective, there are some ways in which we are healthier, given the rise in longevity and lowering of infant mortality, though many argue that outcomes are uneven. If we assume that a society is functional based on the health of its members, we also find that it is more functional for some than others. For a discussion of the disparities of health and health care we turn to conflict theory.

Conflict Theory

The inequality of health and health care discussed earlier in the chapter demonstrates that social location has a significant effect on life chances. People with wealth have easier access to knowledge about health and quality care largely because their economic position affords them opportunities that many others do not have. People with steady employment in the primary labor market with the best-paying jobs are more likely to have health insurance than those in the secondary labor market. Many people in the secondary labor market do not have health insurance, though that may change eventually with health reform. Access to insurance makes a big difference in the ability to get care. As we have seen, race, ethnicity, and gender differences also contribute to the inequality of health and this is reflected in some of the important measures of health: life span, infant mortality, obesity rates, and HIV/AIDS trends. If we were to examine more closely diseases such as diabetes, heart disease, or cancer we would see differences in diagnoses, cures, and survival rates all related to access to care. Why do these disparities exist? What are the structural considerations in this unequal distribution of health and what is the potential for conflict? For this we look at two important components: communities and their environments, and the health-insurance and pharmaceutical industries.

The communities we live in are important to our health. From basic environmental components to access to doctors and healthy food, we can see the impact on health. As we learned earlier, access to healthy food depends in part on our neighborhoods—options for healthy food sources in poor neighborhoods are limited compared to affluent neighborhoods. Similarly, health services are less available in poor urban and rural areas. The rates of obesity are higher among the poor, and diseases impacted by diet such as diabetes are tied to access to healthy food.

Air and water pollution, lead exposure, and even climate change have the potential of harming the poor more than the affluent. This is true domestically and globally. We saw in Chapter 4 that natural disasters have a more devastating effect on poor regions than on developed regions because of the former's limited infrastructures and weak health-care systems. Climate change has the potential for unequal distribution of environmental problems, especially access to clean water. Inequality in these areas may lead to conflict within and between nations as the disparities of health tied to environments become more evident.

The experience of HIV/AIDS points directly to the role of confrontation and conflict during the 1980s and 1990s when scant attention was paid by governments to find treatment and provide effective education. Organized groups of people with AIDS and their supporters confronted politicians and the general public to call attention to the disparity of investment in AIDS research compared to other diseases. They were successful in pushing for more investment in research and treatment, and they continue to work to keep AIDS work funded to this day.

Perhaps the most obvious conflict generated in the health crisis in the United States came with the debate about health reform. The gatekeepers of health-care special interests—insurance and pharmaceutical companies—have demonstrated the strengths of their efforts to maintain their power in the face of reform. These wealthy and influential interest groups lobby hard with legislators, candidates for political office, doctors, and hospitals. We saw earlier in the chapter the great influence of marketing by pharmaceutical companies to maintain their dominant role in treatment. Insurance lobbies have spent hundreds of millions of dollars to influence health-care reform. Millions of dollars were spent on television advertising alone, reaching millions of Americans along with their health-care providers and elected officials. Before the vote on the 2010 Afford-able Care Act, $56 million had been spent in the first half of 2009 alone on advertising by special-interest groups trying to influence the reform effort (Pershing 2009). During 2009, according to the Center for Respon-sive Politics (2010), $3.49 billion was spent by 13,694 lobbyists to influence Congress and the federal government about health reform. Some of the lobbyists are former members of Congress or their staff members. The 2013 government shutdown was largely orchestrated by members of Congress who made a calculated, though unsuccessful, attempt to try to "defund" the Affordable Care Act. Their efforts were financed by large, wealthy interest groups that have spent millions of dollars attacking the law known as "Obamacare."

From a conflict theory perspective, the health-reform debate is a good example of the conflicts that ensue from the unequal distribution of health resources. It has been, and continues to be, one of the most conten-tious political debates so far in the twenty-first century. The powerful insurance and pharmaceutical interests work hard to shape health-care reform to their benefit. Average Americans, and especially the poor, have little opportunity to learn about, much less influence, political decisions except through voting. But when insurance and pharmaceu-tical interest groups spend millions of dollars to promote their version of reform, one can question if citizens are given an opportunity to see all sides of the debate. Considering the unequal distribution of health care, is it any wonder that conflict will continue long into the future?

Micro Theory

Social construction theory has a number of applications when considering health and health care. Whether we define a medical condition as a problem, an epidemic, or a crisis depends in part on what we believe the social ramifications will be if the health problem spreads. Even a definition that has its origins in scientific research, and even a medical diagnosis itself, can change over time in relation to social circumstances. The definition of obesity, which we discussed earlier in the chapter, is universally accepted

---

 Movie Picks 5.9
Sick Around America

The *Frontline* video *Sick Around America* (http://video.pbs.org/video/1099857730/) examines the dynamics of employment and insurance. When people lose jobs, they lose their insurance. Consider how sociological theory helps us understand the crisis of access and cost of insurance.

Thinking Sociologically

- Describe the conflicts presented in the film.
- Which social institutions are impacted by the health crisis in America? How are they impacted?
- Which macro theory best explains the problems sick Americans face? Why?
- Using the sociological imagination, how does the presentation of individual health problems inform us about the social crisis of health care?

Access the live/updated links at http://www.paradigmpublishers.com/resources/goldbergmedia.aspx

in the medical community today, but some people question the validity of the measure and the potential health effects. Much of the debate concerns whether obesity contributes to serious health risks, and how to respond to both the vast media attention obesity has gotten and the rise of a very profitable industry in weight-loss products. Calling obesity an epidemic puts it in a category of disease about which there is no clear agreement. Sociologist Abigail Saguy argues that there is no agreement on many aspects of obesity or even a definition of healthy weight (Sullivan 2005). Obesity is not a static concept, so it is important to recognize the trends in awareness of it as a health problem and to anticipate cultural adaptations as well as research that refine our understanding of it as a social construction.

HIV/AIDS is also socially constructed. Historically, it had several iterations as the medical community tried to understand the virus in the early days of the epidemic. GRID (Gay Related Immune Deficiency) and "gay cancer" gave AIDS an identity unrelated to the virus itself, which only attacks with opportunity—that is, in the wake of risk behaviors. Even after more was known about the virus, the criteria for determining when an HIV diagnosis developed into AIDS was in some ways arbitrary. So much of our understanding of HIV/AIDS today depends on how it was socially constructed over time in the context of the ignorance and fears of the society at large. The definition of HIV/AIDS evolved as greater understanding of the virus emerged. New treatments have further altered our understanding of AIDS. Whereas it was once considered a death sentence, today medicines allow for a greater chance of survival. The idea that AIDS has evolved into a chronic disease has affected attitudes and behaviors, increasing the risk of infection. Since not all infected persons have access to medicines or can tolerate them, constructing it as a chronic rather than fatal disease may have disastrous effects. Social

construction theory gives us insight into the evolving nature of disease as well as our social responses to them. It is a valuable tool for seeing disease in a social context.

Symbolic interaction theory is especially useful in understanding attitudes and labels applied to people who suffer from ill health. We have already addressed how stigma affects an understanding of HIV/AIDS because it is tied to risk behaviors rather than random bad luck. Slurs regarding sexual orientation and risk behaviors make it easy to reject the person suffering from the disease. In the early days of the AIDS epidemic there was a clear line drawn between the "innocent victims"—that is, children, surgical-transfusion recipients, and hemophiliacs—and those whose "irresponsible behavior" marked them as "deserving" the infection—that is, gay men and IV drug users. Similarly with obesity, labeling people as fat, ugly, irresponsible, and deserving of their illness enables others of us to look down on them, deny them sympathy, and limit their treatment. Labeling has a profound effect on the person or group labeled and on society as we communicate about and categorize people.

Symbolic interaction theory also helps us see the value of symbols used to demonstrate the importance of disease, the need for research, and the connections we feel toward those who suffer. Powerful symbols, even very simple ones like the AIDS ribbon, can be used to represent our beliefs and support for things we believe in. This is easily demonstrated with the use of the color pink to represent support of people with breast cancer. It says a lot about a symbol for breast cancer when professional football players don bright pink shoes for games in support of breast-cancer research every fall. Another example with tremendous symbolic meaning is the AIDS quilt. During the height of the AIDS epidemic in the United States, a group of people decided to create a quilt representing loved ones who died of AIDS. Individual

Web Exercise 5.6
The Ultimate Symbolic Gesture
The AIDS Quilt

The Names Project developed a quilt display in which people created panels representing loved ones who died of AIDS. It is now too large to display in its totality—it once covered the entire Mall in Washington, DC. See background information and photos of panels from the quilt and the displays (http://www.aidsquilt.org/). Look at as many pictures of the display as you can. Notice patterns in the symbols on the panels. Consider why people selected certain symbols to represent their loved ones.

- What symbols stand out as representative of people who have died of AIDS?
- What can you learn about an individual when examining a panel?
- How is culture conveyed in the panels?
- What social purpose does making and displaying a quilt panel serve?

Access the live/updated links at http://www.paradigmpublishers.com/resources/goldbergmedia.aspx

panels as well as the quilt as a whole had a powerful message displayed in dramatic fashion of remembrance and reminder of the deadliness of AIDS. The AIDS quilt did more than just visually display information about a person's life. It was a form of interaction and communication among people who saw the quilt. It was symbolically powerful because it was both an individual expression and a social statement about the toll the AIDS epidemic took on our society.

The Future of Health and Health Care

There is a vast amount of information on health trends and the unequal distribution of health care. Sociologists are in a unique position to contribute to an understanding of both the personal and social factors that make up the status of health domestically and globally and to predict future trends. By going beyond medical conditions to a more sociological perspective of disease, we gain insight into patterns of behavior, shifts in cultural values regarding health, the effects

of stigma, the role of stratification, and the political discourse on health reform. This perspective on a macro level enables us to see the structural factors that contribute to the patterns of obesity and HIV/AIDS, as we saw earlier, as well as other diseases not covered in this chapter. We can see how the social construction of disease impacts our understanding of health and illness and how that understanding connects to broad structural patterns. Communication about health and illness, including labeling and symbolic gestures like the AIDS quilt, connect the personal world of the pain of disease to the larger society.

Two basic questions come to mind in relation to the theme of this book: Are the problems of health and health care really a crisis? What can we predict about health and health care in the future?

Is There a Crisis in Health and Health Care?

Let's look at the two health problems discussed in depth in this chapter: HIV/AIDS and obesity. By most measures HIV/AIDS would be considered a crisis for infected people and their family and friends. Fear of death, costly lifelong medication for survival, and altered patterns of behavior are serious factors for individuals. One could argue that sexual practices have changed considerably with awareness of AIDS, even among non-infected people. Condom use and HIV testing have become an acceptable, even expected, practice among many who are sexually active. Depending on a person's relative wealth, insurance status, and where they live in the world, the crisis may be mitigated somewhat by access to support, good health care, and medicine. On a structural level, HIV/AIDS has been devastating for communities and even nations. It is considered a pandemic, that is, a worldwide epidemic. The large-scale loss of life, destruction of families, and economic costs in the billions of dollars have contributed to the ongoing crisis of HIV/AIDS globally. For many years there has been the expectation that a vaccine would be developed to eradicate AIDS, and while many hold out hope for this, it does not appear to be imminent. On a positive note, the crisis of HIV/AIDS has created opportunities to gain a greater understanding of retroviruses applicable to other diseases and it has changed norms in medical settings regarding universal precautions, thus providing cleaner and safer environments for patients and health-care personnel alike. Even though we can expect longer life for those infected individuals lucky enough to get life-saving medication, the costs will be immense and HIV will continue to spread. Most will agree that HIV/AIDS will remain a crisis for individuals and society well into the future.

The question whether obesity is a crisis is somewhat more nuanced. It is more a condition than a disease. Although obesity is associated with heart disease, diabetes, and certain cancers, there is considerable debate about it as a crisis. From a sociological perspective, obesity has contributed to important cultural dynamics, some of which are contradictory. We are more accepting of larger sizes, yet highly critical of people viewed as gluttonous. We eat fast food and we diet. We are sedentary and active. As for the future, there is great concern about the increase in childhood obesity, an important trend that speaks to the fears of increasing health costs and shorter life spans for the next generation. The CDC reports that childhood obesity has increased in all age groups, almost tripling since 1980. Overall, about 17 percent of children ages two to nineteen are obese (Centers for Disease Control 2013c). If today's obese children become obese adults, there will be a crisis both for individuals and society as a whole. Reducing obesity among the young would require considerable cultural shifts in our thinking about food and nutrition, physical activity, and long-term promotion of healthier lifestyles. From a sociological perspective, it is important to watch these trends to predict the future health costs of obesity and its potential as a crisis in the next generation. There does not appear to be any substantive change in behaviors to warrant a prediction that obesity will be reduced in the near future, so we can expect the crisis to build as today's obese children become obese adults.

The Future of Health-Care Reform

Perhaps the biggest unknown for the future of health care is the direction health reform will take in the United States. As we saw earlier in the chapter, the passage of the Affordable Care Act in 2010 was historic. A number of states are challenging the law in court. Enormous sums of money have been spent on lobbying, mostly against reform. Several factors will make a big difference in whether the law will stand. First, how American citizens respond to the provisions as they experience them will influence

Web Exercise 5.7
Media and Health-Reform Advocacy

The Internet is rife with ideas and recommendations for health reform. View the positions of these two organizations on health reform:

The Heritage Foundation (http://www.heritage.org/issues/health-care).
Health Care for America Now! (http://healthcareforamericanow.org/).

- What is the difference, if any, between the goals of each group?
- Who sponsors each group?
- Is there any bias reflected in the information provided on each website?
- Which reform issues do you think are most important?
- What should Americans do to help solve the health crisis?
- Where do you fit into the debate?

Access the live/updated links at http://www.paradigmpublishers.com/resources/goldbergmedia.aspx

acceptance or rejection of reform. Second, the direction of political discourse about the law will influence lawmakers and the public. For now it is contentious and is likely to remain so. There is widespread talk of repeal of the law by those opposed to it while supporters are determined to save the law. Whatever happens, there will be changes to how we experience health care and the debate will go on well into the middle of the twenty-first century.

Looking Backward/Looking Forward

As an issue that is both intimate and universal, the crisis in health and health care has important ties to other topics in this book. Regarding the environmental problems discussed in Chapter 3, there are many health problems associated with the environmental crisis. Exhaust from industry and automobiles has contributed to air pollution throughout the world, and many cities suffer from poor air quality. Respiratory disease is a common result. Environmental problems linked to climate change will have dramatic effects on health as droughts and floods consume

parts of the globe. Small island nations are particularly vulnerable as they lose land and fresh water. As we saw in Chapter 4, people living in fragile or failed states suffer great health problems and have few resources on which to rely. Forced labor in various industries, and contact with oil, metals, and toxic waste in particular, expose workers to risks from which they are not protected. Looking ahead to the chapter on terrorism, the ultimate health hazard is being a victim of a terrorist attack, but there are also residual health problems as we see among the workers at Ground Zero in New York City. It is well documented that many of these workers now suffer from serious health problems from exposure to toxins in the air in the aftermath of the attacks. We should also consider the physical and mental problems associated with wars in Iraq and Afghanistan, including the stress experienced in war and in the aftermath. There is a great deal of documentation of increases in post-traumatic stress disorder (PTSD) and suicide among soldiers and veterans. Finally, in our chapter on technology, we will consider the role of genetics in society, especially regarding issues of identity and the future of reproductive technology. Our growing knowledge about genes and our ability to manipulate them will surely impact the health of many people in the future.

Web Watch

The Internet serves as a handy tool for individuals seeking information on their own health. If you have ever done a search for a condition you are experiencing, you have likely come across a variety of sites selling health products and test kits, recommending cures, scaring you with horrible diagnoses, and perhaps even offering sound medical advice. For our purposes, we will limit suggestions to more substantive research and advocacy websites, some of which are cited in this chapter. As with the other chapters there are also government and international websites listed below. Because health reform is such a volatile topic, students must be careful in viewing sites with political agendas or selling products. Find out who sponsors the site and whether the sponsor has a stake in a particular outcome or has a profit motive.

AARP: http://www.aarp.org/

American Sociological Association medical sociology section: http://dept.kent.edu/sociology/asamedsoc/

The Body: http://www.thebody.com/index/inspire.html

Centers for Disease Control and Prevention: http://cdc.gov

Child Trends: http://www.childtrends.org/

Henry J. Kaiser Family Foundation: http://kff.org/

KaiserEDU.org: Health Policy Explained: http://www.kaiseredu.org/

Obesity Society: http://www.obesity.org/

PEW Research Center: http://pewresearch.org/

Robert Woods Johnson Foundation: http://www.rwjf.org/

Sociosite: Sociology of Health: http://www.sociosite.net/topics/health.php#HEALTH

World AIDS Day: http://worldaidsday.org/

World Health Organization: http://www.who.int/en/

CHAPTER 6

Terrorism and Its Aftermath

A New York City firefighter looks up at what remains of the World Trade Center after its collapse after the Sept. 11 terrorist attack.
Source: US Navy Photo by Photographer's Mate 2nd Class Jim Watson

1995: A truck bomb exploded at a government building, causing many deaths and massive destruction. One hundred sixty-eight lives were lost, some of them young children. Nearly 700 people were injured. The bomb was so powerful that it damaged more than 300 nearby buildings and many cars.

2001: Four airplanes controlled by a group of nineteen terrorists succeeded in destroying two large buildings and damaging another by flying into them. Three of the airplanes successfully hit their targets—government and business buildings— while the fourth crashed in a struggle with passengers who fought the hijackers. A total of 3,120 people were killed, not including the terrorists.

2013: Two bombs exploded at the finish line of a marathon, killing three people and injuring scores of others. The hunt for the perpetrators and their motives crossed international borders.

Which of the above happened on American soil?

All three of these events took place on American soil. When Americans think about terrorism it is only expected that we think first about the 9/11 attacks on the World Trade Center and the Pentagon and the failed attempt in a field in Pennsylvania, the second example above. That day, September 11, 2001, is seared into the memories of most of us who were old enough to watch it unfold on television. The death and destruction, the intensity of loss, the fear, and the mourning are all part of who we are today. For those of you too young to remember 9/11, you may not be fully aware of the consequences of that day but they permeate your lives in important ways that we examine later in this chapter. Some would argue that it is the central defining crisis of your generation both in its immediate effect and in the shape society has taken in its aftermath. Many books and articles have been written about the attacks and the attackers, the planning, the response, and questions about whether it could have been stopped. But it was not the first terrorist attack in the United States, and not all terrorists are foreigners. The 1995 attack described above took place April 19 and destroyed a federal building in Oklahoma City. The terrorists, Timothy McVeigh and Terry Nichols, were militant Americans angry at the government. The third example happened very recently at

the Boston Marathon. There remains confusion about what connections if any the bombers had to terrorist groups or what role religious radicalism may have played. What is clear from that incident is that after a long period of successfully thwarting attacks on US soil, this attack managed to break through the extensive security net developed since 9/11. There have been many other terrorist attacks throughout the world, and many more are expected. The experience, even the anticipation of terrorism regardless of the source, reflects a crisis that impacts the entire globe.

Defining Terrorism Sociologically

The goal of this chapter is to gain a better understanding of terrorism and how it has shaped American domestic policies and global relationships, even its culture and communities. Before we do that, though, we first have to define terrorism. Despite the violence and fear, or maybe because of it, definitions of terrorism are highly subjective. In fact, more than any other topic in this book, terrorism can best be understood as a social construction. There is no objective definition precisely because it means different things to different people at different points in history. How we define it depends on time and place, the perspectives of perpetrators and victims, and of government, community, and individual responses. Applying social construction theory in order to define terrorism helps us see it from different vantage points, yet it is still important to come to an understanding of terrorism and the ramifications of terrorist acts.

Regardless of the difficulty in defining terrorism, in order to gain an understanding of it we must provide a working sociological definition. We will limit our definition to the current era of global terrorism, what Anthony Giddens calls "new style" terrorism that spans the world using new technology that allows for terrorist activities almost anywhere (2006). For our purposes, then, **terrorism** is an act of violence or threat of violence against non-combatant citizens to meet or call attention to political objectives. Terrorists act in this manner because they do not have legitimate power to meet their goals and so they resort to extreme forms of violence that give them a large audience and instill fear among those targeted. They use modern technology including the Internet and cell phones to organize and coordinate acts of terror. They use media to broadcast their goals, recruit members, and take responsibility for the acts they commit, while also hiding their geographic locations. Actual terrorist acts for the most part are not especially technically sophisticated. Car bombs, suicide bombs, kidnappings, and beheadings are common. The attacks on the World Trade Center and the Pentagon required box cutters, the ability to fly airplanes, coordination, and money. The bombs detonated at the Boston Marathon were made from common pressure cookers. Their seeming randomness and anonymity are what strikes great fear in people. Even when a person is not a direct victim of a terrorist attack, the experience resonates in ways that go far beyond the actual physical destruction. There is great concern that terrorists may soon be capable of attacks involving biological, chemical, or nuclear weapons, with much more dire outcomes than acts of terror so far, thus enhancing the fears of ordinary people.

In the remainder of this chapter we address the following:

- A brief overview of major acts of terrorism in the United States and abroad.
- A profile of one of the most active terrorist organizations, Al Qaeda.
- The ways in which terrorism has shaped twenty-first century America in the aftermath of 9/11, including
  ° The impact terrorism has had on the decision to go to war.
  ° Domestic security.

Later in the chapter we also apply sociological concepts and theories as in the preceding chapters.

 Reading Room 6.1
Defining Terrorism Sociologically

Read Austin T. Turk's article, "Sociology of Terrorism" (2004). Consider how terrorism can be defined sociologically. The article examines who the terrorists are and how they are socialized, what role the media plays, and how society responds to terrorism. How does sociology describe terrorism compared to the view of the general public?

Access the live/updated links at http://www.paradigmpublishers.com/resources/goldbergmedia.aspx

Overview of Terrorism

Major Terrorist Attacks on the United States

We have briefly described the three most significant terrorist attacks in the United States in a generation, though Americans had already experienced a serious terrorist attack prior to the Oklahoma City bombing. In 1993 a radical Muslim group attacked the World Trade Center in New York by planting a bomb in the underground parking garage. The building damage was extensive, six people were killed, and over 1,000 people were injured. The bombing was a forerunner of the devastating attack against the same buildings eight years later, but only in retrospect was the significance of the bombing in 1993 realized. At the time a great deal of evidence was uncovered that extensive terrorist attacks were being planned, but the significance was not fully understood. America did not yet feel especially vulnerable to attack, terrorism seemed far away, and with some exceptions we remained largely unconcerned. By contrast, the attack at the Boston Marathon in 2013 demonstrated how quickly officials responded in a remarkable display of sophisticated technology and manpower to find the perpetrators and define the act as terrorism. Media also played a significant role in seeking connections between the bombers and their family and friends, their immigration experience, and their international connections.

Like the other acts of terrorism, the domestic attack in Oklahoma City took Americans by surprise, but it was considered by most to be an isolated, misguided attempt to express grievances against the government. Again, few Americans felt vulnerable. This was equally true of the October 2000 suicide attack on the USS *Cole* off the coast of Yemen, in which seventeen American sailors were killed, and in various other attacks in far-flung places abroad. It was not until September 11, 2001, that Americans felt the full impact of terrorism. Some described it as the twenty-first century's equivalent of the attack on Pearl Harbor, which marked our entry into World War II. In the aftermath of both attacks, there were unprecedented changes on all levels of society: in security, law enforcement, and plans for war; a variety of more cultural responses, especially an intensification of expressions of patriotism and a rising tide of racism; and on the individual level, personal reactions ranging from panic to joining the military to avenge the attacks. On the whole, catastrophic events

---

    Reading Room 6.2
    Timelines of Terrorist Attacks

It is worth exploring the many terrorist attacks against the United States at home and abroad. There are a number of comprehensive historical timelines online. Following is a link that provides a useful timeline:

National Counterterrorism Center Counterterrorism 2013 Calendar and Interactive Map (http://www.nctc.gov/site/).

Consider the targets, the type of weapons, and the perpetrators. Can you make any generalizations to help create a sociological profile of terrorism from these timelines?

Access the live/updated links at http://www.paradigmpublishers.com/resources/goldbergmedia.aspx

Fast Facts 6.1
Global Terrorism 2011

- 10,283 attacks in 70 countries (12 percent fewer than in 2010; 29 percent fewer than in 2007).
- 45,000 victims with over 12,500 killed (5 percent fewer than 2010).
- Regionally, 75 percent of attacks were in South Asia and the Near East.
- Afghanistan experienced the most terrorist attacks, followed by Iraq and Pakistan.
- Most attacks in Africa were in Somalia and Nigeria.

Source: US Department of State (2012b).

reshape our lives and our culture in important ways, and 9/11 was one of those events.

Global Terrorism

If we are to understand terrorism we must see its global reach. In addition to the attacks in America, many more attacks are perpetrated against other countries and groups. These happen all over the world, in developed countries and poor countries, and on nearly every continent. They cross national boundaries, with perpetrators coming from one country and attacking places in another, and the victims are from many different parts of the world. The attacks on 9/11 are an example of this, but so are many other terrorist incidents. We can see a snapshot of terrorist attacks in 2011 in the box on "Fast Facts: Global Terrorism 2011."

Of course each year brings some variation on the types of attacks and locations and purpose, but the similarities are worth exploring. We cannot cover the full range of terrorist attacks or motivations in this book, nor can we address all the responses to the attacks or threats of attacks. Nonetheless, it is helpful to look for patterns in the locations, organizations, and targets. Sociologically it helps to understand the structural context in which terrorism operates.

Web Exercise 6.1
Global Terrorism

Go to the website for Johnston's Archive: Terrorism, Counterterrorism, and Unconventional Warfare (http://www.johnstonsarchive.net/terrorism/). First review the contents and note the definition of terrorism. Select the following: "Map of worst terrorist attacks worldwide." Note that only attacks killing 100 or more people are included. Focus on locations and types of attack.

- What patterns do you see in the geographic distribution of attacks?
- What conclusions can you draw from these patterns?
- Select one incident and find more information on it. Describe the incident.
- Can you tell if this is a reliable website? Explain.

Access the live/updated links at http://www.paradigmpublishers.com/resources/goldbergmedia.aspx

Later in the chapter, we apply sociological concepts to better understand the reasons for terrorism and responses to it. But first we must learn about the terrorists themselves. We now turn to describing Al Qaeda, the group that is responsible for having had the greatest impact on the United States and that is considered to be the perpetrators of the 9/11 attacks, among others. Many American citizens have been lost to their attacks and the response has resulted in major changes in domestic and international policy, including a commitment to go to war.

Terrorist Groups: Focus on Al Qaeda

In a 2011 report, the US Department of State (2012b) designated forty-nine groups as foreign terrorist organizations. As we saw earlier in the Fast Facts box, in that year alone, there were 10,283 deaths globally caused by terrorist activity.

Terrorism has taken many forms and has included a range of people from a variety of cultures and personal backgrounds. While Americans tend to focus on attacks by foreigners in this country, attacks across the globe demonstrate the complexity of terrorism and the motivations of terrorists. What roles do Americans play abroad in the larger dynamics of terrorist activities? What if an American participated in a terrorist attack in another nation?

Despite the many different terrorist organizations, for Americans, Al Qaeda is the best-known terrorist group because of its association with the 9/11 attacks. It was for a time considered the greatest threat to the United States according to the US Department of State (2012a). However, counterterrorism activities have had a significant impact on its strength and ability to carry out major attacks. Osama bin Laden, the organizer of the 9/11 attacks on the United States, was its leader until he was killed by US Navy Seals in 2011. The group emerged out of resistance to the Soviet Union invasion of Afghanistan from 1979 to 1988, and at the time their efforts were supported by the United States. Once the Soviet Union left Afghanistan, the

---

Web Exercise 6.2
Who Are the Terrorists?

Visit these two website reports:

> US Department of State (2012a): *Country Reports on Terrorism 2011,* Chapter 6: "Foreign Terrorist Organizations" (http://www.state.gov/j/ct/rls/crt/2011/195553.htm).
> National Counterterrorism Center (2013): "Counterterrorism 2013 Calendar" (http://www.nctc.gov/site/groups/index.html).

At the NCTC website click on the logo for one of the groups and read about it. (Some groups do not have links available.) Also see the list of terrorists and the interactive map to help locate them in the world.

- What are the goals of the group you selected?
- Where do they operate?
- What is their importance to the United States?
- How did this exercise influence your ideas about terrorism?

Access the live/updated links at http://www.paradigmpublishers.com/resources/goldbergmedia.aspx

Movie Picks 6.1
A Perfect Terrorist

The PBS *Frontline* documentary *A Perfect Terrorist* demonstrates the global nature of terrorism as it explores the experiences of an American man involved in the planning of the Mumbai attacks of 2008 while also acting as an informant for the US government (http://www.pbs.org /wgbh/pages/frontline/david-headley/).

Thinking Sociologically

- What is the relationship of this man to global terrorism?
- Does his multicultural background influence his experiences with terrorism?
- How do his experiences link to other social institutions, especially religion and politics?
- What is the sociological value of examining the experience of one person?

Access the live/updated links at http://www.paradigmpublishers.com/resources/goldbergmedia.aspx

group formed wider goals of spreading Islam throughout the world. This included ridding Islamic countries of non-Islamic influence. In this goal, it focused on the United States and its military and commercial-oil interests in the Middle East. Al Qaeda came to the attention of the United States in 1998 when it bombed American embassies in Kenya and Tanzania. This was the first connection of Osama bin Laden and the Al Qaeda organization to terrorist attacks on US interests. They were later accused of the attack on the USS *Cole* in a port in Yemen in 2000. The most devastating attack was on September 11, 2001 (that is, 9/11), for which Al Qaeda took responsibility. Over ten years the United States had repeatedly tried to find bin Laden in Sudan, Afghanistan, and Pakistan, and it was finally successful in finding him hiding nearly in plain sight in Pakistan. He was killed by a team of US Navy Seals and buried at sea. The information gleaned from his discovery provided important information on past and potential future terrorist attacks. There has been moderate success in dismantling Al Qaeda, which along with other groups continues to pose a threat to the United States.

It is important to understand the motivations of Al Qaeda and similar terrorist organizations. They are committed to a form of Islam that is strictly practiced and aggressive against non-Muslims and even against less-observant forms of Islam. Despite what we may learn from the popular press, Islam comes in a number of variations in the world, from very conservative adherence to traditional practice, to more liberal interpretations of religious teachings. Because most Americans' experiences with Islam are limited to what is known about terrorists, there is significant distortion in understanding the religion itself. Nonetheless, Al Qaeda and other organizations make it clear that they conduct their attacks in the name of Islam. They are referred to as Islamic radicals, insurgents, and fundamentalists, in contrast to more moderate Muslims who do not support committing violence in the name of their religion. The stated reasons for attacking the United States and other Western interests lie in bin Laden's and Al Qaeda's beliefs about Islam and its relationship with non-Muslims. According to them, the presence of non-Muslims in areas considered holy sites in Islam is considered an outrage and requires resistance. They have declared a holy war on the West and believe it is acceptable to kill non-Muslims, even if they are civilians. They also believe that everyone must accept Islam as their religion, even if by force (Religious Tolerance.org 2008).

The trauma of 9/11 and the potential for more attacks in the future have shaped how Americans see the world. This can also be said of any country under siege by such secretive and unpredictable groups. We have briefly explored the range of terrorist attacks and the terrorists themselves, at least as they have affected the United States. Although this review is not sufficient to fully understand the role of terrorism in the twenty-first century, it paints a general picture of the threat that terrorism brings. It was more than a decade since the attacks in New York and Washington, DC, when the attack in Boston occurred. What has been the response from government, communities, and individuals? How are we invested in the parts of the world from which the terrorists came? How have domestic and foreign policy been affected? What threats remain?

The Aftermath of Terrorism

For most Americans and, indeed, for the world, terrorist attacks are understood through the lens of mass media, with its unprecedented coverage. We saw the towers collapse on television repeatedly for weeks after the event. They are iconic images. We watched recovery efforts and memorial services, testimonies of distraught family members and elected officials, and patriotic responses across the country. Americans also received outpourings of sympathy and support from across the globe. This immediate aftermath seemed to draw people together from across a wide spectrum of political views, class positions, and races. For a brief time America seemed to be a community with the shared goal of helping each other through this difficult time. The attack in Boston in 2013 was on a much smaller scale and was resolved quickly but had the nation riveted and supportive of the victims.

In the case of 9/11, once the shock of the attack began to recede, decisions had to be made about how to respond in both big and small ways. As a result, a commitment to war put soldiers in harm's way, new laws tested values regarding privacy rights, and knowledge about the attacks tested religious and ethnic tolerance. If the catastrophic events of 2001 marked America's entry into the experience of global terrorism, the country's response to it will shape American lives in myriad ways for decades to come. Prior to the attacks, few Americans knew much about terrorist groups or why the United States became a target. Since then, newspapers, television reports, and films addressed the problem of terrorism from various political perspectives. One of the most critical and divisive films was Michael Moore's *Fahrenheit 9/11*, which questioned how the government responded to the events of 9/11. The film raised questions about American dependence on Middle East oil and the countries that hold these reserves, whether going to war was justified, and if the terrorist attacks warranted the loss of lives in the conflict.

Next, we briefly examine large-scale decisions about policy and then move to cultural changes.

Political Responses to Terrorism

The government responded to the 9/11 terrorist attacks in several ways:

- President Bush declared the so-called War on Terror in 2001, in which the United States and NATO allies invaded Afghanistan to find bin Laden and destroy Al Qaeda. The invasion of Iraq followed, destroying the regime of Saddam Hussein. At the time of the invasion, the government convinced Congress and the American people that there was a connection between Iraq and Al Qaeda, and further, that Iraq was developing weapons of mass destruction. Each of these official assertions proved to be untrue.

Movie Picks 6.2
Fahrenheit 9/11

Michael Moore's film *Fahrenheit 9/11* was both highly praised and roundly criticized. It raises uncomfortable questions about the role of the United States in addressing terrorism after the 9/11 attacks.

Thinking Sociologically

- Does Moore's film make a compelling argument that the United States should not have gone to war after the events of 9/11?
- How does the film show the relationship between the policy to go to war and its effects on ordinary Americans?
- Do you think the government overestimated the threats of terrorism to the American people?
- The film was made in 2004. How does it resonate today?

Access the live/updated links at http://www.paradigmpublishers.com/resources/goldbergmedia.aspx

- The Department of Homeland Security was formed as an umbrella organization to unite the disparate federal agencies addressing terrorism and other disasters. In addition many top-secret organizations were established since 9/11 to serve security needs.
- The USA Patriot Act enabled increased surveillance of citizens and non-citizens for security purposes.
- The 9/11 Commission studied the event and its aftermath, reported the results to Congress, and recommended a range of actions.

The full import of these actions cannot be examined in depth in these pages. Instead, a brief summary of each is provided so as to set the stage for understanding the aftermath sociologically.

The War on Terror

In a rapid response to the attacks of 9/11, President Bush declared the War on Terror by sending military troops to Afghanistan, whose Taliban-controlled government was accused of harboring the group (Al Qaeda) that had attacked the United States. This was an international effort that included NATO troops seeking to capture the terrorists, especially bin Laden. At the same time, there was increasing concern that Iraq was developing weapons of mass destruction (WMDs), and the United States invaded that country as well in 2003. The regime of Saddam Hussein was toppled and he was eventually captured, put on trial, and executed. There has been a great deal of Iraqi resistance to the presence of the American military as well as jockeying for power among Iraqis. As of 2013, the war in Iraq, now wound down, had claimed the lives of a total of 4,409 American troops. The war in Afghanistan has claimed 2,085 American troops so far (US Department of Defense 2013). There have also been many thousands of Iraqi and Afghan casualties of the wars. The number of American troops in Iraq was dramatically reduced in 2010, and more have been sent to Afghanistan to continue operations there.

There has been a great deal of criticism of the War on Terror about whether it was

A US Marine uses the scope on his weapon to scan the area while providing security during Operation Steel Dawn II, a clearing operation in Barham Chah, Helmand province, Afghanistan, Oct. 30, 2010. The Marines are assigned to the 4th Light Armored Reconnaissance Battalion.

Source: US Marines

invade Iraq based on disputed claims of evidence that Iraq was developing weapons of mass destruction and that Iraq had ties to Al Qaeda's 9/11 attacks on the United States. The US government has been widely criticized for either lying about the threats or being unable to provide substantive proof of the claims. The media has also been criticized for not carefully investigating the claims. In addition, the United States established a controversial detainment center for suspected terrorists at its naval base at Guantanamo Bay, Cuba, causing many questions about the possibility of American torture of prisoners during interrogations.

either necessary or helpful in reducing the likelihood of future attacks. There was little initial criticism, especially regarding Afghanistan. Later, though, a great deal of criticism was directed at the decision to

The loss of lives, including the thousands of Iraqis, the destabilization of the government and hence of the region, and the lack of clarity about how to end the conflict have contributed to the widespread criticism of the war. By 2010, President Barack Obama initiated a pullout from Iraq, but the country

---

 Movie Picks 6.3
Behind Taliban Lines

This PBS *Frontline* video examines the efforts of Taliban insurgents to attack American troops (http://www.pbs.org/wgbh/pages/frontline/talibanlines/view/). These are villagers who are organized by and support the Taliban. Their efforts are thwarted by minimal technology and poor communications.

Mixed-Media Extra

See additional material on the film's website. Read the "Afghan Policy Review" link (http://www .pbs.org/wgbh/pages/frontline/talibanlines/).

Thinking Sociologically

- Describe this insurgent Taliban group, especially their organizational structure.
- What are their objections to Western influence?
- Why are they all men?
- What is the responsibility of the journalist who spent time with the Taliban?

Access the live/updated links at http://www.paradigmpublishers.com/resources/goldbergmedia.aspx

Watch Online 6.1
Inside Guantanamo

Watch the National Geographic video *Inside Guantanamo*, which shows the experiences of prisoners as well as guards.

Access the live/updated links at http://www.paradigmpublishers.com/resources/goldbergmedia.aspx

remains unstable and the war continues in Afghanistan. The main goal of the war in Afghanistan is counterinsurgency, an effort to help citizens rid their society of the Taliban. Internal power struggles, broken infrastructure, and widespread corruption take their toll on the effort. For American soldiers, the threat of attacks, frustration with communication issues with Afghan citizens, and slow progress create a confusing situation. We discuss the experiences of the soldiers in more depth later in the chapter.

Homeland Security and Other Security Organizations

The Department of Homeland Security came into being in 2002 to bring together the bodies responsible for domestic protection, especially from terrorist attacks. The expressed purpose of the new agency was to control national borders, especially to keep terrorists from entering the United States; to respond to national emergencies; to improve the detection of weapons of mass destruction (chemical, biological, and nuclear); and to provide ongoing analysis of threats to the country (US Department of Homeland Security History Office 2008). The experience of 9/11 made it evident that there were many independently operating government agencies who were not communicating with each other about the threats to the country. There were no clear guidelines about how information should

be processed or to ensure that it was taken seriously. This agency would consolidate information and ensure proper communication. One of the responsibilities of the agency is to inform the public of the threat level at any given point of time. Initially, the Homeland Security Advisory System used a color-coded system, from green for a low level of threat to red for a severe threat. The level of threat varied, but it typically had been at the yellow, or "elevated," level for a long time. By 2011 the use of the threat-level format was discarded as ineffectual. A new system called the National Terrorism Advisory System labels threats as imminent or elevated (US Department of Homeland Security 2011).

Criticism of the Department of Homeland Security centers mostly around its failure to adequately secure airports and other mass transit, its management of cyber security, and, indeed, its overall poor management (Hall 2004; Condon 2008). After the Boston Marathon attack in 2013, new questions were raised about the effectiveness of communication about the suspects between government agencies at federal and state levels and amid warnings from abroad.

Homeland Security is one part of the infrastructure built around providing greater security. A *Washington Post* series "Top Secret America" (2010) examined the many agencies, private companies, and people who are part of this new industry. The fact that 850,000 people have top-security clearances exemplifies the

Movie Picks 6.4
Obama's War

Obama's War, a PBS *Frontline* program, shows a detailed, graphic, and intimate portrait of America's involvement in Afghanistan since the election of President Obama in 2008 (http://www.pbs.org/wgbh/pages/frontline/obamaswar/). Problems associated with communication, drugs, and cultural differences abound.

Mixed-Media Extra

Links to extensive additional information on the topic are on the PBS website. Since the film was made in 2009, explore more recent events in Afghanistan with your own Internet search.

Thinking Sociologically

- What are the goals of Americans in Afghanistan?
- What are the dynamics between Americans and Afghanis?
- How does this film contrast to the film *Behind Taliban Lines* (Movie Picks 6.3) in relation to motives, technology, and cultural touchstones?
- From your understanding of culture, can counterinsurgency work with people from such different cultures?
- What power dynamics between Americans and Afghanis are portrayed in the film?
- Describe the global politics surrounding the war.

Access the live/updated links at http://www.paradigmpublishers.com/resources/goldbergmedia.aspx

Web Exercise 6.3
"Top Secret America"

The *Washington Post* series "Top Secret America" provides a detailed examination of the growth of the security industry post-9/11 (http://projects.washingtonpost.com/top-secret-america/). There is a lot to explore on the website. Watch the opening video and read the articles. Then focus on areas of interest to you.

Also watch the PBS *Frontline* video *Top Secret America—9/11 to the Boston Bombings* (http://projects.washingtonpost.com/top-secret-america/).

- Find your home town or college location on the interactive map. Were you aware of security work at or near this location?
- How does the size of the security effort impact its effect?
- Do you think the security infrastructure constitutes a new social institution?
- How are ordinary people affected?
- How is the overall social structure affected?
- How do you think the Boston Marathon bombers escaped the security network?

Access the live/updated links at http://www.paradigmpublishers.com/resources/goldbergmedia.aspx

size of the effort. The series asks: Is it possible to manage security on this scale?

The USA Patriot Act

The USA Patriot Act was signed into law in October of 2001, just a month after the 9/11 attacks. Clearly the government and the American people wanted to act quickly to confront terrorism and limit future attacks. The law has provisions that go far beyond any previous laws enabling surveillance of citizens and non-citizens:

> The Act gives federal officials greater authority to track and intercept communications, both for law enforcement and foreign intelligence gathering purposes. It vests the Secretary of the Treasury with regulatory powers to combat corruption of U.S. financial institutions for foreign money laundering purposes. It seeks to further close our borders to foreign terrorists and to detain and remove those within our borders. It creates new crimes, new penalties, and new procedural efficiencies for use against domestic and international terrorists. (Doyle 2002, 1)

There has been a great deal of controversy about this law from its inception. Whether it goes far enough to seriously combat terrorism, or conversely, goes too far and is an invasion of privacy of innocent citizens is a constant debate.

The 9/11 Commission

The formal name of the 9/11 Commission is The National Commission on Terrorist Attacks Upon the United States. It was formed in 2002 as a bipartisan group to investigate the events of 9/11 as well as the circumstances leading up to and following the attacks. Additionally, it recommended actions to prevent future attacks. The report runs several hundred pages, providing details of the terrorist attacks, a description of terrorists, the development of counterterrorism, and more. Some criticism was leveled at the report for not delving deeply enough into what was known before the attack. It

---

Web Exercise 6.4
What Is the Truth about the USA Patriot Act?

Read the following documents that present contrasting views of the USA Patriot Act:

"America's Surveillance Society," by the American Civil Liberties Union (https://www.aclu.org/sites/default/files/images/asset_upload_file381_37802.pdf), and
"Dispelling Some of the Major Myths about the USA PATRIOT Act," from the Department of Justice (http://www.justice.gov/archive/ll/subs/u_myths.htm).
Read both documents carefully to see the contrasting views of the USA Patriot Act.

- How do the documents differ?
- What other types of surveillance does the ACLU document discuss?
- Do you think surveillance provides protection from terrorism?
- Would you agree that the need for surveillance outweighs privacy or is privacy more important?

Access the live/updated links at http://www.paradigmpublishers.com/resources/goldbergmedia.aspx

The final report of the 9/11 Commission.
Source: US Government Printing Office

remains to be seen if its recommendations will be carried out. Criticism is leveled both at the report itself and by the commissioners who say their recommendations are not being carried out.

Social Consequences of Terrorism

Beyond the government's response in the immediate aftermath of the 9/11 attacks, there

were patterns in the reactions of citizens and communities, especially for those dealing directly with the attacks. The cleanup efforts and plans for the site of the attack in New York generated a great deal of debate. Some argued the site is sacred and needs to be a memorial in its entirety, but a new building on this expensive piece of Manhattan real estate is already nearing completion. At the Pentagon, the building has been repaired and a memorial site has been erected. There is construction of a memorial at the site where the fourth plane crashed before it could cause more destruction.

There has been a strong anti-Muslim backlash especially around the anniversary of the attacks each September. In the immediate aftermath in 2001, President George W. Bush made it explicit that Islam is not to blame for the attacks, but anti-Muslim attitudes have persisted. Among the clearest recent examples are the threat to burn a Koran during the 2010 anniversary of 9/11, and objections to the building of a mosque two blocks from the World Trade Center site in New York City. There have also been growing anti-Muslim attitudes and actions globally, especially in Europe where there are many Muslim immigrants. We will look further into these responses and anti-Muslim prejudice later in the chapter.

Sociology of Terrorism

Prior to 9/11, little attention was paid to terrorism among sociologists, and even

Reading Room 6.3
The 9/11 Commission Report

Read the full *9/11 Commission Report* (http://www.9-11commission.gov/report/), or selected chapters, or the "Executive Summary."

It is worth spending some time reading material in the report. It will help those who are not familiar with the details of the events of 9/11 to understand the immensity of the experience.

Access the live/updated links at http://www.paradigmpublishers.com/resources/goldbergmedia.aspx

Pentagon Memorial (9/11).
Source: US Department of Defense

after that, few sociologists have tackled the issue. Despite its limited response, sociology can offer an analysis of the social context, on both the macro and micro levels. Turk (2004) describes the role of sociology in studying terrorism this way: "the distinctive objective is to develop an explanation of its causation, the dynamics of its escalation and de-escalation in relation to other forms of political violence, and its impact on the stability and change of social orders." (See Reading Room 6.1 for more details.) We can begin to consider terrorism sociologically by using the concepts and theories we have applied to other crises in this book.

Terrorism and the Sociological Imagination

What can sociology offer to help sort through these experiences? We will start, of course, with the sociological imagination. You are a college student who perhaps remembers 9/11 as a child, or maybe only heard of it. In what ways does it matter to you? Do you live in a large city? Ride mass transit? Fly? Are you a foreign student with a visa to study in the United States or are you an immigrant? Do you use a cell phone? the Internet? Have you considered serving your country in the military, or perhaps using military service

as a way to get an education? Think about how you personally fit into the post- 9/11 world. As Mills has argued, your personal "troubles" tie you to the larger social experience, so the more you understand the role terrorism plays in society, the better you will understand your place in the world. Certainly the people most directly affected by 9/11, and more recently by the Boston Marathon bombings, were those who died and their relatives and friends. There is no clearer example of a personal trouble than losing someone who died in such a horrifying way. In New York scores of firefighters died that day and as people mourned their loved ones, the loss of life generated a remaking of the fire department, new systems of communication, funds for stricken families, and increased respect for the job by people who may have rarely thought about the dangers faced by firefighters. The hundreds of firefighters who lost their lives were certainly individuals with their own stories and personal troubles, but as a whole they became something important socially. That's the point of the sociological imagination. From political leaders to the least powerful, all are affected in some way. Even if you never experience terrorism directly, it still has meaning for you. It has shaped modern society and it shapes you.

Understanding the Cultural Context of Terrorism

Changes in Material and Non-Material Culture

Dramatic transformations such as those that took place after the attacks on 9/11 invariably have an important effect on culture. This is true globally, but for now we focus on the American experience. As for material culture, the development of barriers to

⊕ **Web Exercise 6.5**
   Generation 9/11 and the Sociological Imagination

Read these articles:

"Generation 9/11" by Kay Randall (http://www.utexas.edu/features/2005/generation/).
"9/11's Children Grow Up" by Claudia Kalb (http://www.newsweek.com/911s-children
   -grow-79477).

Consider what the research tells us about how college students responded to 9/11, and how younger children responded.

• What were some of the personal and community responses of college students to 9/11?
• Were college students' reactions similar to or different from those of other people?
• What factors contributed to how younger children responded?
• Apply your sociological imagination to describe your own reaction to 9/11.
• Is there a "Generation 9/11"?
• How did your generation respond to the Boston Marathon bombing of 2013?

Access the live/updated links at http://www.paradigmpublishers.com/resources/goldbergmedia.aspx

protect airline pilots, government buildings, and military installations is ubiquitous, and most college students who do not remember another landscape take them for granted.

Sophisticated machines to scan baggage and people boarding airplanes are also now embedded in how we conduct our lives. Unseen security systems such as cameras and machines to detect explosives are a given. Indeed, security cameras on Boston streets were instrumental in quickly identifying the perpetrators of the bombing at the marathon. Material culture is supported by the knowledge, skills, beliefs, and practices of members of society. To support these new technologies, people are trained in detection and in the knowledge necessary to intercept messages intended for potential terrorists. Even untrained citizens are reminded by signage along highways to report suspicious activity.

Both the material infrastructure and the non-material worldview of society have dramatically changed in a few short years. Norms of behavior in public places are circumscribed by security needs. Lines at security checkpoints before boarding airplanes or going into government buildings are examples of the new normative behavior. We allow strangers to poke through our private belongings and even to scan our bodies to look for explosives or weapons. In many homes after 9/11, safe rooms were created, stocked with water and other provisions in case of attack, and duct-taped to seal the rooms from anthrax or toxic gases. These efforts reflect a cultural shift in accepting the likelihood of future attacks. What stands out in regard to values and attitudes, the non-material aspects of culture? There was a surge of patriotic expression after the 9/11 terrorist attack ranging from widespread flying of American flags, to enlisting in the military, to reevaluating the role of the United States in global affairs. This was combined with a siege mentality and an unaccustomed feeling of vulnerability. As the years have passed, some of the more dramatic responses have receded, but much has remained in the daily lives of ordinary people. Feelings about vulnerability remain, and responses to that

Web Exercise 6.6
Cultural Change After 9/11

Read "The Subtle Changes Since 9/11" by Stephanie McCrummen (http://www
.washingtonpost.com/wp-dyn/content/article/2006/09/10/AR2006091001300.html).
Consider how ordinary Americans' lifestyles have changed in the years since 9/11.

- Describe the material and non-material adaptations made by the people in the story.
- Are these just individual changes or do they reflect cultural change?
- Do you think these changes are representative of the culture in general?
- Does it make a difference if you live near or far from possible terrorist target sites?
- How many of the 9/11-related changes are things you do routinely today?
- What effect, if any, did these changes have in the aftermath of the Boston Marathon bombing?

Access the live/updated links at http://www.paradigmpublishers.com/resources/goldbergmedia.aspx

vulnerability are reflected in our beliefs and behaviors, including the response to the Boston Marathon bombing.

Individualism in the Context of Terrorism

In previous chapters, we have seen the power of the American value of individualism. It is embedded in our culture and expressed in many aspects of social life, so much so that acts of violence are usually attributed to the individual psychological makeup of the perpetrators rather than social circumstances. The belief that individual grievances and mental illness are the primary causes of violent attacks prevents us from seeing them potentially as political acts. We see this in analyses of crimes, but even in the case of the Oklahoma City and Boston Marathon bombings, much of the discussion was about the psychological state of those involved. This is also true when discussing suicide bombers, whom we often think of as disturbed. It could be argued that by emphasizing the individual psychological makeup and motives of terrorists, we miss the relevance of the social context that gives cohesion to their ideas and their acts of violence. The

value we hold regarding individualism may blind us to larger motives and keep us from fully understanding the culture from which the terrorists come and the motives that drive them to commit violent acts even at their own peril. As sociologists, we must keep in mind the power of culture from the point of view of both terrorists and victims.

Subcultures and Countercultures

Another aspect of culture relevant to the experience of terrorism is the subgroups that are affected differently by the experience. People serving in the military and others who are immersed in providing security are considered subcultures. They share the values of the larger society, but they also have their own knowledge, beliefs, and skills that are directly connected to the war or efforts to stop terrorist attacks. The terrorists themselves make up their own segment of society, especially in a global sense. Are they a subculture or a counterculture? This would depend on one's perspective. Those supporting terrorism might claim that—with their training, communications systems, and political goals—terrorists are a subculture of a larger culture who wish to rid their society of intrusion by the West, as seen in the video *Behind Taliban Lines* (Movie Picks 6.3). Suicide bombers, especially, stand out for their willingness to end their lives for their beliefs, in actions they call martyrdom. Terrorists are also seen as members of a counterculture, going against the norms of the majority in society who oppose terrorist acts. There is endless discussion about whether Islam supports or rejects the ideas and actions of terrorists demonstrating that cultural orientation matters in assessing the significance of terrorism.

Inequality and Terrorism

It may seem that terrorism is not connected to inequality. After all, terrorist attacks kill all kinds of people. Those who died at the World Trade Center had jobs ranging from low-paid restaurant workers to high-end financial managers. Every major race and ethnic group and many religions, including Islam, were represented among those who died. The same is true of many other attacks. While terrorism may be focused on a specific entity, say an embassy or a military post, many bystanders are also victims. In the Oklahoma City bombing, the attacker described the deaths of children as "collateral damage." Nonetheless, as in all areas of society inequalities do exist in the context of terrorism, so examining inequality is of special sociological interest when discussing the aftermath of 9/11. Later in the chapter we will apply conflict theory to examine how inequality can breed terrorism. Here, though, we focus on two issues in the United States that are of particular importance. First, we look at the military men and women who are deployed in the war. Second, we discuss the expressions of prejudice and acts of discrimination against Muslims and people from the Middle East.

Inequality and the Military Response

In the United States, military service is voluntary. This was not always so. In fact, for most of American history, until 1973 a draft required men to register for military service and to serve when called upon. Today men are still required to register at the age of eighteen, even though the draft no longer exists. Women have always been excluded from the requirement to serve in the military in the United States. The draft was supposed to be a great equalizer of men. It didn't matter who you were or what your class or race was, you had a theoretically equal chance of being drafted. In reality, however, men with money and influence were often able to keep out of harm's way if they so chose. The last war in which there was a draft was the Vietnam War, and the draft, along with other factors, helped make the war very unpopular and contributed to the antiwar movement of the 1970s. Because it had the potential to affect nearly every young man, the war hit very close to home for most citizens. Things are very different now. Because we have an all-volunteer military, much has changed in our experiences with war and our attention to the men and women who serve there. Since women were not drafted, their service in previous wars was limited to support roles. Today both men and women volunteer and serve in a variety of military tasks that put them both at risk. According to the US Army (2012), women make up 15.7 percent of the total army today, which is greater than in previous years but still much lower than the percentage of women in the general population. Among women enlisted in the Army, 29.4 percent are black and 13.2 percent are Hispanic. For the Navy, 31 percent are black and 22 percent are Hispanic (US Department of Defense 2010).

A 2004 study examined the demographic breakdown of those who serve. In studying "the propensity to serve," fewer people were inclined to enlist in more recent years of the volunteer military as compared to the early years. Factors that contributed to the likelihood of enlistment included "parents' education (children of college-educated parents are less likely to serve), high school grades (those with higher grades are less likely to serve), college plans (college students are less likely to enlist), [and] race and ethnicity (African Americans and Hispanics are more likely to serve than whites)" (Segal and Segal 2004, 9). These characteristics are clearly tied to social class but are by no means definitive. Historically, during the period of the draft, and now, with the volunteer armed forces, research shows that both the wealthiest and the poorest tend not to serve. Rather enlistees come from the middle of the socioeconomic ladder. Research by Lutz (2008) found that enlistees were more likely to come from families with lower income than higher income, as the military might provide career opportunities they otherwise would not have in civilian life. In fact, socioeconomic factors were more predictive of military service than race or immigrant status:

> among race, socioeconomic status, and immigration status, socioeconomic status is the only significant predictor of having ever served in the military. Class differences in military enlistment likely reflect differences in the non-military occupational opportunity, structured along class lines. This research shows that the all-volunteer force continues to see over-representation of the working and middle classes, with fewer incentives for upper class participation. (Lutz 2008, 185)

Economic incentives will remain a factor for the all-volunteer army. The recession in the first decade of the twenty-first century enabled the military to successfully recruit people who were out of work or unable to find jobs. While there are actually very few data available on recent military enlistment beyond sex, race, and ethnicity, it is important to continue to examine the role that inequality plays in determining the makeup of military personnel.

Reporting about the experience of the armed forces in Iraq and Afghanistan in the mainstream media shows a dedicated group of well-trained men and women, some of whom serve multiple years away from home. Advances in protective gear and medical treatment mean that many injured service people survive terrible wounds and must receive long-term treatment once home. There is much concern about unseen brain injuries as well as post-traumatic stress, both invisible but serious issues. Also of concern is the adaptation to civilian life and families as well as the ability to find and keep a job. The post-war experiences of veterans are important to explore to see whether their experiences provide opportunity or leave them disaffected and unable to enter the mainstream. From a sociological point of view, then, it is important to consider inequality both when considering who participates in war and how they are treated once they return from war.

Anti-Muslim Responses

Another important area of inequality is found in the expressions of anti-Muslim sentiment and related discrimination that has arisen especially after the 9/11 attacks. Many people equate the attacks with the religion, though there is no evidence that the terrorists spoke for the religion as a whole. The fact that the 9/11 terrorists were Muslim and claimed they were acting on behalf of their religion complicates the reaction to the attacks. The term **Islamophobia** was coined to represent the anti-Muslim attitudes that have grown up, not only in the United States but throughout the non-Muslim world. From rhetoric to attacks on individuals and places of worship, there have been many expressions of hatred and anger against Muslims. The Council on American-Islamic

Movie Picks 6.5
The Ground Truth: After the Killing Ends

This documentary follows the life of men and women who served in the war in Iraq. From recruitment to deployment to the aftermath of service, interviews with participants in the war provide much food for thought. This film can be searing and difficult to watch.

Mixed-Media Extra

Listen to or read "A Soldier's Journey from Iraq to Grad School," the NPR *Morning Edition* interview with Demond Mullens (http://www.npr.org/templates/story/story.php?storyId =16272276). Mullens was featured in The Ground Truth and later became a sociology student after struggling when he returned from the war.

Thinking Sociologically

- Describe the people interviewed in the film.
- What are their main thoughts about the war?
- What problems do they face when they return home?
- Would you consider these veterans a subculture?
- How do they socially construct the experience of war from their perspectives? Is it different from your own perspective?
- Is there evidence of class, race, or gender inequality?
- What connection does Demond Mullens make between his experiences and sociology?

Access the live/updated links at http://www.paradigmpublishers.com/resources/goldbergmedia.aspx

Relations (2009/2013) reported that there were 2,728 civil-rights complaints in 2008, and 116 reports of "anti-Muslim hate crime complaints."

In 2010, leading up to the anniversary of 9/11, a plan to burn a Koran by a minister in Florida evoked national and global responses. There was fear that the act would incite attacks on soldiers fighting abroad, and more attacks on civilians. Aside from the actual potential burning, the incident provided a backdrop for discussions about freedom of speech and the role of the media in fanning the flames of hatred. Other burnings

Reading Room 6.4
Islamophobia

Read about the impact of Islamophobia in the United States at the website for the Council on American-Islamic Relations (https://www.cair.com/islamophobia.html). Consider how beliefs about Islam translate into action. Why do you think anti-Muslim beliefs and discrimination have increased rather than decreased after 9/11?

Access the live/updated links at http://www.paradigmpublishers.com/resources/goldbergmedia.aspx

and acts of destruction involving the Koran have taken place without such a large-scale response. Ground Zero, the site of the ruins of the World Trade Center, has also become embroiled in the backlash against Muslims. A plan for an Islamic center two blocks from the site was ferociously debated by politicians and citizens alike. Some argue it is an affront to the people who suffered in the attacks, while others see it as an attempt by moderate Muslims to reach out to the larger community. Other attempts to build mosques in the United States have been met with strong opposition. Ironically, at the Pentagon, where one of the terrorists' planes struck, an interfaith center was created where people from all religions pray. It generated no opposition. The social context for anti-Muslim sentiment is the vulnerability people feel and the suspicions they harbor about people who fit stereotypes of Muslim extremists, which can create breeding grounds for racism and Islamophobia. In Europe, there are new laws that curtail Muslim practices, such as the French ban on head coverings in some public arenas like schools. There is growing dissatisfaction with the patterns of immigration of Muslims into Western Europe and their seeming lack of interest in adapting to European culture. It is worth watching the global impact of anti-Muslim sentiment in the years to come.

Applying Sociological Theory

Both macro and micro theories are useful in sorting through the experience of terrorism. On the macro level, important structural changes have taken place and the application of both functional theory and conflict theory can be used to better understand the institutional responses as well as the inequalities that expose power differentials that lead to conflict. As for micro theory, we have already indicated the difficulties in defining terrorism as a social construction, so we

will look at that in more depth. We will also explore the power of communication using symbolic interaction theory as it applies to the act of terrorism and the fear it engenders.

Does Terrorism Serve a Social Function?

There are different ways to look at terrorism from a functionalist perspective, such as one from the terrorist's point of view and another from the response to terrorism at the receiving end. Prior to 2001, terrorist attacks against US interests have typically been focused on a specific goal, such as the release of prisoners. In those cases, the taking of hostages functioned to force a favorable response. Today the goals are less clear, and at the same time more broad. The attacks on 9/11 did not involve negotiations of any sort but the goal was to put the United States on notice about the terrorists' grievances regarding the presence of the West in Muslim countries and their hopes to spread their form of Islam throughout the world. It is argued that the function of such attacks is to frighten the public and to force them to reconsider their role in the Islamic countries.

From the point of view of those at the receiving end, as we saw earlier in the chapter, new laws, agencies, and policies have been created in order to prevent or at least limit future attacks. An immense security apparatus is in place. There are serious questions about the relationship of its size to the ability to thwart new attacks as we saw in the 2013 Boston bombing. There are also questions about the effects of security technologies and laws on the privacy rights of citizens. Nonetheless, the functions of such organizations and the purpose of their policies are to deter terrorism. A functionalist analysis would argue that in order to keep society in equilibrium—that is, free from catastrophic attacks—these new additions are necessary. Similarly, the war efforts in Afghanistan and Iraq were designed to eliminate terrorism at its source. Whether this is effective remains to be seen. All of these actions are to ensure that society is not destabilized as a result of terrorism. Has it worked? Until 2013, there were no successful attacks in the United States since 2001, though there have been quite a few attempts in the intervening years. There is the general belief that security systems work well as long as they adapt to new attempts at terrorism, but because they can never guarantee perfect safety, no one is complacent about the future.

It is also worth examining the response to terrorist attacks through social institutions. Consider how each institution was impacted by 9/11 and what has happened in the ensuing years. We have already discussed the changes in political institutions and the military. With the new security infrastructure, the economy is impacted with the development of new technologies and employment in these industries. Religious organizations speak out about fears of terrorism and respond to anti-Muslim rhetoric and action—both for and against it. As we saw in Web Exercise 6.6, families continue to make decisions to stay away from perceived threatening situations. Perhaps most directly relevant to families are those who have family members serving in the military.

Long absences, injuries, and death are built into the lives of those who serve in the war, and this has profound effects on family life.

Overall, functional theory helps us see how society responds to a crisis. In a word, large-scale terrorism as we saw on 9/11 is dysfunctional to society. How institutions respond and how society changes to meet new needs represent the approach of functionalism. Functionalism can help explain how the response to the Boston attacks was evidence of changes in the institutions supporting first responders as well as local and federal policing agencies. We have shown the limitations of functional theory in earlier chapters. Here too, we can see how society never stands still, and therefore we must acknowledge the importance of seeing social change as a permanent part of society, not just a response to a crisis. For that analysis, we turn to conflict theory.

Does Inequality Breed Terrorism?

Terrorism does not come out of nowhere. We may find it abhorrent but we still must look for the reasons why people act in such a dramatically destructive way. Since conflict theory is based on understanding the unequal nature of relationships, we should

---

 Web Exercise 6.7
The Functions of Rebuilding

View the website for the video *America Rebuilds II: Return to Ground Zero* to see what actions took place five years after the 9/11 attacks (http://www.pbs.org/americarebuilds2/). Read the "People Profiles" and "The Challenges Ahead" links. Also be sure to look at some of the other related links. There are many photos as well as video clips.

- What functions does creating a memorial serve?
- Why is there a debate about what is to be built on the site of the World Trade Center?
- Using functional theory, does this effort constitute a rebalancing in the aftermath of a social dysfunction?

Access the live/updated links at http://www.paradigmpublishers.com/resources/goldbergmedia.aspx

Reading Room 6.5
"The Evolution of Islamic Terrorism: An Overview"

Read the summary of the rise of modern Islamic terrorism starting in the mid-1960s to the present on the PBS *Frontline* website "The Evolution of Islamic Terrorism: An Overview" by John Moore (http://www.pbs.org/wgbh/pages/frontline/shows/target/etc/modern.html). Consider the role of failed states, liberation movements, the rise of religious militancy against the backdrop of the end of the Cold War, and political change in the Middle East. How much does this history inform you about the current terrorism threat?

Another useful reading on the history of terrorism is "Terrorism in Historical Perspective" by Fred Halliday (http://www.opendemocracy.net/globalization-madridprevention/article_1865.jsp).

Access the live/updated links at http://www.paradigmpublishers.com/resources/goldbergmedia.aspx

consider the history of colonialism discussed in Chapter 4 to help us see the inequalities and resulting conflicts in the volatile regions from which terrorism emerges. The post-colonial nations in the Middle East in particular influenced the rise of contemporary terrorism. Throughout the Middle East there were anti-Western political movements that were initially mostly secular and leftist, and many of them opposed the creation of the state of Israel in 1948. These secular movements gradually became more religious as they organized to use terrorist tactics to meet their aims. A combination of the end of the Cold War, the rise of Islamic states like Iran, and the growth of extremist groups gave rise to much instability in this region. Reading 6.5 provides a detailed account of the beginning of this form of terrorism.

It is important to understand the nature of the inequalities that might help explain the attacks. According to conflict theory, inequality of power results in conflict. People typically do not resort to terrorism if there are legitimate alternatives to meet their perceived needs. Because they are disenfranchised from their own governments and other means of expressing their interests, terrorists are not in a political or material position to respond to inequities through legitimate channels. The great divide in political power, military hardware, and technology between the terrorists and those they attack help explain why they take desperate measures. And, indeed, they are effective because they are unanticipated and cruel. They are not a nation-state against which war can be declared, and their attacks are global in nature. Thus they are very difficult to confront because terrorists do not represent legitimate political entities, and the places from which they operate have weak and often corrupt governments. A conflict theorist would argue that terrorism will continue as long as the inequities persist in the regions where terrorists operate, and between these regions and the rest of the world. There are strong ideological and religious convictions that go along with terrorism, so resolving this conflict will take extraordinary efforts to address the global divides that have been created.

The Social Construction of Terrorism in Context

Earlier in the chapter we saw how the definition of terrorism is itself a social construction. The specific history of the rise of terrorism matters very much to its definition. From Reading 6.5, we saw the connections between the political dynamics in the post–Cold War Middle East and the rise of terrorism. In that context, it does not seem a surprise that there would be anger and resistance to Western influence, both political and economic. To the disenfranchised populations, terrorism may seem a good choice, especially now coupled with religious zeal. This volatile mix helps us understand the nature of terrorism and the willingness of some to commit it, even at the loss of their own lives. What is most valuable about the application of social construction theory is the understanding that there is a social context for even the most heinous acts in modern times. Understanding that context enables us to address it realistically.

Symbolic Interaction:
Communicating Difference

Systems of communication within and across cultures present sociologists with rich examples of the importance of symbolic interaction. While we pay close attention to the words of terrorists and those who oppose them, much can be said without words when culturally agreed-upon symbols are conveyed. Social organizations are especially rife with symbolic representations of their purposes, with deliberate artwork and words to convey meaning to others, and terrorist organizations are no exception. Even terrorist attacks or threats of attacks have symbolic value to the perpetrators. Terrorists do not believe an attack will make them victorious. Rather, terrorism conveys an important message of fear that helps define both the terrorists and their targets.

Symbolic interaction theory helps us see how cultural ideas and practices are communicated within and between societies. It is especially useful when cultural change may be rapid. One area of importance is demonstrated in the heated arguments about the role of Islam in Western society. To what extent do Muslims integrate into mainstream life? How much should they adhere to traditional practices while living in predominantly non-Muslim countries? For example, there has been an ongoing debate about the role of the head coverings of Muslim women. There are varieties of coverings from full body veils to simple headscarves, but what is most important about these coverings is the meaning they convey to the user and the observer. From the vantage point of different cultures, these simple pieces of cloth carry important meaning. For instance, there is a question among feminists whether the covering is liberating or oppressive and that concern partly reflects who gets to define the meaning of the covering. It is a complicated issue.

Haddad's study "The Post-9/11 Hijab as Icon" examines the reasons why young American Muslim women choose to wear the head cover known as the *hijab*. Haddad argues that "the hijab has become a symbol of an American Islamic identity—a public affirmation of trust in the American system that guarantees freedom of religion and speech. At the same time, it has also become a symbol of anti-colonial solidarity and resistance to efforts to eradicate Islam in an American environment that is increasingly seen as anti-Islamic" (2007, 253).

Al Qaeda in Iraq.
Source: Anti-Defamation League

Web Exercise 6.8
Interpreting Terrorist Organization Symbols

Go to the "International Terrorist Symbols Database" on the website of the Anti-Defamation League (http://archive.adl.org/terrorism/symbols). Read the introduction and look carefully at the symbols representing the different organizations.

- What symbols and colors do the groups share in common?
- What symbols are unique to specific organizations?
- From the symbols alone, what can you tell about a group's purposes?

Click on several of the symbols to read further about the groups.

- Are the descriptions of the groups' goals and activities represented in the symbols?
- What are some of the symbolic representations of the 9/11 memorials? of the wars in Iraq and Afghanistan?
- Are all the symbols you observed forms of communication? If so, how?

Access the live/updated links at http://www.paradigmpublishers.com/resources/goldbergmedia.aspx

The decision to wear the hijab can reflect religious or political commitment, and to outsiders it can convey otherness and generate fear and anti-Muslim stereotyping or discrimination. It has taken on much more symbolic meaning with the acceleration of terrorism even though there is no connection between head coverings and terrorist attacks. In France, a law was passed in 2010 banning overt symbols of religious expression in public, including banning women from wearing full veils in public. Head coverings for religious reasons raise important questions about how cultural practices are carried out and their symbolism represents much of what is understood about religion and opposition to it.

Symbolic interaction theory provides sociologists with a way of understanding the varieties of communications that may come in the form of conciliation, threats, tolerance, or fear. Mass media, especially the Internet, has sped up our access to a range of communications for and against extremist groups of all kinds, news about terrorism, and observations of attacks in real time, as was so clearly demonstrated in the Boston Marathon attack and its aftermath. How we digest the vast amounts of information and communicate across borders on such volatile issues is the subject of twenty-first-century symbolic interaction theory. Interpreting the shared meanings of symbols is an important contribution to furthering our study of terrorism and its aftermath.

Looking to the Future

The attacks of September 11, 2001, are the touchstone of America's experience with terrorism and they have already begun shaping the twenty-first century in myriad ways. As we have seen in this chapter, it is a crisis with both immediate and long-term repercussions. Few doubt that other attacks will happen in the future and some may even be more disastrous, but 9/11 stands out largely because as a society we were so much in the dark about massive terrorism and it was so shocking to watch it unfold. Warnings went unheeded because people lacked the imagination that such a cataclysmic event could happen and there was no workable organizational structure in place to quickly put the pieces together that would point to an imminent attack or to respond to it effectively. In the aftermath, a great public effort has been made to understand the events and respond to them: engaging in war, creating new security practices, changing the physical landscape with all manner of barriers, and enhancing oversight of systems of communication. Within ten years of the 9/11 attacks, major known terrorists have been captured and killed, most notably Osama bin Laden. How people respond to these changes depends on their social location: New Yorkers, ordinary citizens, active military, and citizens of Iraq and Afghanistan all have perspectives that shape their experiences with terrorism and its aftermath. These alterations to our social and material world will be with us for at least a generation or more. Sociology can provide a means of understanding both the events themselves and how people respond to them.

Looking Backward/ Looking Forward

Nothing as cataclysmic as large-scale terrorism goes unnoticed in other areas of social life. Our discussion of fragile and failed states in Chapter 4 gave us insight into the unrest that comes from lack of power, both for disenfranchised citizens and for countries beholden to the West for their economic and/or political survival. The relationships of the United States and other Western nations with those countries from which most terrorists come are fraught with political problems of major consequence. Iraq, Iran, Pakistan, and Afghanistan have the most immediate impact because of their roles in terrorism and war or threat of war. Saudi Arabia, Yemen, Libya, and other Middle Eastern states play an important role in brokering both peace and war, but also because their oil resources are much needed by the West. As the recent unrest in this region unfolds as it has most recently in Egypt and Syria, there are many unresolved problems that will surely impact the future of terrorism. Understanding the global nature of political power helps us see the importance of terrorism.

Chapter 5 covered health and health care. A very direct effect of 9/11 was on the health of first responders to the emergency and the people involved in the cleanups of New York and the Pentagon. Initially it was believed that the dense air filled with debris would not be harmful over the long run. Since then, many people who worked on the site of the

---

 Watch Online 6.2
"9/11 Heroes Now Sick and Dying"

Watch the brief video "9/11 Heroes Now Sick and Dying" on the Reuters website (http://www.reuters.com/video/2009/09/09/9-11-heroes-now-sick-and-dying?videoId=111089). Consider the relationship between terrorist attacks and health. In New York, the health of the 9/11 first responders is impacted. In Boston, several hundred survivors of the Boston Marathon attack suffered loss of limbs and other permanent injuries that will affect their lives and those of their families.

Access the live/updated links at http://www.paradigmpublishers.com/resources/goldbergmedia.aspx

World Trade Center and nearby areas have suffered serious respiratory and other health problems. As it turned out, there were many toxins in the air for quite some time, and little was done to protect workers.

Another health concern involves members of the military who served in Iraq and Afghanistan. Protective equipment and efficient medical care helped many injured soldiers survive, but their injuries, some unseen, are in many cases severe. In addition to amputations, burns, and other obvious injuries, there have been many brain injuries, the importance of which has only recently been recognized. Treatment is only partly effective, and too often is rendered only if soldiers and their families push for care. In addition, many veterans suffer from post-traumatic stress, a health problem about which some people are skeptical. The difficulty in adjusting to life away from combat can be harrowing for the veterans and their families. Suicides, family strife, and violent episodes mark many of the experiences of soldiers once they come home. There has been criticism that the country was unprepared for the care of these veterans and many have languished with untreated health problems.

Our next chapter is about technology. An important connection exists between the efforts to curb terrorism and the new technologies. While these technologies are truly innovative, questions are raised about their uses and in particular about their effects on the rights to privacy. In mid-2013, the extent of the National Security Agency's access to phone and email records of American citizens was revealed to be far more extensive than many previously thought. The need to balance national security with individual privacy will be with us for many years to come.

Web Watch

Information about terrorism can be found throughout the Internet, from government agencies, to advocacy groups, terrorist-organization websites, international bodies, and news sources. Below are a few of the sources that can provide information on terrorism and responses to it. Because terrorist acts take place quickly, it is worth reading about them on reliable news sources, including those from the locations where they took place. Terrorist websites are often taken down as soon as they are put up, so it is difficult to find them online. Below are some websites that can help investigate terrorism more fully:

Council of American-Islamic Relations: http://www.cair.com/

Hearts and Minds: Information for Change, "Anti-Terrorism Links": http://www.heartsandminds.org/links/terror.htm

Open Democracy: Free Thinking for the World: http://www.opendemocracy.net/

UN Action to Counter Terrorism: http://www.un.org/terrorism/

US Department of State: http://www.state.gov

US Department of Homeland Security: http://www.dhs.gov

CHAPTER 7

Privacy and Identity in an Age of Crisis

The Role of Technology in Shaping the Twenty-First Century

Millennials are the first generation of digital natives with their easy
adaptation to technology and dependence on it for daily life.
Source: Roberta Goldberg

Students come to college today with a great deal of technological hardware—computers, cell phones, game machines, MP3 players, and so on—and they are quite experienced at using it. How technology is used depends on more than just availability and know-how. It also depends on decision-making, a sense of responsibility, thoughts about consequences, perspective, affordability, and considerations of privacy—in other words, social factors. In 2010, when a college student broadcast his roommate having sex with another man in his dorm room, did he violate the privacy of the people he videoed? Did he breech social norms? Could he imagine the consequences: that his roommate would shortly commit suicide, after first saying good-bye on a social-networking site? What

172

was missing in the student's calculation about the outcome this video might produce? Everyday technology is used in both positive and questionable ways, by individuals, corporations, political groups, hospitals, police, governments, and international bodies. How is its use decided and who decides the value and legitimacy of its use?

From a sociological point of view, the above scenario raises important questions about the connections between technological capability, knowledge, culture, and power. We explore these throughout this chapter. We mostly think of technology in a positive way in terms of the advancement of society. For college students today, technological innovations help them succeed academically and provide various ways to conduct their personal lives. Many of you access syllabi online, communicate with professors through email, and submit papers and take exams online. The newest phone applications, the coolest games, the hi-def experience on hundreds of television channels, access to the latest music, and the time spent on social-networking sites are all indications that technology serves many of our social needs. Some would say it has shaped our needs and changed our culture.

Technology is indispensable to students and the rest of us, but what of the larger social implications of this technology? We will start with the big picture. In the preface of this book, two observations were made that resonate with the ideas in this chapter: first, the world is getting smaller, and second, time seems to move faster and faster. The reasons for these feelings are tied directly to technological capability and the human skills necessary to use it. Our communication and transportation systems do indeed give us the sense that the world is smaller. This can be positive in terms of opportunities to share ideas and experiences across the globe. But as we saw in the opening vignette, the public airing of an individual's sexual behavior also makes the world smaller in a way that results in negative consequences. The speed of technology, which is increasing as you read this,

contributes to the sense of the faster passage of time. Technology enables machines to work faster than individuals and societies can process information and that may contribute to cultural lag between the technology and cultural values and norms. For example, later in this chapter we examine how the implementation of technology to secure us against terrorist attacks raises important questions about privacy rights. We will also see how advancements in reproductive technology can raise ethical questions about reproduction and identity that have significant impact on society.

You may wonder how this topic fits into a book about social crises. Technology in itself is not a crisis nor does it produce one by itself. It is simply a tool of the people who use it. From a sociological point of view, technology is a reflection of the society out of which it has developed. Yet its use is so much a part of the crises we experience that it is worth exploring the ramifications of the exponential growth of new technologies and their effects on society. We will find mixed results depending largely on who controls the technology and the purposes to which it is put. There are many different technological changes worthy of discussion, but we will focus on two specific areas—security and privacy, as well as genetics and identity—to show how technology plays an important role in the social crises faced today.

The goal of this chapter then is to demonstrate the important connections between technology as machinery, the social needs it works to meet, and the intended and unintended consequences of using technology. This is a complicated topic and there is much overlap between the two issues this chapter will address. We begin with an overview of the effects of technology in general, then move on to our focus on the two topics indicated above.

A Brief Overview of Technology

We all know how important technology is to modern life but because of our fascination with the newest gadgets, we sometimes fail to consider the relationship of technology to its social purpose. Technology is used at all levels of society to conduct business, government, educational, political, and personal life. It does not exist separately from the social needs it is built to meet. From earliest human civilizations, technological innovations have met the physical and social needs of people in those societies. Simple handheld implements to produce food, wells for fresh water, plows to enable large-scale farming, hunting tools, weapons, and of course, the wheel, all served to meet social needs through early human history. Many of these technologies helped to spur significant economic and political changes. The Agricultural Revolution was made possible by innovative use of land, plows, and animals. The printing press enabled large numbers of people to share information. Militarily, the armies and navies with the most advanced weapons won the most wars. Over the past two centuries the Industrial Revolution changed what was produced, how it was produced, and the dynamics between employers, employees, and consumers. The phenomenal growth of manufacturing in the industrial period changed the world's economies dramatically and enabled the rise of modern capitalism that meets new social needs for consumer goods as well as large-scale social development. Industrial production of textiles met a consumer-driven need for clothing and related items. Steel manufacturing helped create cities. The internal-combustion engine used in automobiles led to new highway systems.

In all these examples, the technologies were created to meet the social needs of the time. Although technology responded to social needs, it also created opportunities for new knowledge and experiences and in so doing helped to create new needs.

Western society today is considered post-industrial in large part because the production of information and services now dominates the economies of the developed world. Post-industrial technology has enabled the tremendous growth in communication, in the sharing of ideas, and the processing of finance, politics, health care, and education systems that are the hallmarks of modern society. This shift from producing material goods to non-material services has been made possible by the technologies of the twentieth century, particularly the computer. The technological revolution today has indeed changed the world forever much like the Industrial Revolution did in its time. We will look more closely at the relationship between culture and technology later in the chapter, but for now it is important to remember that technology is part of material culture that serves social needs but it is also part of non-material culture, being shaped by and helping to shape values, experiences, and norms. Technology cannot be understood apart from the social reasons for its existence. From a sociological point of view what is most relevant is the purpose for which the technology is used, who has access to it, who controls it, and its benefits and its drawbacks.

Technology, Security, and Privacy

We begin by examining two areas in which technology impacts the privacy and identity of individuals. The first is government surveillance after 9/11 and the other involves private business efforts for security and marketing purposes. Sometimes these two efforts overlap, as is suggested by the pervasive

Security cameras are ubiquitous
in the twenty-first century.
Source: Roberta Goldberg

presence of surveillance cameras today. Both
government and private businesses use cameras for crime prevention and detection and
to protect property. Although it is impossible
to know how many cameras are in use, as
their locations are often hard to see, there
have been attempts to count cameras. In
New York City, for example, there are at least
4,313 cameras in the subway system alone,
and a 2005 count of Lower Manhattan estimated over 4,100 cameras, "one for every 84
residents" (Palmer 2010). Many more cameras have been added since 2005, including
the cameras required outside of nightclubs
and more police cameras throughout the
city. Many cities have a similar distribution
of security cameras. There are also cameras
to catch speeders and red-light runners,
cameras that capture license-plate numbers
(automatic number plate recognition), and
now with GPS systems and programs like
E-ZPass, travelers can be easily tracked.
Most of us assume that all the reasons for
these cameras are good: catch criminals and
terrorists, protect the public, and keep civil
peace. The rapid identification of the Boston
Marathon bombers in 2013 through video

images exemplifies the usefulness of security
cameras. If citizens are kept safe from terrorists and criminals through surveillance,
is there a down side?

Government Surveillance through Technology

We first return to our previous chapter on
terrorism and its aftermath to explore the
role of government surveillance in society
today. We saw in Chapter 6 that one of the
most significant outcomes of the 9/11 attacks
was an increase in surveillance in order to
thwart future terrorist attacks and to appre-
hend active terrorists. The development of
technology applied to this endeavor has been
unprecedented. Data mining, surveillance
cameras, the use of DNA and biometrics (discussed later in the chapter), GPS technology,
and body scans are some of the technologies put in place after 9/11. There is special
emphasis on transportation, especially flying,
and for good reason. The use of airplanes in
the 9/11 attacks was dramatic. A number of
other attempts at terrorism have also involved
transportation both before and after 9/11,
including bombs placed in packages from
Yemen bound for Chicago in late 2010.
In Europe, rail and subway systems have
been subject to attack and several attacks on
subways and heavily populated cities in the
United States have been thwarted. In other
parts of the world—India, Iraq, Afghanistan,
and much of the Middle East and Africa—
terrorism is a continuing threat. Over time,
the increasingly sophisticated terrorist plots
have required increasingly sophisticated
security measures. For example, removal of
potentially dangerous substances from lug-
gage, checked baggage, and shoes, and conducting body scans at airports, are in direct
response to specific attempts at terrorism.
Body scans are an especially good example
of the use of technology to meet the goals
of securing the air-transportation system,

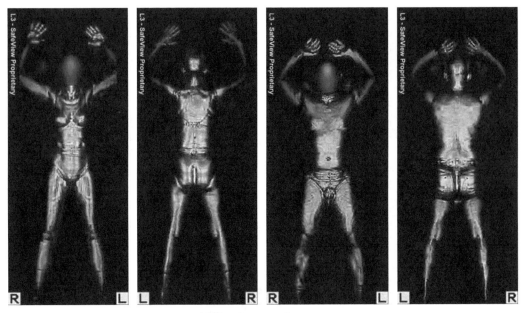

Millimeter wave images.
Source: Transportation Security Administration Blog

though public protest influenced the removal of the most revealing scanners in 2013.

Questions about the loss of privacy have emerged from the use of this body-scanning technology as it exposes the body under clothing in the process of a search for weapons. It is argued that this technology is justified in the interest of security and basic safeguards are in place to protect the personal privacy of airline passengers. As you can see in Web Exercise 7.1, even safeguards can be breached. It is understood that greater security means less privacy. Since protection of personal privacy has long been valued in American society, there are questions about how much more secure these activities will make us and whether Americans are willing to sacrifice privacy for security. Indeed, resistance to the use of body scanning has led to innovations that are less invasive.

Security of transportation systems is only one part of the government effort to prevent terrorism. As we saw in Chapter 6, there are many federal agencies involved in trying to prevent more terrorist attacks. States and private businesses are also part of an information-sharing network that compiles and analyzes data on individuals. Much of your private information is now online and access to it is enhanced by technology. If you drive, borrow money, use a bank or credit card, or rely on a cell phone it is likely that your personal information is stored in "fusion centers" whose purpose is to share information using computers about potential terrorism and other crimes. Mostly run by local and state agencies, but also involving the military, the federal government, and private contractors, there were seventy-nine fusion centers in the United States by July 2009 (Intelligence Fusion Centers 2009).

The availability of advanced software technology has enhanced the ability to collect massive amounts of data. In 2013, it was revealed that the National Security Agency (NSA) has been secretly collecting data on Americans and others from a range of electronic sources, especially phone and email communications. Risen and Light-blau (2013) report that "90 percent of the data that now exists in the world has been created in just the last two years. From now

Web Exercise 7.1
Digital Strip Search: Too Far?

Read "TSA Tries to Assuage Privacy Concerns about Full-Body Scans" by Philip Rucker in the *Washington Post* (http://www.washingtonpost.com/wp-dyn/content/article/2010/01/03 /AR2010010301826.html?sid=ST2010010301836). View the accompanying infographic for visuals about the full-body scans at airports. Also read "Feds Admit Storing Checkpoint Body Scan Images" by Declan McCullagh at CNET News (http://news.cnet.com/8301-31921_3-20012583 -281.html) and "TSA Meets 'Resistance' with New Pat-Down Procedures" by Suzanne Ito on the ACLU Blog of Rights website (https://www.aclu.org/blog/national-security/tsa -meets-resistance-new-pat-down-procedures).

- What are the advantages and disadvantages of full-body scans?
- Why do some people oppose their use?
- Which do you think is more socially acceptable, body scans or pat-downs?
- Is the concern about privacy legitimate?
- Should everyone be scanned equally or only those flagged by the TSA? Who might those flagged people be?
- Using your sociological imagination, consider how you would respond when faced with the choice of a full-body scan or a pat-down. How would your personal experience connect to the larger issue of security?

Access the live/updated links at http://www.paradigmpublishers.com/resources/goldbergmedia.aspx

until 2020, the digital universe is expected to double every two years." Given the predicted increase in data, we can assume that surveillance of the data will also increase. The forms and extent of surveillance raise important questions about the role of government in securing the nation in contrast to the protection of privacy as guaranteed by the Constitution.

Surveillance for Profit and Politics

Security is not the only reason your private lives are carefully scrutinized. There are economic and political reasons as well. The private use of personal data creates a great deal of information on your food or clothing preferences, your entertainment choices and other consumer activities, as well as your political preferences. This information provides a wealth of data for businesses and political organizations to focus on your lifestyle and shape their marketing so as to enhance the likelihood of favorable purchases or political choices. Again, since technology is a tool, it is developed to meet the needs of particular segments of society who can purchase or otherwise use the technology to their advantage.

Cybersecurity and Cybercrime

A more far-reaching issue related to security and privacy is cybersecurity, and here we see considerable connections between government, private business, and individuals. For businesses, the risks taken with computer use involve cybercrimes such as stealing money, customer identification, or health records. There is also a risk of sabotaging utilities, especially electric and water systems, which would cause major disruptions across society.

Movie Picks 7.1
Spying on the Homefront

Watch the PBS *Frontline* video, *Spying on the Homefront*, to see the how America's response to terrorism involves domestic spying (http://www.pbs.org/wgbh/pages/frontline/homefront/). The video can be watched in five segments. Consider the evolution of domestic spying and the debate about greater security and loss of privacy.

Mixed-Media Extra

Click on the links "The New Era of Pre-emption/Prevention" and "Interviews" for more details about domestic spying

Thinking Sociologically

- In what ways does domestic spying change the assumption of privacy in the United States?
- What is the dynamic between domestic spying and political institutions?
- How does the government engage private business to collect information on citizens?
- How does the technology of spying impact the information collected?
- Who decided how this technology is used?
- Can there be an acceptable balance between security and privacy?
- How are you personally affected by domestic spying?

Access the live/updated links at http://www.paradigmpublishers.com/resources/goldbergmedia.aspx

At the government level, hacking into federal agencies, including the military, is a special risk. There have been attempts in all these areas and vulnerability is high despite efforts to stop cyberattacks. These attacks, often called **cyberwar**, are often carried out by foreign governments seeking protected information. The FBI reported in 2008 that about two dozen countries have tried to attack US government computers (Federal

Web Exercise 7.2
The "Numerati" Are Watching You

Listen to the NPR interview with Stephen Baker on "Our Digital Lives, Monitored by a Hidden 'Numerati'" (http://www.npr.org/templates/story/story.php?storyId=95166854).

- How is technology used to learn about your personal life?
- How is this form of marketing different from traditional marketing?
- What does Baker mean by the term *tribes*? Is this good sociology?
- What are the cultural attributes most important in understanding purchasing experiences? political orientation?
- What is the connection between data mining and consumerism? and security?
- Is your privacy compromised by these activities?

Access the live/updated links at http://www.paradigmpublishers.com/resources/goldbergmedia.aspx

Web Exercise 7.3
Cyberwar/Cybercrime

Watch the *60 Minutes* segment "Cyber War: Sabotaging the System" to explore how computer hacking has attacked government agencies and utility infrastructures on a large scale (http://www.cbsnews.com/video/watch/?id=6578069n). Also check the "Web Extra" links. Consider how the idea of cyberwar emerges from the technology developed to maintain our systems.

For an example of the global nature of cybercrime read the *Washington Post* story, "ATM Thieves Conducted Massive Cyberattack," by Zachary A. Goldfarb (http://articles.washingtonpost.com/2013-05-09/business/39142997_1_prepaid-debit-cards-heist-gift-cards).

- How does our dependence on technology open the door to cyberwar?
- What is the dynamic between cyberwarfare and cybercrime?
- What conflicts exist between private corporations' drive for profit and the need for security?
- What is the connection between cybercrime and globalization?
- How vulnerable are you to cyberattacks or identity theft?

Access the live/updated links at http://www.paradigmpublishers.com/resources/goldbergmedia.aspx

Bureau of Investigation 2008). Considering that almost all government business is done using computers, much is at risk. In 2009 the military created a Cyber Command whose main purpose is to protect their computers from cyberattacks that could potentially hurt military operations. Cyberspying and cyberwarfare are now parts of the global social landscape.

For individuals, the issue of **cybercrime** demonstrates how the use of technology can both enhance and disrupt one's personal identity. Personal identity theft is a specific type of crime that affects many people. The US Department of Justice (n.d.) defines it this way: "Identity theft and identity fraud are terms used to refer to all types of crime in which someone wrongfully obtains and uses another person's personal data in some way that involves fraud or deception, typically for economic gain." According to the Bureau of Justice Statistics, in 2010, 8.6 million households (that is, 7 percent of all US households) were victims of identity theft, 64.1 percent of which involved misuse of existing credit

cards. The remainder included fraudulently opening new accounts and other use of personal information (Langton 2011). You put a great deal of personal information online when you pay bills, do banking, buy products, and interact on social-networking sites. You would have a hard time completing your college education without putting personal information on your computer. These activities are increasingly common and very convenient. In addition to your own activities, the government, your university, and the businesses where you purchase products all keep information about you online, and so they are vulnerable to hackers.

The use of technology is paradoxical. On the one hand, computers provide access to valued information and education, and make it easier to conduct daily life. Cybersecurity helps to track terrorist activities and prevent attacks. Technology also helps solve crimes. On the other hand, technology enables criminals to use computers to steal from government, businesses, schools, and individuals, and to intrude in the private

> **Fast Facts 7.1**
> **Cybercrime**
>
> - 336,655 complaints to the FBI in 2009 for online crime.*
> - $559.7 million lost in 2009 to cybercrime.*
> - Personal information of an estimated 50 million people exposed since 2005 through computer access by unauthorized users.**
> - Of security breaches reported since 2005, 50 percent occurred at colleges.**
>
> *Sources:* *The Federal Bureau of Investigation (2010); **LaClaire (2006).

lives of citizens. The above examples help demonstrate the sociological perspective that the use to which technology is put depends on many social factors. If technology remains vulnerable to attack we can expect to experience a range of crises that are made worse because of our dependence on computers and related technology:

- Reduced ability of the government to function, including national security.
- Inability for financial institutions to operate.
- Inability to deliver utilities, transportation, fuel, and other basic necessities.
- Shutting down of everyday business practices.
- Personal ruin from identity theft.

Further, if technology used for security purposes undermines privacy, there will be significant challenges to personal freedom. The future of technology depends on both the material products and technical skill that enable its application, and on the people who use it for good or ill.

We have explored the ways in which modern technology is applied to security, crime, and privacy. The next section looks further into issues of identity to see ways in which technology is used to define who we are. We explore more specifically how technology is used in the application of our knowledge of genetics and in the related area of reproductive technology.

Genetics and Identity

It may seem odd to bring the science of genetics into a sociological discussion of identity and technology. Most of us have little knowledge about genetics—perhaps if you have taken a biology course or have a special interest in this science you may know more than the average sociology student or professor. There is a great deal of research in the area of genetics and there is an equal degree of controversy over the application of this new knowledge to modern living. Animal cloning and genetically modified food are two of the most volatile subjects that have arisen in the debate about genetic engineering, which

FBI Headquarters, Washington, DC.
Source: Federal Bureau of Investigations

involves manipulating the genetic material in a living organism to create a new, desired outcome. Some believe that genetic engineering will solve the problems of food shortages, whereas others fear it will harm the food supply. There are concerns about environmental harm as well as treatment of animals. In any case, genetically engineered food is here to stay and the knowledge of breeding, cloning, and other forms of manipulation impact people both directly and indirectly. What we eat, how we think about food, and an overall acceptance of genetic manipulation become part of our technological know-how that can then be applied to all living things, including humans.

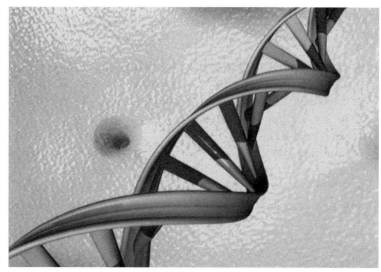

DNA double helix.
Source: National Human Genome Research Institute

Social Implications of Genetic Research

One of the most important scientific projects spanning the twentieth and twenty-first centuries is the Human Genome Project (HGP). The goal of this project was to map the genes that make up the biology of human beings. It was a daunting task, but to date the HGP has produced a great deal of information about the genetic sources of human attributes. There is great promise that it will help us learn more about our species for many years to come. How that knowledge is put to use is the subject of sociology.

We do not discuss the science of genetics here, but rather the social ramifications of the knowledge gained by genetic research and the technological applications that matter to the issue of identity. What makes genetics so interesting from a sociological perspective is how the science and the technology created around it are applied to individuals and social groups. If you are not already convinced of

---

Reading Room 7.1
The Human Genome Project Update

A good place to become familiar with research on genes is at the Human Genome Project Information website (http://www.genome.gov/10001772). Be sure to view the links for current discussions on the status of the project, its ability to predict links to disease, and the future use of the knowledge gained from the project.

Access the live/updated links at http://www.paradigmpublishers.com/resources/goldbergmedia.aspx

the sociological importance of this topic, consider these questions:

- Should parents be able to select genetic characteristics of their offspring for improved outcomes such as health, height, sex, intelligence, or personality characteristics?
- How long should embryos be preserved and for what purpose?
- Should people be told if they carry a gene for an incurable disease?
- How might the definition of *family* be affected if there are multiple participants in the reproductive process (such as egg or sperm donors, and surrogate mothers)?
- Is there a future in human cloning? Is it ethical?
- How important is genetic information and who should have it? The individual? Family members? The government? Employers?
- Should genetic information be used for identification? employment?

These are basic sociological questions that speak to the connection between what is technologically possible, socially ethical, and culturally valued. While we cannot cover all these topics in this chapter, they give you an idea of how this technology opens the door to many social uses. The speed with which genetic knowledge and the technology of genetic engineering have developed has left questions about ethics, law, and values in the dust. There are no definitive answers to these questions and as the technology associated with genetics continues to develop at a rapid pace, we are not likely to catch up any time soon. Sociology can help us extract the social meaning of this new world of genes and identity by examining the relationship between technological capability and the social forces that influence it.

As we examine this material, remember that technology develops out of social need and depends on the people who have the resources and means to develop it. How technology associated with genetics is used and by whom will determine the direction that will be taken socially. The application of genetics to social life will have a profound effect on how we understand human experience, how much our genes are used to determine our identity, and what society will do with that information. We begin with a brief overview of the social construction of genetics, then move on to the ways genetics has become important in reproductive technology and overall identity, and the crises that may ensue. The discussion of identity then circles around to an earlier topic in this chapter, the question of privacy.

Genetics as a Social Construction

The simple fact that so much money—$2.7 billion (US Department of Energy 2010)—and effort were put into tracing the human genome speaks to the importance we have given to knowledge about genetics. The decision to pursue this knowledge was not inevitable but rather a choice based on the importance given to biological attributes over other ways of understanding humans. Much can be gained from this knowledge, especially in the area of health and well-being. The more informed people are about their inherited genetic traits the better they can make decisions about lifestyle, reproduction, treatments for disease, and other valued choices. It seems a very good thing.

Beyond the evident scientific and health reasons for this knowledge, what does the HGP say about our emphasis on genetic inheritance? Consider this basic sociological question: What is more important to understanding human behavior—nature (genes) or nurture (social environment)? Perhaps you have discussed this in your psychology or sociology classes before, but you might revisit the question again as you read this chapter. How do we decide which characteristics matter in a person? How are those characteristics formed? Culturally speaking, there is much evidence that nature is more valued than nurture. "Blood is thicker than water" means that pregnancy and birth are considered superior to adoption, and loyalty to blood relatives is more important than friendships. Most Americans take adherence to this attitude at face value, rarely questioning its validity. This belief in the power of biology influences the directions that knowledge about genetics will take us and how we decide to use it. In her study of genes and society, Rothman (1998) describes genetics as more than science, as an ideology within a historical and political context, in other words, as a social construction. Without that context, we cannot understand the profound effect the new technologies will have on us.

If we accept that the technology is a tool that will take society in new directions, we need to think about the use to which that technology is put, who decides how it is used, and the changes it creates in society. There are many avenues to explore, but perhaps one of the best examples of how this technology is both personal and social is the area of reproductive technology.

Reproductive Technology

Most American families have biological children and most believe that children are an integral part of family life and a legacy for the future. Although children are highly valued, infertility has increased over time. Alternatives to natural conception, pregnancy, and birth abound today and new technologies have been developed to meet the desire for blood-related children. One obvious choice for infertile couples is adoption and many choose this route to parenthood. However, there are also a variety of technological options to provide a biological child of at least one genetic parent in a couple that is otherwise unable to conceive or bear children. This is appealing precisely because of the belief that a genetic connection to a child is the preferred route to parenthood despite the health risks and the cost of using technology to bear a child. Artificial insemination is one of the oldest relatively low-tech options, with the sperm donor being a woman's partner or another man, usually a stranger, arranged through a sperm bank. For lesbians wishing to have children biologically, this is the most

---

 Web Exercise 7.4
Genes, Technology, and Society

Go to the interactive PBS website Bloodlines: Technology Hits Home to consider the use of technology in six cases concerning genetic manipulation (http://www.pbs.org/bloodlines/). Click on each case under the link "Making Precedent" to view the role of science and technology and the choices people might make. Clips from the film Bloodlines can be viewed in this link under "Watch a clip."

- Describe the ways in which these cases combine science, technology, and society.
- Which social institutions influence decisions about the use of technology for genetic manipulations?
- Are some people or groups more powerful than others in deciding the use of the technology?
- What cultural values are questioned in the cases presented?
- In the context of this technology, how is defining human life genetically a social construction?

Access the live/updated links at http://www.paradigmpublishers.com/resources/goldbergmedia.aspx

Fast Facts 7.2
Uses for Genetic Testing

- Matching people for "DNA-compatible mates" (Weiss 2008).
- Testing for whether someone is "shy or adventurous" (Weiss 2008).
- Requiring college athletes to test for sickle cell anemia (Stein 2010).
- Genetic testing to determine a child's athletic potential in specific sports (Macur 2008).
- Genetic selection for certain characteristics: genetic diseases, sex, "savior siblings," and "cosmetic traits" (Center for Genetics and Society n.d).

common way to conceive. Various forms of either traditional or gestational surrogacy—in which the surrogate mother is or is not related to the embryo, respectively—may be utilized. There are also a number of medications used to increase fertility, some of which increase the likelihood of multiple births. Newer, more expensive, and invasive options called assisted reproductive technology (ART) include in vitro fertilization, egg and embryo transfers, and a number of other techniques in this rapidly developing technology. Along with the technology many lucrative businesses have emerged to help provide an assortment of reproduction options.

Aside from the array of technical possibilities for conception and birth, there is increasing interest from prospective parents in choosing specific biological characteristics from one's own embryos or in choosing a potential donor. There are about 900 genetic tests available, of which many are used to screen embryos and babies in the womb (US National Library of Medicine, National Institutes of Health 2010). Genetic testing of embryos for inherited diseases has become relatively common and is generally accepted practice when parents have those diseases or a genetic predisposition for them. A number of businesses have begun to offer genetic tests

for a range of concerns outside of medical issues. The science of genetics is relatively new and there is no guarantee that the results are valid, yet that has not stopped companies from offering tests for a variety of traits or people from purchasing them.

Many questions have been raised about the use of genetic testing as there are many possibilities for both use and abuse. There are no clear ethical or legal guidelines regarding which diseases or which other characteristics should be screened, and once screened, what to do with the information. Among ethicists, there is great concern that genetic testing will be used by people with resources to build babies with preferred genetic traits that could potentially result in increasing the inequalities that already exist in society. There is also concern about the ways in which genetic material can be used for identification purposes, thus further challenging the rights to privacy already compromised by the security surveillance systems discussed earlier in this chapter.

The relatively new field of biometrics uses "biological (anatomical and physiological) and behavioral characteristics that can be used for automated recognition." These "include fingerprint, face, iris, voice, signature, and hand geometry" (National Science and Technology Council Committee on

Technology 2006). Other more sophisticated characteristic recognition is being developed. Although some of these techniques, like fingerprinting, have been in use for a long time, the methods of collection and digital storage allow for greater use of large amounts of data for different purposes. For example, the FBI began a program in 2007 to develop a database using biometrics to identify people. And although some characteristics are already in use, "in the coming years, law enforcement authorities around the world will be able to rely on iris patterns, face-shape data, scars and perhaps even the unique ways people walk and talk" (Nakashima 2007). There is concern that collecting and retaining these data will further limit the privacy of citizens even beyond security and crime prevention. The potential for using biometrics commercially has already been recognized in banking, credit cards, social services, education, and almost anywhere identification is needed. With this rapidly advancing technology it is worth considering the social uses to which it will be put in the near future. Combined with the rapid growth of genetic technologies to shape humans biologically, what social outcomes can we imagine?

Technology through a Sociological Lens

The role of technology in society and the potential for myriad problems becomes abundantly clear when examining the issues of security, surveillance, and genetics, and the related concerns about identity and

---

 Movie Picks 7.2
Gattaca

The movie *Gattaca* depicts a fictional society in the near future in which one's identity is almost never left to chance, beginning with specific genes selected at conception to determine one's place in society. Biometrics allows for constant monitoring at work and at play. Consider how familiar this world is to you.

Mixed-Media Extra

If collecting data about your political or shopping habits seems intrusive, what would happen if your ideas could be "read"? Watch the *60 Minutes* segment, "Mind Reading" (http://www.cbsnews.com/video/watch/?id=5119805n).

Also, read the article "FBI Building System That Blows Away Fingerprinting" to see the real world of biometrics (http://news.idg.no/cw/art.cfm?id=E7DD109B-1A64-67EA-E4D0CD2824087487). Be sure to watch the slide show.

Thinking Sociologically

- How is technology used to control important aspects of social experience?
- Which aspects of the technology depicted in *Gattaca* are already used today?
- How does genetic manipulation affect culture?
- How is inequality redefined?
- What is the connection between identity and social control?
- Who gains the most from the technology of "mind reading" in the *60 Minutes* video?

Access the live/updated links at http://www.paradigmpublishers.com/resources/goldbergmedia.aspx

privacy. It may appear that technology is the driving force that has created this new world, but we must remember that technology develops out of a social need whose use is determined by social experience, expectations, knowledge, and power. While today's technology consists of all manner of sophisticated equipment, it is society that spurs it onward to develop in one direction rather than another and to apply its use in a social context. It may help resolve crises or it may contribute to them, depending on the use to which it is put. To understand the role of technology sociologically we will turn to the concepts of culture, norms, inequality, and interaction, and we will apply sociological theory to this phenomenon that is helping to define the twenty-first century. We begin by applying the sociological imagination to see the dynamic between you, technology, and the society at large.

Technology and the Sociological Imagination

Let's return to the opening vignette at the beginning of this chapter. Many people were appalled at the incident that exposed the sexual activities of a college student and were disturbed about its terrible outcome. It seems an extreme example of how social networking is used, but it suggests important questions: Where is the line drawn between anonymity, privacy, and social expression when using technology? How fast and how widely can information travel? Although this incident involved only a few devastated friends and family, within a day most people with access to the Internet or a television knew about it. What was private became public. Thus, it is a microcosm of the effects of technology in a society that has not fully digested the implications of its use. The application of technology for personal use is part of the larger social context that

includes the other issues discussed in this chapter: surveillance, privacy, genetics, and identity. In other words, whether the use to which this technology is put is small or large, it is its social acceptance that unites these experiences.

Consider your personal connection to technology. How dependent on technology are you? What can be learned about you in cyberspace? How much thought do you give to the information you put online? Do you think about your privacy when using a bank card or credit card or your university ID, or when you put pictures of yourself or your friends online and update your status? When you submit work to your professor electronically, how do you feel about the real possibility that it might linger forever in cyberspace? Are you aware of your interaction with government surveillance? These questions are not as easily answered as they may seem. Sometimes we are not even aware of the implications of our use of this technology because we are so immersed in it. To gain some perspective on your dependence on technology, consider what you would do without your personal connection to technology (see *Anti*-Web Exercise 7.5).

Applying the sociological imagination to understand technology places you squarely in the middle of the greatest technological revolution since industrialization. Think about the variety of uses to which technology is put, from the micro world of the individual user to the macro world of global surveillance, cybersecurity, and biometrics. Although it is easy to reflect on your personal use of technology, the sociological imagination enables you to see beyond your own technosphere to see yourself in a global context that is immersed in the technology upon which modern society depends. Understanding the impact of this technology brings us to a consideration of its impact on culture and the configurations that make up social structure.

***Anti*-Web Exercise 7.5**
Can You Survive without Your Technology?

List all the types of technology you use regularly (e.g., cell phone, computer, TV, car, MP3 player, GPS). Keep a twenty-four-hour log recording how long you use each one and what you use it for. Select the one you use the most and don't use it for twenty-four hours.

- Are you surprised by your involvement in technology?
- What did you do when you could no longer use your favorite?
- Did you cheat?
- Which of the technologies you use gives government or businesses access to your personal information?
- Use your sociological imagination to connect your personal dependence on technology to the larger social system. Could you function without it?

Access the live/updated links at http://www.paradigmpublishers.com/resources/goldbergmedia.aspx

Culture and Technology

The rapid movement into the digital age required a revolution in material culture. The creation and development of microchips and the software that enables the use of computers has been transformative. The many machines that track, record, and otherwise trace your existence from birth to death are not only a permanent fixture in our culture, they will become faster and more sophisticated in ways we cannot imagine today, as will the systems of communication. As we know, material culture is tied to non-material culture, so it is important to consider the knowledge, skills, beliefs, and values associated with these technologies.

Digital Native Culture

Most college students are digital natives, well-versed in the technology with an easy command of its language, folkways, and mores, and have seamlessly integrated it into

their lives. The adaptation of non-material culture to the material culture is reflected in the skills needed to function in a digital world, but it also impacts lifestyle, values, and norms, the very factors that make up culture. The amount of time people spend online has increased dramatically and this is especially obvious among digital natives. Today's teens and young adults value their time online for both social and educational purposes. That leaves less time for face-to-face interaction and physical activity and it changes how school work is performed. Values related to privacy change as more personal information goes online, surveillance cameras abound, bodies are exposed in airport scanning machines, and genetic material is recorded and stored. The cultural lag between what information is gathered and how we use it is considerable. In the process of adapting to these new cultural experiences, there remain questions about the use to which the technology is put. Exposure of sexual behavior, online bullying, and other questionable activities remain problematic

---

Web Exercise 7.6
Digital Native Culture

Read "Digital Native or Digital Immigrant, Which Language Do You Speak?" by Brad Cunningham (http://www.nacada.ksu.edu/Resources/Clearinghouse/View-Articles /Digital-natives-and-digital-immigrants.aspx). Next, watch the video "Digital Dossier" (http://www.youtube.com/watch?v=79IYZVYIVLA). Consider how the technology you use impacts the way you see the world.

- Do you agree with Cunningham that the technology you use for communication is an extension of yourself? Explain.
- Describe the difference in how you use technology compared to your parents, grandparents, and professors.
- How does being a digital native change cultural values and norms?

Access the live/updated links at http://www.paradigmpublishers.com/resources/goldbergmedia.aspx

---

in this new age of reduced privacy. As for passing knowledge from one generation to the next, an important component of culture, perhaps as far as the material culture goes, is that today's younger generation has much to teach their parents.

Although a new world of social networking has a profound effect on culture, we also should consider the cultural changes brought on by opportunity to use genetic testing and reproductive technology to determine characteristics of babies. The desire for more perfect children reflects a deep-seated desire for and cultural bias toward biological perfection. Otherwise, why do people pay so much money and suffer physical discomfort to determine embryonic and prenatal health? When given a choice, people will want a healthy baby with much potential. How we define health and potential will be redefined as the technology develops. No doubt as the technology becomes more affordable and easier to use, there will be greater acceptance of genetic modification that reflects social values. Who has access to these important technological changes is the subject of inequality.

The Connection between Technology and Inequality

As we have emphasized throughout this chapter, the very design of any technology is tied to social needs. There are important questions as to who defines those needs, who pays for the technology, who uses it, and for what purposes. We can assume that people with the most resources and skills dominate the distribution and use of technology, and so it is important to look at the inequalities of class, gender, race, and ethnicity regarding technology. First, we explore inequality of access to one of the most important tools of the twenty-first century, the Internet. Second, we consider the connections between surveillance, privacy, genes, and inequality.

Unequal Internet Access

The term *digital divide* commonly refers to differential access to and use of computers, and the implications of that for success in school and work and opportunities for information sharing. In Chapter 1 we saw that

Movie Picks 7.3
Growing Up Online

Watch the *Frontline* video *Growing Up Online*, which shows the immersion of teens into social networking (http://www.pbs.org/wgbh/pages/frontline/kidsonline/). Consider the connection between families, education, personal relationships, and the Internet.

Mixed-Media Extra

Check the link "Inside the Revolution" at the video website for in-depth interviews, especially with sociologist C. J. Pascoe.

Thinking Sociologically

- What factors are most important in understanding the social dynamics of online communication?
- Compare the positive and negative aspects of teens online as presented in the video.
- How do the social institutions of the family and education change with the use of this technology?
- Are race and gender important considerations when examining teens' involvement online?
- Describe the impact of social networking on cultural values and norms.
- Does this video suggest a cultural revolution?

Access the live/updated links at http://www.paradigmpublishers.com/resources/goldbergmedia.aspx

there are important global divisions in access to media, including Internet usage. The digital divide between the most developed and least developed nations is large. Here we focus on the United States where 73.5 percent of the population lives in households with Internet access (US Census Bureau 2010). As the box "Fast Facts: Internet Equality" shows, income and educational levels inform us about access to the Internet, as do race, ethnicity, and geography. Access to the Internet does not appear to be a gender issue, though how it is used may differ between men and women.

A report by Child Trends (2012) found a link between Internet access, income, and education when examining Internet use among children. By 2010, 85 percent of children had access to computers at home. Data from 2003 indicate that nearly all (96 percent) children from homes with incomes over $75,000 had access to the Internet, while in households earning less than $15,000 only 43 percent had Internet access. Parents' education levels also indicated that the higher a parent's education, the more likely that their children have access to computers and the Internet at home. In 2010, while only 57 percent of children whose parents had less than a high-school education had computers in the home (29 percent had access to the Internet at home), 97 percent of children whose parents had at least a college education had computers at home (71 percent had Internet access). According to the Child Trends study, "there is little evidence that having a computer at home improves students' academic performance, or narrows achievement gaps associated with race or socio-economic status" (2012, 2).

Fast Facts 7.3
Internet Equality

- 90.2 percent of people with at least a college degree live in households with Internet access but only 38.8 percent of those with less than a high-school degree do so.*
- 82 percent of households with incomes of $75,000 and over have broadband access while 35 percent of households whose income is less than $50,000 have access to broadband.**
- 80.3 percent of employed people live in households with Internet access while only 67.8 percent of the unemployed and 62.4 percent of those not in the labor force do so.*
- There is a 15 percent digital gap in household broadband access between whites and other race and ethnic groups (whites: 55 percent; minorities: 40 percent).**
- 54 percent of urban households and 39 percent of rural households have broadband access.**
- 74 percent of men and 73 percent of women live in households with Internet access.*

Sources: *US Census Bureau (2010); **One Nation Online (n.d.).

However, Brown and Martin, also of Child Trends, found that children's Internet access is tied to academic success and that computer literacy is important for later success in the workplace. Even though many children of various backgrounds have computer access today, "such skills are generally better developed among youth from more advantaged backgrounds" (2009, 4).

Overall, the digital divide appears to be diminishing. According to Smith (2010), there are some significant trends in computer and Internet usage:

- There is a narrowing racial gap in Internet and broadband use, but the gap persists in desktop-computer ownership: 65 percent for whites and 51 percent for blacks. Laptop ownership is about equal.
- Although Latinos use the Internet almost as much as whites, those who are not born in the United States are much less likely to use it.
- Racial minorities are more likely to own mobile phones and use them for a greater variety of functions than whites.
- Although racial minorities are less likely to go online than whites, they are more likely to use social networking sites and twitter.

The research on Internet access indicates that the digital divide persists but to a lesser extent than in the past. These remaining disparities of access to the Internet have major implications for education, news, and communications. As more and more of the information we receive is found on the Internet, those without access are being left out.

We now turn to inequalities in relationship to surveillance, privacy, and genes.

Surveillance, Privacy, Genes, and Inequality

What factors increase the chance that people will be subjected to greater or less surveillance or loss of privacy? In most cities, the use of surveillance cameras and data-driven technology is defended as a tool in fighting crime, although the original purpose of this technology was to address the threat of terrorism. While many support the use of these types of surveillance as crime rates have dropped where cameras are present, some question whether they violate privacy rights. For instance, some videos from surveillance cameras are broadcast on the Internet. Recent research on the use of this technology in fighting crime has resulted in increases in racial profiling since 2001 (Favro 2009).

In the case of genetics and biotechnology there are two related areas to consider:

- The cost of genetic testing and reproductive technology is very high, so only those with the most resources will be able to take advantage of them.
- By manipulating genes, we can make reproductive choices regarding sex and other characteristics that may give some offspring greater advantages over those without those choices.

This scenario implies that the use of advanced biotechnology will serve to reinforce traditional class, gender, and race inequalities by providing opportunities for enhancing the characteristics of children for the greatest social advantage. The current use of genetic testing and reproductive technology favors reduction in the chances for certain diseases. As we saw earlier, sex selection, athletic potential, and personality characteristics are also considered valid considerations. For people seeking sperm and egg donations, choosing on the basis of the IQ or education levels of donors presumes a preference for intelligence. For all of these characteristics, though, only people with considerable resources can afford these procedures, limiting access to upper levels of the social class spectrum and mostly whites. Although in some ways reproductive technology creates opportunities, in other ways it reinforces the status quo. As long as some groups of people or characteristics are favored

in society, those will be the choices made when we reproduce.

Examining Technology through Sociological Theory

Macro sociological theories contribute to understanding these amazing changes to the technological landscape by looking at the impact of technology on social structure. Both functionalism and conflict theory can be used to see how technology impacts society and the changes that occur as a result of its use. At the micro level, technology has had a dramatic effect on the interplay between individuals and society. We have already explored technology as a social construction earlier in the chapter and saw how the preference for biological explanations for human behavior has helped to shape the technology associated with genetics. Symbolic interaction theory addresses the enormous changes in communication brought to us through computers, especially social media. We therefore address macro and micro theories in turn.

Functionalism: Technology as Functional Adaptation

We have seen how the technologies discussed in this chapter have developed to serve specific functions. For functionalist theory the great expansion of surveillance after 9/11 demonstrated how in a moment of crisis society worked to stabilize itself. The structural adaptations that took place after 9/11 were, from a functionalist perspective, an example of how social change occurs. Many agree that the new technologies developed to safeguard against terrorism have mostly worked well, with the exception of the Boston Marathon attack in 2013. There have been no other successful attacks to date, though there have been some attempts. Thus it appears that technological innovations have served to rebalance the society and subsequently maintain equilibrium. It has been pointed out, however, that several of the attempted attacks were thwarted not by technological surveillance but by alert citizens, so it is not clear that the application of these technologies has sufficiently, or even efficiently, functioned as hoped. Similarly, the move to greater genetic understanding and the application of that knowledge to serve a social need through reproductive technology indicates that this technology serves a necessary function for the social good. Questions remain, however, about the balance between technological capability and societal responses to these innovations that raise ethical and legal questions.

For functionalist theory each of these examples suggests that society always seeks balance, so it is no surprise that the uses to which these technologies are put reinforce the status quo. We see no substantive change in the basic structural underpinnings of society as a result of new technology. Challenges to privacy and identity are seen as unfortunate but necessary actions in the effort to create a more secure and stable society. Yet, as noted above, there are important questions that fester. We turn to conflict theory to examine them and other issues pertaining to power and conflict.

Conflict Theory: Technology, Power, and Privacy

In every example of technological development addressed in this chapter, we can see the effects of inequality. Who has access to new technologies and who decides how it is used are essential questions asked in conflict theory. What are the implications of technological inequality for the distribution of power and the potential for conflict? The question of privacy is probably the most obvious, as it is related to a variety of new systems of surveillance to fight terrorism and crime. After 9/11, airport screening was enhanced and cockpit doors reinforced. These measures seemed adequate until terrorists employed other measures to attempt to bring down planes—shoe bombs, underwear bombs, liquid and plastic explosives—and with each of these, the response has been greater security at airports.

Each response to the escalation in attempts at terrorism has raised questions about security and privacy. The implementation of sophisticated body scanners at airports is a case in point. Even as soon as body scanners were introduced pilots and passengers alike have argued that they are intrusive health hazards and treat people like criminals. Conflict between the need for security as defined by the government and the need for privacy as defined by the public exemplifies the ongoing debate about security and privacy. Because the flying public must choose between physical exposure and intimate patdowns, these security measures raise greater indignation than the less-intrusive technologies that affect privacy, but they are all part of the larger issue regarding safety and privacy. Further, a conflict theorist would suggest that terrorism will not disappear with the use of newer technology—that only delays the next attempt. The conflict between terrorists and the rest of us is resolvable only if the root causes of terrorism are addressed. That raises a much larger—and more difficult to solve—question about social inequality.

There are other examples of inequality and the potential for conflict that raise questions about privacy. From cameras to data mining to genetic mapping, the traditional expectations of privacy are undermined. From a conflict theory perspective, the distribution of surveillance technology and the uses to which it is put reflect structural inequalities but also strengthen the power of those who command the technology, whether that power resides in government or corporations. Whether fighting terrorism or crime, or marketing to consumers, or even stealing identity, the development and use of technology reinforces basic inequalities and suggests the potential for conflict.

In the future will technology be used to maintain inequality or will it work for the common good? Technology has recently been used to support revolutionary and democracy movements against powerful dictatorships in the Middle East. Social media has played an important role in communicating dissent and calls to action from Tunisia to Yemen to Egypt to Syria and to Libya. Powerful, wealthy, and long-tenured rulers have been overthrown with the help of technology that conveys the power of groups who have previously been quashed by the ruling parties. The call for demonstrations or armed resistance, as well as the media attention to these movements, have contributed to a substantive change to Middle East politics, for example. Ubiquitous cell-phone videos among other forms of technology have enabled the world to see what has come to be known as the "Arab Spring" despite efforts to control the distribution of information by besieged dictatorships.

Inequality is also found in the application of technology to genetics, and particularly in reproductive technology. Understanding the genetic makeup of humans easily leads to questions about which traits are socially desirable and undesirable: sex, physical appearance such as height and skin color, and intelligence can potentially be manipulated to ensure greater social acceptance. In other words, cultural values that enhance inequality are easily projected in the selective use of technology. Further, who can afford to use this expensive technology in building a family? The financial cost of carrying out such manipulation serves to sustain class inequality. Those with the fewest resources stand to lose the most, while those with the most resources stand to gain the most in their access to and use of technology.

We must understand how technology fits into the structure of society, but it is also important to see how technology affects how we interact with each other within and across societies. For that we turn to symbolic interaction theory.

Symbolic Interaction Theory:
Technology and Communication

Given your personal experience with computers, and especially the Internet, it should come as no surprise that how and what we communicate has been dramatically impacted by technology. As digital natives, college students are entirely comfortable with the new forms of communication. Faster is better, shorter is better, wider distribution is better. Email, tweeting, texting, ebooks, online research, Skype—each of these creates a world of communication that is embraced throughout our society and increasingly, globally. New words, abbreviations, emoticons, and such have become part of our language. These symbols of communication will continue to evolve as the technology makes communication faster and more efficient. This development by itself is neither good nor bad, it is simply new. As with all of our discussion of technology, it is the use to which it is put, by whom, and how we interpret it that matter if we want to understand it sociologically.

Symbolic interaction teaches that communication with others helps us form our concept of "self," a definition of who we are in our social environments. This is referred to as the "looking-glass self," a social mirror by which we evaluate how others respond to us. How does this change when we communicate online? Zhao's study of teens' online communication finds that people develop two selves: offline and online. This has important effects for teens, especially, who are in the process of forming their identities and who use both offline and online experiences to create the "self." The anonymity of the "digital self" enables people to hide identities, play games, and be more intimate than would be expected face to face (Zhao 2005, 401). That is, until the person communicating is revealed, either intentionally or unintentionally. The potential for misunderstanding and even tragedy increases dramatically as communication sweeps through online communities.

Let's return to the opening vignette of the college student who committed suicide when he discovered that a video of him having sex with another man was broadcast. Why was it filmed and broadcast? What was communicated? Why did he kill himself? What line was crossed? Has the technology outstripped our ability to understand its effects? Do we care? While this example shows the terrible consequences of the invasion of a person's privacy, it is not the only one. Many people are bullied online and some also commit suicide. Sexting, sending pictures of genitals via cell phones, seems to be a form of entertainment. These are experiments with the formation of the "self" that will continue into the future as technology develops faster and broader ways of interacting.

Much of the new communications technology is wonderful. It is easier for family members to stay in touch, to find old friends, to meet people with common interests, to perform academic research, to learn about politics or science or religion. It will grow faster and be more innovative in the future in ways we cannot imagine. It will also raise more questions about privacy and security and identity and will challenge how we communicate with each other. Symbolic interaction theory helps us understand how the self develops in a social context, how we communicate, and what is important in that process. The use of technology, especially social networking, is a major force injected into twenty-first-century personal and public dynamics.

Looking Backward: Connecting Technology to Twenty-First-Century Crises

The crises we studied earlier in this book—the environment, global issues, health care, and terrorism—are each intertwined with technology in ways that can contribute to or diminish the effects of these crises. It is important to understand the uses of technology in relation to these crises. Even the technology that facilitates the use of media throughout this text demonstrates the power of technology to enable us to learn through mixed media, the Internet, and films. This could not be possible without the tremendous development of new technologies that so encompass our lives. Technology also contributes to crises in some very direct ways. The actual material that makes up the technology—the metals, the plastics and wires, and the deliberate built-in obsolescence that leads to discarding old products—creates toxic waste that increases with each new gadget or upgraded computer. So we come full circle to address an unambiguous relationship of technology to some of the major crises addressed in the book: the creation of environmental and health hazards that mostly affect people in the least developed nations. As we go through the twenty-first century, what is our responsibility for the technology and the waste it produces?

Although the issue of high-tech trash is linked in specific ways to the crises in the environment, the developing world, and health, there are many other examples of the ways in which technology is connected to the crises we have studied. Technology both contributes to and helps address these crises. Climate change and oil depletion cannot be understood or solved without sophisticated technology. The development of alternative fuels and the drive to reduce carbon emissions require advances in technology. Our knowledge of global issues would be much

Web Exercise 7.7
What about Your Tech Trash?

Read the *National Geographic* article "High-Tech Trash" (http://ngm.nationalgeographic
.com/2008/01/high-tech-trash/carroll-text) and view the accompanying interactive
site's links. Consider the ways in which high-tech waste is a health hazard and contributes to
environmental problems.

Watch "The Story of Electronics," which describes the problems of electronic waste
(http://storyofstuff.org/movies/story-of-electronics/).

- How is the problem of high-tech trash a global problem?
- Describe the health and environmental problems that result from this trash.
- Why is high-tech trash more of a problem than traditional trash?
- In what ways does inequality factor into the problem of high-tech trash?
- What responsibilities do businesses that create technology products have regarding their trash?
- As a consumer of technology, what is your responsibility for the trash you create?

Access the live/updated links at http://www.paradigmpublishers.com/resources/goldbergmedia.aspx

more limited without the ability to communicate across thousands of miles. Advances in computers have helped spread news about child soldiers and human trafficking, about which we would otherwise have little or no knowledge. Health care today is high-tech in many respects but health-care problems also result from technology. For example, there is a debate about the health effects of radiation from cell phones and computers in our daily use of technology. Tracking terrorists and securing society depends heavily on technology, as we saw in the hunt for the Boston Marathon bombers, but these technological advances also open the door to impingements on privacy and exposure of many sorts of confidential information. In late 2010, the exposure of secret government documents by Wikileaks raised myriad questions about the right to know, national security, and international diplomacy. Studying technology sociologically provides a perspective to evaluate this vital component of society that will dominate the entire twenty-first century.

Looking Forward: Where Will Technology Take Us?

Ask your parents and grandparents if they could have imagined the technology we have today compared to what they experienced when they were young. Most of the technology you use with great expertise and assume is part of our social fabric did not exist for the average citizen even twenty years ago. What will it look like in another twenty years? Advances in computers, genetics, media, and other newer technologies will have profound effects on your lives. Increasingly sophisticated security measures will attempt to protect you from terrorists and criminals. The problems of cybercrime may or may not be resolved. Your genes will probably be public knowledge and may affect your chances for employment, but emerging technologies of genetic medicine may also increase your life span and enhance your health. Your reproductive choices will multiply. There will be fewer buttons to push and more cyber communication. Paper, and perhaps money, will become irrelevant. It is hard to speculate about the technology itself, and in any case what matters sociologically is not the material equipment but the use to which it is put—whether it enhances life or destroys it; whether the structural inequalities that exist today continue to exist; if how we communicate improves our understanding of ourselves and our world. We will have to wait and see. Keep your eyes open!

Web Watch

As you would expect, many websites address technology and society. Given the rapid pace of technological change, it is well worth exploring these sites, some of which are listed below. They address both the new technologies and the legal and social impact these technologies will have as we move through the twenty-first century.

American Civil Liberties Union: http://www.aclu.org

Biometrics.gov: http://www.biometrics.gov/ReferenceRoom/Introduction.aspx

Center for Genetics and Society: http://www.geneticsandsociety.org/

Computer Crime and Intellectual Property Section, United States Department of Justice: http://www.cybercrime.gov/

Electronic Privacy Information Center (EPIC): http://epic.org/

FBI, Cyber Crime: http://www.fbi.gov/about-us/investigate/cyber/cyber

Genetic Engineering and Its Dangers (Ron Epstein): http://online.sfsu.edu/~rone/GEessays/gedanger.htm

Privacy Rights Clearinghouse: http://www.privacyrights.org/

Youth and Media: http://youthandmedia.org/

Crises in Perspective

Agency and Action

We have just completed an exploration of some of the most dramatic examples of the social problems we face in the twenty-first century. They were chosen because they provide important evidence of the major social crises that are occurring now and that will affect society for at least a generation. They are both immediate and long term, and they are interconnected in many ways. Although the problems we studied are daunting, by applying sociological concepts and theories we can understand them better and plan for the future as individuals and as a society.

When examining these crises there is the risk of feeling helpless and despairing. In fact, sociology students often tell their professors that sociology is depressing: they study a lot of bad things about society and few of the good things. Not all sociology professors adopt a social-problems approach, but for those who do, it is hard to avoid difficult topics. And why should we? At the beginning of this book we saw how the founders of sociology used science to study society for a specific purpose: to understand the problems and make a better world. In keeping with that goal, we will end this book with some ideas of how we can use sociology to address the crises discussed in these chapters and how you might make a difference.

Let's start with the concept of **agency,** which helps us to understand our roles in society as active participants. Despite feeling that problems overwhelm or envelop us, we can consider how we conduct our lives and respond to problems. A strong case has been made in this book that social structure largely determines how society is shaped and who shapes it. Social institutions provide the means to serve social needs and the stability required for society to function. Structural inequalities provide both opportunities and limitations based mainly on the dynamics of social class, gender, race, and ethnicity. How, then, do we respond to these entrenched structures?

Social structure seems formidable compared to the role of individuals, but sociology recognizes that individual action also shapes society. Human beings have the will to act and in so doing, influence society. This is agency. In other words, a society does not exist independent of the people who inhabit it. And those people are actors who observe and make decisions about issues large and small. Symbolic interaction theory points out that we define ourselves in relation to society, but we also make independent choices for ourselves within the social context. We act in accordance with our sense of self and where we see ourselves in the larger social picture. How else to explain social movements such as the civil rights and women's movements of the twentieth century, and the recent widespread opposition to dictatorships in the Middle East? In each case, despite significant personal risk even in the face of powerful opposition, people chose to be agents of their destinies.

Social action then is the dynamic between individuals and social structure. All of us have the ability to make choices. We can do this largely because we develop our concepts of our "selves" in a social context, but with the free will to make decisions in any number of directions. Agency is the ability to do just that. We are agents of our own behavior, influenced by society but independent decision-makers nonetheless. This does not mean that our decisions are random, however. In fact our decisions fall within parameters based on our social experience and knowledge as well as social limitations. In this context, the sociological imagination makes a great deal of sense. Who am I? Where do I fit in? How does history shape

society? How does society affect me and how do I affect society?

For each of the problems we investigated in this book, you can be an agent; you can develop a perspective and act according to your knowledge and beliefs and your place in society. Before you decide to act, though, you have a responsibility to be well-informed. Indeed, the central goal of academic learning is to provide a knowledge base that gives students the tools needed to make good decisions about their own lives and to frame the ideas to which they are committed. You have learned about several important social problems in this book and have developed ways to analyze these problems sociologically. This knowledge will enable you to make decisions for yourself and as a member of a community, to take action in ways that are meaningful to you. There are many different avenues for action from personal changes to political ones in which you can partake: making personal choices for yourself and your family, supporting your community, educating others formally or informally, volunteering for an advocacy organization, donating money, even having a career that addresses a social problem.

Hopefully you now have enough ideas about the problems addressed in this book

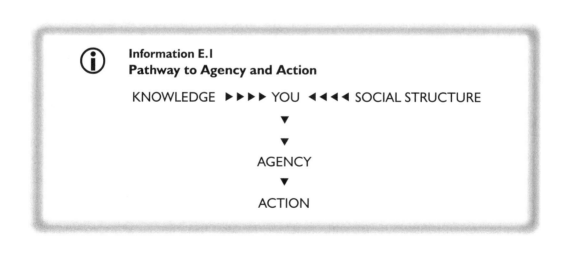

Information E.1
Pathway to Agency and Action

KNOWLEDGE ▶▶▶▶ YOU ◀◀◀◀ SOCIAL STRUCTURE

▼

▼

AGENCY

▼

ACTION

that you can make your own decisions about whether you want to advocate for a particular issue and the ways in which you may choose to participate. Whether you choose to take action or not, you are the agent that makes that decision. Having agency is being human. In the rest of this chapter we present ways to consider agency and the possibility of advocating in relation to each of the crises discussed in the book.

The Environmental Crisis

Probably the most difficult part of understanding the environmental crisis is cutting through the highly politicized information on climate change and oil depletion in the popular media to get to the scientific findings. It is difficult to address such a complex issue given the structure of our industrial base and transportation systems as well as the power of the political interest groups who work hard to argue that climate change is a myth and to forestall legislation limiting global warming. Similarly, the debate over depletion of oil, our major source of energy, is highly politicized and global in nature. Nonetheless, many people and organizations act both in their own self-interest and in an effort to change social directions to improve the future of climate on the planet and to seek alternative energy sources. It is not just individuals who have accepted these realities. Some large corporations, including automobile manufacturers and energy companies, have moved to help reduce carbon emissions. In some ways they are ahead of the political process that is still mired in controversy over the reality of climate change. The production of electric cars and the development of renewable energy are two big changes on the horizon promoted by corporations and government. On a smaller scale, personal choices about what you buy and what you throw away or recycle, or the

transportation you use, may seem minor, but such actions involve changes in lifestyle that entail shuffling priorities and some amount of inconvenience. Many people today are aware of the value of recycling efforts, for example. A step above personal responsibility is to reach out to your community at school or at home to enhance recycling efforts. Another example is the "buy local" movement, which encourages support of local farms while also reducing the need for transportation of crops, thus helping local economies while reducing CO_2 emissions. Environmental clubs abound on college campuses, and environmental committees are found in places of worship and in community centers. If you want to go beyond a personal effort, there are many environmental organizations who advocate for a variety of ways to improve the environment.

Crises in a Fragile World

The crises in the least developed regions of the world seem far from us who seem protected by distance and cultural divides. Chapter 4 demonstrates, however, that the fragile world is not so far away. The plight of child soldiers and the problems of human trafficking and genocide, all prevalent today, contribute to an unstable world. In each case, we could see the impact on the people directly involved, but also on the rest of us from our relative positions of safety. What is your role in addressing this problem? If you watched the film *Invisible Children*, you saw how ordinary college students stepped out of their comfort zone and journeyed to a tragically destabilized region. They not only brought back information, they established a nationwide effort to spread information about children caught up in civil war. Refugees, like the lost boys of Sudan, and victims of human trafficking

Watch Online E.1
The Ultimate Roller Coaster Ride: A Brief History of Fossil Fuels

Watch this brief video from the Post Carbon Institute (http://www.postcarbon.org/blog-post /176080-the-ultimate-roller-coaster-ride-a). Think about where you fit into the future of fossil fuels. Can you participate in the four actions the video suggests for a post-carbon future? What cultural changes will occur? What are the global connections that could promote a post-carbon future?

Access the live/updated links at http://www.paradigmpublishers.com/resources/goldbergmedia.aspx

and ethnic cleansing are found throughout the developed world, trying to put their lives back together. It would not take a lot of effort to find refugees in your communities and religious organizations who provide direct assistance to refugees and who lobby to improve conditions. No doubt there are students in your university whose lives have been directly touched by the problems of the least developed regions of the world as well as organized efforts to support victims of human trafficking and genocide. This support can range from personal to political, on the micro and macro levels of society.

Health and Health Care

Your personal health and the economics and politics of health care are perfect examples of the direct relationship between the individual and society. When you are sick, you need to find health care. If you are a full-time university student, you have access to the health center on your campus. What if you need to go to a hospital or what if a family member is faced with a health condition requiring a great deal of expensive care? How will you navigate the complexities and costs facing you? The social structure of health care really does matter in direct ways in your lives. The

Watch Online E.2
Invisible Children Updates

The Invisible Children website (http://invisiblechildren.com/) has a number of videos at the "Multimedia" link that update viewers on the projects focusing on the effects of war on the children of Uganda. It also asks visitors to join their various projects in support of their goals.

- Do you think there is a role for American students in addressing the needs portrayed on the website?
- How is this advocacy similar to or different from advocacy for disadvantaged children in the United States?
- Is this advocacy an example of applying sociology to social crises?

Access the live/updated links at http://www.paradigmpublishers.com/resources/goldbergmedia.aspx

passage of the Affordable Care Act in 2010 does not end the debate about access and cost of care. Indeed, this debate is likely to follow you throughout most of your life. If you are young and healthy, it is difficult to focus on this issue, but it is important to stay informed to see how the political impact of the law and attempts to rescind or revise it may impact you, your family, and your community.

There are a number of ways to address health care, starting with advocating for your own care and that of your family and friends. Understanding your insurance policy, expecting good medical care from practitioners, and knowing your rights as a patient are a starting point, and this can make the difference between good care and bad care. Tending to your personal health requires knowledge about protection from a range of mild to serious diseases and medical conditions. As we saw in Chapter 5, obesity and HIV/AIDS are preventable yet remain serious problems. Agency in the form of healthy lifestyles and regular HIV tests if you are sexually active are important contributors to your health. On a more macro level, understanding how inequality impacts the underinsured and uninsured, which we addressed in Chapter 5, gives us a broader view of what the impact of access to care

means for the life chances of people in various positions in society. Even people in the relative comfort of the middle class can have their lives thrown into turmoil by a health crisis or chronic condition and therefore run the risk of losing their economic security. We saw with the recent debate about health-care reform the important role that agency and advocacy play. With an informed position on this issue, you can make a difference in the outcome for health-care reform.

On a global scale, health care also resonates as a major issue of concern. Connecting global poverty, life expectancy, and illnesses such as HIV/AIDS to inequality in health and access to care is sociologically important. With so many health concerns in our own society it is difficult to see a role to play in addressing health care far away. Nonetheless, it is worth exploring those connections both to understand the relationship between health and global poverty and the role advocacy might play in helping address these inequalities.

Terrorism and Its Aftermath

The attacks of 9/11 marked an important moment in US history, and there is the

---

 Reading Room E.1
Patient's Bill of Rights

There have been a series of Patient's Bills of Rights over the years. Most recently, one was developed as part of health-care reform. Read "Fact Sheet: The Affordable Care Act's New Patient's Bill of Rights" (http://www.cov.com/files/Uploads/Documents/HHS%20Fact %20Sheet%20%28coverage%20limits%29.PDF) (2010) to see how the new law will impact you. You should also follow the ongoing debate about health-care reform to see which of the provisions are being challenged and why.

- Which provisions are important to you personally?
- Which do you think help or hinder health care for yourself and others?

Access the live/updated links at http://www.paradigmpublishers.com/resources/goldbergmedia.aspx

Reading Room E.2
Be the Change, Save a Life

The website Be the Change: Save a Life is sponsored by ABC News and addresses a number of health problems in the developing world (http://saveone.net/). In addition to describing the problems, it also suggests ways ordinary citizens can support health initiatives.

Explore the site and consider in what ways the site promotes advocacy:

- Do you think this is an effective way to address global health problems?
- Do people in developed societies bear any responsibility in helping provide better health care in more fragile societies? Why or why not?

Access the live/updated links at http://www.paradigmpublishers.com/resources/goldbergmedia.aspx

tendency to view what followed as the "aftermath." This is a bit presumptuous because, as was made clear by the Boston bombing twelve years later, 9/11 was not the end of terrorism. It was the beginning of a new era of challenges to address the acts of terror, the actors, and the social factors that make terrorism so important today.

The role of sociology, and of you as agents of your destiny, is to understand terrorism on several levels. First, of course, is to contemplate the basic experience of terrorism as personally horrifying and frightening. On a personal level, what choices do you have when you travel or attend a sporting event or a concert? How do you weigh the value of security against the value of privacy? Agency in this case means that you will make decisions in the context of your relationship to terrorism depending on your experience with it or feelings about it. You may choose to limit your exposure to potential terrorist acts by avoiding flying, for example. Or, if you do fly, you may accept or reject security measures that some interpret to be invasions of privacy, especially the latest technology in body scanning. These acts of individual agency take place in a social context in which choices are directly connected to a person's fears of terrorism and sense of privacy.

Indeed, the widespread negative response to full-body scans at airports has helped influence attempts at finding acceptable alternatives. Though at the time of publication there are few organized advocacy efforts in this arena, it is a good example of how agency can turn into advocacy when large numbers of people take a strong position on something they care about. National Opt-Out Day scheduled for the day before Thanksgiving, 2010, was an example of a citizen's movement that, although it was generally seen as ineffective, demonstrated an effort to organize around the issue of security and privacy in the post-9/11 era.

Of course it is not sufficient to see terrorism only as a personal problem. As with our other topics, one must see terrorism broadly in a social context. Despite the inclination to see terrorism as random, it is important to understand the social dynamics that make terrorism likely and make people vulnerable. Understanding this can impact how we conduct our lives, both individually and socially. As we learn about terrorist organizations, their grievances, their goals, and their support systems, we can discern patterns that make sense sociologically. Only with that are we able to see terrorism in its proper context and respond effectively.

Reading Room E.3
Holiday Travel: National Opt-Out Day

Read the *Washington Post* Live Q&A session with Kate Hanni of FlyersRights.org as people express their opinions about the use of body scanners at airports (http://www.washingtonpost .com/wp-dyn/content/discussion/2010/11/24/DI2010112401939.html).

Consider the need for information, concerns about privacy and radiation, and related issues.

- How is agency expressed in these conversations?
- How has the threat of terrorism changed our outlook on privacy?

Access the live/updated links at http://www.paradigmpublishers.com/resources/goldbergmedia.aspx

Technology

Perhaps this topic resonates most with college students. You are immersed in new technology—some say it is an extension of you—and you will feel its effects every day of your lives. As a form of communication, as a system of identification and security, or as a breach of privacy, the role of technology in your lives is unprecedented compared to earlier generations. And yet, in twenty years it will have an even greater impact. We can understand the importance of technology by applying the sociological concepts that show the relationship of technology to society even as it moves in new directions. By doing so, you can develop your own sense of "self" in that context and make important decisions about how you will participate in the world of twenty-first century technology.

Technology is a double-edged sword. On the one hand, you will have more information about your health, better reproductive choices, greater longevity, and more access to information and global experiences. All these things bring opportunity for more satisfying lives. On the other hand, your privacy will likely be compromised by technology, bringing with it the commercialization of genes and ethical dilemmas regarding

important technological breakthroughs such as cloning and genetic engineering. Problems with technology also resonate with the other topics covered in this book. While technology has contributed to global climate change, it has the potential to help solve it as well. Technology has the promise of developing more sources of nutrition for fragile regions of the world. At the same time technology is used to extract natural resources in ways that may harm local populations. In the area of health, medical breakthroughs and more effective treatments could not be achieved without sophisticated technology, yet the extension of life through technological solutions does not solve the question of quality of life. While technology helps to contribute to our security in an effort to control terrorist activity, its use also has the potential of compromising privacy. Sociologically, the best way to predict the uses of these many new technologies is to understand who has power over the technology and who has access to it. As an agent in your own life, understanding where you fit in relation to the many new technological innovations depends on your location in this social context.

This last chapter ties sociological analysis of some of the most difficult problems we

Reading Room E.4
The Future of Technology

Explore the website Future for All (http://www.futureforall.org/). Read about some of the predictions for changes in technology over the next few decades.

- Do you think these predictions are plausible?
- Can you see yourself living in this world?

Check out especially the link to the "Global Seed Vault" in the right-hand column.

- Is this an example of agency?

Also read the "Future of Privacy."

- What role can people take to protect their privacy, or should they?
- How is the experience of technology going to be different for people in different walks of life?
- Is there a way to ensure that the benefits of technology are shared equally?
- Consider your personal connection to technology and the relative benefits and problems you may face in your lifetime.

Access the live/updated links at http://www.paradigmpublishers.com/resources/goldbergmedia.aspx

face with ways to personally address them. With this knowledge, you can choose a path that makes you a fuller participant in the world around you. Even as some problems recede, others will become dominant. New crises will likely arise. How will you respond to these issues? The sociological imagination was emphasized throughout this book because it is so important to understanding your relationship to the larger social landscape. You will face many personal "troubles" in your future, and you will see "troubles" facing others both near and far. Applying the sociological imagination will help you manage as individuals and give you tools to contribute to the social good.

Glossary

Achieved Status: Status acquired by a person due to some voluntary action. Some major achieved statuses include **occupation**, **education**, marriage, parenthood, and home ownership. Compare **Ascribed Status**.

Agency: The ability for people to act on their own behalf when determining the best course of action for themselves and their group.

AIDS (Acquired Immunodeficiency Syndrome): A disease diagnosed when the **HIV** virus has multiplied to the point that the body can no longer resist "opportunistic infections" that cause serious deterioration in the body's ability to survive. Without recently developed antiviral drugs the likelihood of survival is slim.

Ascribed Status: The status a person is born with or that is not altered by social circumstances: **sex**, age, **race**, and **ethnicity** are important ascribed statuses. Compare **Achieved Status**.

Bureaucracy: In modern society most large social institutions, and some small ones, are organized systematically using written policies, formal means of employment, job descriptions, and other formalized systems to run large-scale operations. Corporations and governments are, by necessity, bureaucratic institutions. Max Weber developed a

theory about the importance of bureaucracy in modern society.

Child Soldiers: Individuals under the age of eighteen who participate in combat or as support for combat. The widespread use of children starting in late twentieth-century conflicts is unique in the history of warfare, and it persists today despite objections from international bodies like the United Nations and many child-advocacy groups.

Conflict Theory: A theoretical perspective that examines conflicts arising from the unequal distribution of resources and power that emerged with the growth of industrial capitalism. Essential to conflict theory is the idea that **inequality** creates social dynamics in a drive to seek greater equality. Society is always in flux as some conflicts are resolved while others emerge. Compare **Structural Functionalism**.

Conspicuous Consumption: A reflection of one's **social status** by displaying to others what is purchased, thus demonstrating what is believed to be the person's well-being to his or her social network.

Counterculture: Components of **culture** that oppose the **norms** of society by creating their own set of norms in opposition to, and marginalizing themselves from, the mainstream. In some cases society responds by criminalizing their activities. Extremist groups such as terrorist groups, gangs, and racial supremacist groups are examples of countercultures. A counterculture can also be less extreme, such as groups that support legalizing recreational use of marijuana. Compare **Subculture**.

Cultural Diffusion: The exchange or sharing of goods and knowledge across cultures. Mass media today is one of the most important contributors to cultural diffusion.

Cultural Lag: A delay in the cultural adaptation to technological change as advances in technology develop more quickly than a society's ability to respond to those changes.

Cultural Relativity: The understanding that there is a great deal of variation of norms, beliefs, and values across cultures and that no one society can claim that its own culture represents universally correct values and norms.

Culture: Language, customs, norms, beliefs, and attitudes shared among a group of people in a society. It is passed down from generation to generation. It is a way of experiencing and seeing the world from the perspective of the people sharing it, a society. See also **Material Culture** and **Non-Material Culture**.

Culture Shock: The experience of being introduced to new cultures with limited or no familiarity with the new culture.

Cybercrime: The commission of crimes using computers to steal identities or money from individuals and institutions.

Cyberwar: The use of computers in attacks on government facilities and utilities to try to cause significant disruption to society or discover protected information. Cyberwarfare

is carried out by governments and non-government entities.

Developing Nations: Also known as "least developed countries," they are primarily agricultural but are beginning to industrialize. There is a great deal of poverty throughout this sector. They have weak governments and heavy investments from abroad to develop and extract natural resources and to influence economic and political stability. Internal civil wars, inability to respond effectively to natural disasters, and weak infrastructures mark this group. Much of Africa, parts of Asia and the Middle East, as well as Haiti are considered developing nations.

Digital Divide: Differential access to computers and the Internet. Such unequal access occurs between most and least developed nations, and between social classes, races, ethnic groups, and geographical regions within countries.

Discrimination: An act that singles out a group or an individual member of a group for unequal treatment.

Dual Labor Market: The dual labor market is made up of two distinct sectors of the workforce in which most occupations fall: the **primary sector** and the **secondary sector**. These categories are distinguished by differences in pay, job security, and related factors.

Education: An important component of **social stratification**. The level of formal education a person achieves helps determine his/her position in a stratified society.

Epidemiology: The study of the connections between illnesses as medical concerns and the social factors that contribute to the patterns diseases take in various populations.

Ethnic Cleansing: Singles out specific ethnic groups and may include killing, but it generally involves taking over ethnic neighborhoods or regions and the forcibly removing members of ethnic groups to "cleanse" an area of that group. Compare **Genocide**.

Ethnicity: A category that represents a group of people who share a cultural heritage, including a place of geographic origin and language. It may also include other cultural attributes associated with social institutions such as family lifestyle and shared religious practices.

Ethnocentricity: A sense of superiority of one racial or ethnic group over another group. The concept of **racism** is often used interchangeably with *ethnocentrism*.

Failed States: Countries facing extreme poverty and violence and that cannot meet the basic needs of society. Compare **Fragile States**.

Folkways: Norms that are less restrictive and more flexible than **mores**. Often referred to as *customs*.

Fragile States: Politically and developmentally unstable countries, often at war, with weak institutions and governance. Compare **Failed States**.

Functionalism: See **Structural Functionalism**.

Gender: The social roles that result from the social interpretation of biological attributes associated with **sex**.

Gender Socialization: The teaching of boys and girls the accepted social roles of their sex that takes place in families, schools, religious institutions, and the broader culture.

Genocide: As defined by the United Nations, acts to destroy a national, ethnic, racial, or religious group in whole or in part. Specific means of committing genocide include killing members of the group, causing serious bodily or mental harm to group members, and imposing conditions of life on the group calculated to bring about its physical destruction. Compare **Ethnic Cleansing.**

Highly Industrialized Nations: Post-industrial countries that have strong capitalist economies and stable political systems that are mostly democratic. Some manufacturing takes place in these countries, but much of the economy is based on information processing and service industries. Examples include the countries of Western Europe, the United States, Canada, Japan, and Australia.

HIV (Human Immunodeficiency Virus): A virus that is typically spread by unprotected sexual contact or sharing of intravenous needles, though also through blood transfusions, or during birth or maternal nursing. HIV in itself is not a fatal disease, but the virus reduces the effectiveness of the immune system, thus increasing the likelihood of dying of infections, at which point a person is determined to have **AIDS**.

Human Trafficking: Forced or deceitful recruitment or transportation of persons for purposes of exploitation. Such exploitation might include prostitution or other sexual exploitation, or slavery or other forced servitude, among other forms.

Income: Compensation mostly earned through a job in the form of wages or salary. Other sources of income include interest, dividends, and government sources such as Social Security and public assistance.

Individualism: An attribute of **non-material culture** that emphasizes individual rights over group or community rights. Individualism is considered a traditional American value.

Inequality: Differential access to resources and means of livelihood for individuals or groups of people in society. All societies have some form of inequality based on the economic structure of society.

Islamophobia: Anti-Muslim attitudes that have arisen throughout the non-Muslim world. Islamophobia includes expressions of hatred and anger against Muslims and physical attacks on individuals and places of worship.

Institutional Discrimination/Racism: Discriminatory practices that have been established over time that discriminate even in the absence of overt **racism**.

Least Developed Nations: see **Developing Nations**.

Life Chances: Life chances determine the opportunities and limitations people experience based on their location in a system of **inequality**. Among the important life chances are the chance for **education**, for health, for the likelihood of incarceration, and for a good job.

Macro Theory: Structural theories as they address the significant structures that make up our social world. These structural theories are the backbone of modern sociological theory today, including **structural functionalism** and **conflict theory**. Macro theory was first developed by early sociologists such as Auguste Comte, Herbert Spencer, Emile Durkheim, Karl Marx, and Max Weber. Also known as macro sociology.

Material Culture: Tangible aspects of the **culture** of people in a society. It emerges from the ways in which people meet basic needs for food, shelter, and overall sustainability. Housing, clothing, forms of transportation, food, and technology are some of the most important aspects of material culture. Compare **Non-Material Culture**.

Materialism: The desire and drive to own things, and the meanings people derive from that ownership.

Micro Theory: Micro theory examines how people perceive themselves and communicate with one another. **Symbolic interaction theory** is the central micro theory in sociology. Also known as micro sociology

Mid-Level Industrialized Nations: Also considered "rapidly developing countries," they have transforming economies aided by strong ties to Western capitalist nations. Some of these nations have emerging democratic political structures but overall less-stable political systems than the highly industrialized nations. China, India, and Russia are the best examples of these countries.

Mores: Norms that are written laws and unwritten requirements to which people are expected to strictly adhere.

Negative Sanctions: Penalties for violating **norms**, especially **mores**.

Non-Material Culture: Ideas and knowledge about the world around us. What we think of as justice, honor, morality, religion, and beauty—our values and attitudes, along with the skills and knowledge necessary to meet our needs—make up our non-material culture. Compare **Material Culture.**

Norms: The expected behaviors of people who share a **culture**. Compare **Folkways** and **Mores**.

Obesity: Along with being overweight, obesity is a label for ranges of weight that are greater than what is generally considered healthy for a given height. The Centers for Disease Control and Prevention provides specific definitions of obesity based on an adult body-mass index, derived from a person's weight and height, with alternative definitions for children and adolescents.

Occupations: The jobs held by people. Occupations are an important category in determining **social class** and **social status**.

Patriarchy: The dominance of men over women in society.

Peak Oil: The point globally at which the amount of oil extracted from the earth is outpacing the overall supply of this finite resource. Many believe that the world has reached this peak.

Political Power: Power is the ability to influence others, even against their resistance. Political power helps determine the political direction of a society. In a stratified society, people with the most wealth generally have the most political power.

Post-Industrialized Nations: Countries also known as "highly industrialized" whose economies are based in information processing, communications, and service industries.

Poverty: The lack of resources necessary to meet basic needs. There is no definitive measure of poverty, but the US government uses a specific measure that takes into account the cost of buying necessities and income. See **Poverty Line** and **Poverty Threshold**.

Poverty Line: An income line below which people are determined to be eligible for public assistance based on their poverty status. The monetary value of the poverty line changes yearly and assistance varies by state.

Poverty Threshold: Determined by calculations of the Census Bureau based on a formula originally developed by the Social Security Administration and tied to the cost of food. This threshold determines the guidelines used by the government to draw a **poverty line**.

Prejudice: A belief or set of beliefs directed toward a group including racial or ethnic groups. These beliefs are usually negative, though not always, and are unrelated to any real or individual traits.

Prestige: A synonym for **social status**.

Primary Sector: In the **dual labor market**, the primary sector provides the highest pay, the most security and autonomy, and the best benefits. It also requires the most formal education. Compare **Secondary Sector**.

Race: A group of people whose geographic origins may indicate certain physical characteristics and whose unique historical experiences tie them to specific identities of importance to the society in which they live. Race is a social construction that is based on an interpretation of biological characteristics such as skin color, hair texture, and other physical characteristics that are socially significant in a given society.

Racism: Beliefs or actions that reinforce **inequality** by being directed toward a group or individuals within a group based on their race alone.

Rapidly Developing Nations: See **Mid-Level Industrialized Nations.**

Sanctions: Rewards and punishments deemed by society to reinforce **norms**.

Secondary Sector: In the **dual labor market**, the secondary sector provides lower pay, less security and autonomy, and lower benefits than the **primary market**. Employees typically have less education than their counterparts in the primary sector, but may get specialized training for certain jobs.

Sex: The biological attributes that determine whether someone is male or female and the related reproductive roles of each sex. Compare **Gender**.

Social Class: The most fundamental component of **social stratification** in modern society. Social class is most often measured by **income**, **occupation**, **wealth**, and **education**. In a modern stratified society, there are significant class differences among people.

Social Construction of Reality: Understanding social experiences depends at least in part on the perspective of the people experiencing it, the moment in time, and the culture of a particular group. History, culture, and social location can influence what is perceived to be social reality. Reality is considered socially constructed when the perception of an event of social experience changes over time or is perceived differently by different groups.

Social Institutions: Institutions make up the structure of every society, though how institutions are shaped and how they function vary from society to society and over time. All societies have the following social institutions in some form: economics, politics, family, **education**, and religion. In modern societies mass media, health, and military institutions are important.

Social Status: A person's social rank or **prestige** based on subjective judgment. Status is associated with **social class**, but is not the same thing.

Social Stratification: The layering of society based on unequal access to resources. The term *social stratification* can be used interchangeably with the term **inequality**.

Sociological Imagination: One of the most significant and enduring concepts in sociology, developed by C. Wright Mills. The sociological imagination places personal experience within the larger social and historical context to allow people to understand their place in the world. The sociological imagination demonstrates how sociology can help link personal "troubles" to social circumstances and events. The sociological imagination looks at how structural changes in society impact our individual lives and the lives of others.

Stereotype: A belief that associates whole groups or members of a group with unfounded assumptions about that group or its members. Stereotypes often are associated with **prejudice** and **discrimination**.

Structural Functionalism (or Functionalism): Functionalism examines the structure of society and how different parts function, both of these factors being useful in understanding social life. Functionalist theory argues that for societies to function, there must be a certain amount of equilibrium in major social institutions. When that equilibrium is disturbed, dysfunction creates the likelihood of social change.

Subculture: Components of culture that, while adhering to a society's overall normative expectations, may layer on other expectations that are specific to a group but not in opposition to the larger society. Subcultures may include religious or ethnic groups, occupations, youth culture, and so forth. Compare **Counterculture**.

Symbolic Interaction Theory: Symbolic interaction theory studies how we use language and other forms of communication to reflect who we are, give meaning to our circumstances, and meet our social needs. George Herbert Mead and Charles Horton Cooley were major symbolic interaction theorists.

Terrorism: An act of violence or threat of violence against non-combatant citizens to meet or call attention to political objectives.

Wealth: The assets held by a person or group. Personal wealth includes assets such as bank accounts and stock and real-estate investments, minus debt. Wealth can be acquired through inheritance, investments, and savings. Wealth is an important determinant of one's position in a stratified society.

References

350 Science. n.d. http://350.org/en/about/science. Retrieved 5/27/13.

Adusei, Lord Aikins. 2009. "Why Are We Still Poor?" *Modern Ghana News*, May 27, 2009. http://www.modernghana.com/news/218434/1/why-are-we-still-poor.html. Retrieved 7/16/10.

Altman, Drew. 2012. "Pulling It Together: Reflections on This Year's Four Percent Premium Increase." The Henry J. Kaiser Family Foundation. http://kff.org/health-costs/perspective/pulling-it-together-reflections-on-this-years/. Retrieved 5/11/13.

American Sociological Association Section on Environment and Technology. 2012. http://www.envirosoc.org/visitors.php. Retrieved 3/21/13.

AP. 2009. "US Income Gap Widens as Poor Take Hit in Recession." http://www.cnbc.com/id/33067886. Retrieved 1/30/10.

Avert.org. n.d. "HIV and AIDS in Western and Central Europe." http://www.avert.org/aids-europe.htm. Retrieved 5/11/13.

———. 2010. "HIV and AIDS in Africa." http://www.avert.org/hiv-aids-africa.htm. Retrieved 9/20/10.

———. 2013. "South East Asia HIV & AIDS Statistics: Thailand." http://www.avert.org/aids-hiv-south-east-asia.htm. Retrieved 5/11/13.

Barry, Patrick. 2004. "A Chilling Possibility." Science at NASA. http://science.nasa.gov/headlines/y2004/05mar_arctic.htm. Retrieved 5/4/12.

Bishaw, Alemayehu, and Trudi J. Renwick. 2009. "Poverty: 2007 and 2008 American Community Surveys." *American Community Survey Reports*. US Census Bureau (September). http://www.census.gov/prod/2009pubs/acsbr08-1.pdf. Retrieved 2/1/10.

Braasch, Gary. n.d. "World View of Global Warming: The Photographic Documentation of Climate Change." http://www.worldviewofglobalwarming.org/pages/arctic.html. Retrieved 6/7/13.

Brown, Brett, and Pilar Martin. 2009. "Adolescents and Electronic Media: Growing Up Plugged In." *Child Trends Research Brief,* May 2009. Publication #2009-29. http://www.childtrends.org/Files/Child_Trends-2009_05_26_RB_AdolElecMedia.pdf. Retrieved 11/12/10.

Callan, Patrick. 2008. "The 2008 National Report Card: Modest Improvements, Persistent Disparities, Eroding Global Competitiveness." In *Measuring Up: The National Report Card on Higher Education*. The National Center for Public Policy and Higher Education. http://measuringup2008.highereducation.org/print/NCPPHEMUNationalRpt.pdf. Retrieved 1/20/13.

Cawthorne, Alexandra. 2008. "The Straight Facts on Women in Poverty." Center for American Progress. http://www.americanprogress.org/issues/2008/10/pdf/women_poverty.pdf. Retrieved 2/22/10.

CBC News. 2008. "The Crisis in Darfur, a Timeline." http://www.cbc.ca/news/background/sudan/darfur.html. Retrieved 5/28/13.

CBS News. 2009. "Fast Food Linked to Child Obesity." http://www.cbsnews.com/2100-204_162-591325.html. Retrieved 5/10/13.

Center for Genetics and Society. n.d. "About Genetic Selection." http://www.geneticsandsociety.org/section.php?id=82. Retrieved 11/9/10.

Center for Responsive Politics. (OpenSecrets.org.) 2010. "Lobbying Database." http://www

.opensecrets.org/lobby/index.php. Retrieved 10/3/10.

Center for Science in the Public Interest. 2004. "Obesity Is One of the Greatest Health Challenges of Our Time." www.cspinet.org/new /pdf/sdtaxes_obesity_factsheet.pdf. Retrieved 9/14/10.

———. 2012. http://www.cspinet.org/. Retrieved 6/10/13.

Centers for Disease Control and Prevention. n.d. "HIV Basics: Basic Statistics." http://www.cdc .gov/hiv/basics/index.html. Retrieved 9/21/10.

———. 2007. "Disease Burden and Risk Factors." Office of Minority Health and Health Disparities. http://www.cdc.gov/omhd/AMH/dbrf .htm. Retrieved 9/23/10.

———. 2009. "Leading Causes of Death." http:// www.cdc.gov/nchs/fastats/lcod.htm. Retrieved 9/13/10.

———. 2010a. "Defining Overweight and Obesity." http://www.cdc.gov/obesity/defining .html. Retrieved 9/13/10.

———. 2010b. "HIV in the United States: An Overview." http://cdc.gov/hiv/topics/surveillance /resources/factsheets/us_overview.htm. Retrieved 9/20/10.

———. 2010c. "Overweight and Obesity." http:// www.cdc.gov/obesity/index.html. Retrieved 9/13/10.

———. 2011, 2012, 2013. "FastStats." (Multiple links: Infant Mortality; Life Expectancy; Leading Causes of Death; Health Insurance Coverage.) http://www.cdc.gov/nchs/fastats/default .htm. Retrieved 5/10/13.

———. 2012. "Health Insurance Coverage." http://www.cdc.gov/nchs/fastats/hinsure.htm. Retrieved 5/11/13.

———. 2013a. "Epidemiology of HIV Infection through 2011." http://www.cdc.gov/hiv/pdf /statistics_surveillance_Epi-HIV-infection.pdf. Retrieved 6/10/13.

———. 2013b. "HIV among African Americans." http://www.cdc.gov/hiv/pdf/risk_HIV_AAA .pdf. Retrieved 5/12/13.

———. 2013c. "HIV in the United States: At a Glance." http://www.cdc.gov/hiv/pdf/statistics _basics_factsheet.pdf. Retrieved 5/10/13.

Central Intelligence Agency. 2013. "The World Factbook." https://www.cia.gov/library /publications/the-world-factbook/rankorder /rankorderguide.html. Retrieved 5/27/13.

Chen, Michelle. 2010. "Gendering the Birthright Citizenship Debate." *Huffington Post*, August

10. http://www.huffingtonpost.com/michelle -chen/gendering-the-birthright-_b_687794 .html. Retrieved 8/23/10.

ChevronToxico: The Campaign for Justice in Ecuador. n.d. "Health Impacts." http:// chevrontoxico.com/about/health-impacts/. Retrieved 5/12/12.

———. 2005. "Crude Reflections." http:// chevrontoxico.com/news-and-multimedia /2005/0424-crude-reflections.html. Retrieved 5/16/12.

Child Soldiers International. 2008. "Child Soldiers Global Report 2008." http://www.child -soldiers.org/global_report_reader.php?id =97. (Link #5 factsandfigures2031629.pdf.) Retrieved 6/3/10.

Child Trends. 2012. "Home Computer Access and Internet Use." http://www.childtrends .org/?indicators=home-computer-access. Retrieved 10/26/13.

Cohn, D'Vera. 2010. "Race and the Census: The 'Negro' Controversy." In *All Things Census* (1/21/10). Social and Demographic Trends. Pew Research Center. http://www .pewsocialtrends.org/2010/01/21/race-and-the -census-the%E2%80%9Cnegro%E2%80%9D -controversy/. Retrieved 5/4/13.

Condon, Stephanie. 2008. "Critics: Homeland Security Unprepared for Cyberthreats." CNET News, September 17, 2008. http://news .cnet.com/8301-13578_3-10043665-38.html. Retrieved 10/19/10.

Congressional Budget Office. 2008. "Growing Disparities in Life Expectancy." Economic and Budget Issue Brief, April 17. http://www .cbo.gov/ftpdocs/91xx/doc9104/04-17 -LifeExpectancy_Brief.pdf. Retrieved 9/22/10.

Council on American-Islamic Relations. 2009 (updated 2013). "Executive Summary." 2009 Civil Rights Report: Seeking Full Inclusion. http://cair.com/civil-rights/civil-rights-reports /2009.html. Retrieved 5/14/13.

Cunningham, Brad. 2007. "Digital Native or Digital Immigrant, Which Language Do You Speak?" NACADA Clearinghouse of Academic Advising Resources. http://www.nacada.ksu .edu/Clearinghouse/AdvisingIssues/Digital -Natives.htm. Retrieved 6/5/13.

Cutter, Susan. 2006. "The Geography of Social Vulnerability: Race, Class, and Catastrophe." Social Science Research Council. http:// wasis.ou.edu/docs/Cutte_2005.pdf. Retrieved 6/5/11.

Daly, Matthew. 2010. "BP Spent $93M on Advertising after Gulf Spill." AP, September 2. http://www.boston.com/business/articles /2010/09/02 /after_gulf_spill_bp_spent_93m _on_ads/. Retrieved 5/27/13.

DeCicco, John, and Freda Fung. 2006. "Global Warming on the Road: The Climate Impact of America's Automobiles." The Environmental Defense Fund. http:// www.edf.org/sites/default/files/5301 _Globalwarmingontheroad_0.pdf. Retrieved 6/12/13.

Denning, Paul, and Elizabeth DiNenno. 2010. "Communities in Crisis: Is There a General- ized HIV Epidemic in Impoverished Urban Areas of the United States?" Centers for Disease Control. http://cdc.gov/hiv/topics/surveillance /resources/other/print/poverty.htm. Retrieved 9/21/10.

Domhoff, G. William. 2013 (updated Feb. 2013). "Wealth, Income, and Power." WhoRules America? http://www2.ucsc.edu /whorulesamerica/. Retrieved 4/11/13.

Dor, Avi, Christine Ferguson, Casey Langwith, and Ellen Tan. 2010. "A Heavy Burden: The Individual Costs of Being Overweight and Obese in the United States." The George Wash- ington University School of Public Health and Health Services, Department of Health Policy. http://www.gwumc.edu/sphhs/departments /healthpolicy/pdf/HeavyBurdenReport.pdf. Retrieved 9/21/10.

Doyle, Charles. 2002. "The USA Patriot Act: A Sketch." CRS Report for Congress, April 18. Congressional Research Service. The Library of Congress, http://www.fas.org/irp/crs /RS21203.pdf. Retrieved 10/18/10.

Environmental Defense Fund. 2002. "Clearing the Air on Climate Change: Carbon Emissions Fact Sheet." http://apps.edf.org/documents/2209 _CarEmissionsFactSheet.pdf. Retrieved 5/27/13.

———. 2007. "Global Warming Facts." http:// www.edf.org/article.cfm?contentID=5816. Retrieved 6/12/13.

Fairfield, Hannah. 2009. "Why Is Her Paycheck Smaller?" New York Times, March 1. (Published 2/28/09). (A version of this article appeared in print on March 1, 2009, on page BU4 of the New York edition.) http://www.nytimes .com/2009/03/01/business/01metrics.html ?_r=2. Retrieved 4/12/11.

Faris, Stephan. 2009. "The Last Straw." Foreign Policy: The Failed States Index 2009. http:// www.foreignpolicy.com/articles/2009/06/22 /failed_states_index_the_last_straw. Retrieved 6/9/10.

Favro, Tony. 2009. "Critics of surveillance cameras fear racial profiling in US cities." City Mayors Society, June 11, http://www.citymayors.com /society/us-security-cameras.html. Retrieved 5/12/11.

Federal Bureau of Investigation. 2008. "The Cyber Threat Today." http://www.fbi.gov/news /stories/2008/october/cyberthreat_101708/ ?searchterm=cyber%20threat%20today. Retrieved 11/4/10.

———. 2010. "IC3 2009 Annual Report on Internet Crime Released." March 3. http:// www.fbi.gov/news/pressrel/press-releases/ic3 -2009-annual-report-on-internet-crime -released?searchterm=IC3+2009+. Retrieved 11/4/10.

Federal Trade Commission. 2007. "2006 Identity Theft Survey Report." http://www.ftc.gov /os/2007/11/SynovateFinalReportIDTheft 2006.pdf. Retrieved 11/4/10.

Fleshman, Michael. 2004. "Women: The Face of AIDS in Africa." Africa Renewal 18 (3): 6. http://medilinkz.org/old/Features/Articles /Oct2004/women_aids04.asp. Retrieved 5/10/13.

Food Research and Action Center. 2010. "Hunger and Obesity? Making the Connections." http:// www.frac.org/pdf/Paradox.pdf. Retrieved 9/14/10.

Free Press. n.d. "Who Owns the Media?" http:// www.freepress.net/ownership/chart/main. Retrieved 12/15/10.

Gamson, Joshua, and Pearl Latteier. 2012. "Do Media Monsters Devour Diversity?" In The Contexts Reader, edited by Douglas Hartmann and Christopher Uggen. New York: W. W. Norton and Co., pp. 107–114.

Giddens, Anthony. 2006. "Sociology and Terror- ism." Sociology, 5th Edition (interview). http:// www.polity.co.uk/giddens5/news/sociology -and-terrorism.asp. Retrieved 1/2/09.

Gilbert, Dennis. 2011. The American Class Struc- ture in an Age of Growing Inequality. 8th ed. Los Angeles: Pine Forge Press.

Global Education Project. n.d. "Exploration- Discovery-Consumption" (graph). World Energy Supply. http://www.theglobaleducationproject

.org/earth/energy-supply.php. Retrieved 3/7/11.

Global Policy Forum. n.d. "Failed States." http://www.globalpolicy.org/nations-a-states/failed-states.html. Retrieved 6/14/10.

Goldfarb, Zachary A. 2013. "ATM Thieves Conducted Massive Cyberattack." *Washington Post*, May 9, http://www.washingtonpost.com/business/economy/atm-thieves-conducted-massive-cyberattack/2013/05/09/0c3c3a1c-b8ec-11e2-92f3-f291801936b8_story_1.html. Retrieved 5/18/13.

Goldstein, Amy. 2010. "New Formula to Give Fresh Look at U.S. Poverty." *Washington Post,* March 3, A02.

Goodridge, Elisabeth, and Sarah Arnquist. 2009. "A History of Overhauling Health Care." *New York Times,* March 21. http://www.nytimes.com/interactive/2009/07/19/us/politics/20090717_HEALTH_TIMELINE.html?_r=1&. Retrieved 6/10/13.

Green, Ronald M. 2008. "Building Baby from the Genes Up." *Washington Post*, April 13. http://www.washingtonpost.com/wp-dyn/content/article/2008/04/11/AR2008041103330_pf.html. Retrieved 4/13/08.

Haddad, Yvonne Yazbeck. 2007. "The Post-9/11 Hijab as Icon." *Sociology of Religion* 68 (3): 253–267.

Hall, Mimi. 2004. "Ex-Official Tells of Homeland Security Failures." *USA Today,* December 28. http://www.usatoday.com/news/washington/2004-12-27-homeland-usat_x.htm. Retrieved 10/19/10.

Halliday, Fred. 2011. "Terrorism in Historical Perspective." Open Democracy. http://www.opendemocracy.net/globalization-madridprevention/article_1865.jsp. Retrieved 5/14/13.

Hammond, Ross A., and Ruth Levine. 2010. "The Economic Impact of Obesity in the United States." Economic Studies Program: The Brookings Institution, Washington, DC. http://www.brookings.edu/~/media/research/files/articles/2010/9/14%20obesity%20cost %20hammond%20levine/0914_obesity_cost _hammond_levine.pdf. Retrieved 9/16/10.

Harkinson, Josh. 2009. "Despite Pledge, Exxon-Mobil Still Funding Climate Change Deniers." *Mother Jones,* July 1. http://www.motherjones.com/blue-marble/2009/07/despite-pledge-exxonmobil-still-funding-climate-change-deniers. Retrieved 5/27/13.

HealthyPeople.gov. 2013. "No Leisure-Time Physical Activity, Adults, 1997–2010." http://www.healthypeople.gov/2020/topicsobjectives2020/nationalsnapshot.aspx?topicId=33. Retrieved 5/10/13.

Henry J. Kaiser Family Foundation. 2009. "Key Health and Health Care Indicators by Race/Ethnicity and State." http://kaiserfamilyfoundation.files.wordpress.com/2013/01/7633-02.pdf. Retrieved 9/23/10.

———. 2011. "Poverty Rate by Race/Ethnicity." Kaiser State Health Facts. http://kff.org/other/state-indicator/poverty-rate-by-raceethnicity/. Retrieved 5/29/13.

———. 2012. "Employer Health Benefits: 2012 Summary of Findings." http://kaiserfamilyfoundation.files.wordpress.com/2013/03/8346-employer-health-benefits-annual-survey-summary-of-findings-0912.pdf. Retrieved 5/29/13.

Hoberman, J. 2009. "The Decade in Film: A Timeline." *The Village Voice,* December 2. http://www.villagevoice.com/content/pringVersion/1557964. Retrieved 1/9/10.

House Committee on Natural Resources. 2011. "Markey Report: Big Five Oil Companies Approach $1 Trillion in Profits for the Decade, Yet Still Rely on 100 Year-Old Subsidies to Sell $100 Oil." February 2. http://democrats.naturalresources.house.gov/press-release/markey-report-big-five-oil-companies-approach-1-trillion-profits-decade-yet-still-rely. Retrieved 5/27/13.

Inequality.org. n.d. "Inequality Data and Statistics." http://inequality.org/inequality-data-statistics/. Retrieved 6/11/13.

Institute for Research on Poverty. 2013. "What Are Poverty Thresholds and Poverty Guidelines?" http://www.irp.wisc.edu/faqs/faq1.htm. Retrieved 5/26/13.

Intelligence Fusion Centers. 2009. "Public Intelligence." http://publicintelligence.net/intelligence-fusion-centers/. Retrieved 11/1/10.

Intercounty Connector (ICC). 2011. http://www.iccproject.com/. Retrieved 8/5/11.

Internet World Stats. 2012. "Internet Usage Statistics: The Internet Big Picture: World Internet Users and Population Stats." http://

www.internetworldstats.com/stats.htm. Retrieved 4/9/13.

IRIN. 2003. "In-Depth: Child Soldiers: AFRICA: Too Small to Be Fighting in Anyone's War." UN Office for the Coordination of Humanitarian Affairs. http://www.irinnews.org /IndepthMain.aspx?IndepthId=24&ReportId =66280. Retrieved 6/3/10.

———. 2013. "In-Depth: Fighting for the Rights of Child Soldiers." http://www.irinnews.org /indepthmain.aspx?indepthid=94&reportid =94664. Retrieved 6/18/13.

Isaacs, Julia B. 2010. "The Effects of the Recession on Child Poverty." Brookings: Center on Children and Families. http://www.brookings .edu/~/media/research/files/papers/2010/1/04 %20child%20poverty%20isaacs/0104_child _poverty_isaacs.pdf. Retrieved 5/26/13.

Ito, Suzanne. 2010. "TSA Meets 'Resistance' with New Pat-Down Procedures." ACLU Blog of Rights, November 3. http://www.aclu.org/blog /technology-and-liberty/tsa-meets-resistance -new-pat-down-procedures. Retrieved 12/10/10.

Kalb, Claudia. 2009. "Generation 9/11." *Newsweek,* September 8. http://www.newsweek.com /2009/09/07/generation-9-11.html. Retrieved 10/20/10.

Kates, Jen, Tina Hoff, Sarah Levine, Alicia Carbaugh, and Carolina Gutierrez. 2013. "A Report on Women and HIV/AIDS in the U.S." The Kaiser Family Foundation. http:// kaiserfamilyfoundation.files.wordpress.com /2013/04/8436.pdf. Retrieved 5/12/13.

Khan, Mafruza. 2003. "Media Diversity at Risk: The FCC's Plan to Weaken Ownership Rules." Corporate Research E-Letter No. 35, May (updated 6/20/03). http://www.corp-research .org/archives/may03.htm. Retrieved 12/16/09.

LaClaire, Jennifer. 2006. "Hackers Target University Computer Assets." *TechNews World,* May 30. http://www.technewsworld.com/story/50799 .html?wlc=1288894067. Retrieved 11/4/10.

Langton, Lynn. 2011. "Identity Theft Reported by Households, 2005–2010." Bureau of Justice Statistics NCJ 236245. http://www.bjs.gov /index.cfm?ty=pbdetail&iid=2207#. Retrieved 5/19/13.

Lendman, Stephen. 2010. "Child Slavery in Haiti." *Dissident Voice,* February 3. http:// dissidentvoice.org/2010/02/child-slavery-in -haiti/. Retrieved 3/14/10.

Lundy, Janet. 2010. "Prescription Drug Trends." Kaiser Family Foundation. http:// kaiserfamilyfoundation.files.wordpress .com/2013/01/3057-08.pdf. Retrieved 5/10/13.

Lutz, Amy. 2008. "Who Joins the Military? A Look at Race, Class, and Immigration Status." *Journal of Political and Military Sociology* 36 (2): 167– 188. http://surface.syr.edu/cgi/viewcontent .cgi?article=1002&context=soc. Retrieved 10/21/10.

MacDorman, Marian F., and T. J. Mathews. 2008. "Recent Trends in Infant Mortality in the United States." NCHS Data Brief No. 9, October 2008. Centers for Disease Control and Prevention. http://www.cdc.gov/nchs/data /databriefs/db09.htm. Retrieved 9/23/10.

Macur, Juliet. 2008. "Born to Run? Little Ones Get Test for Sports Gene." *New York Times,* November 30. http://www.nytimes.com/2008/11/30 /sports/30genetics.html. Retrieved 12/1/08.

Max, Arthur. 2009. "Climate Talks Resume with New Emissions Pledges." Associated Press, August 10. http://www.utsandiego.com /news/2009/Aug/10/eu-climate-talks-081009 /?#article-copy. Retrieved 5/27/13.

McCrummen, Stephanie. 2006. "The Subtle Changes since 9/11." *Washington Post,* September 11. http://www.washingtonpost .com/wp-dyn/content/article/2006/09/10 /AR2006091001300.html. Retrieved 5/7/12.

McCullagh, Declan. 2010. "Feds Admit Storing Checkpoint Body Scan Images." CNET News, August 4. http://news.cnet.com/8301-31921 _3-20012583-281.html. Retrieved 8/4/10.

Miller, Mark Crispin. 2002. "What's Wrong with This Picture?" *The Nation,* January 7. http://www.thenation.com/article/whats -wrong-picture-0?page=0,0. Retrieved 1/2/08.

Mills, C. Wright. 1959 (2000). *The Sociological Imagination: Fortieth Anniversary Edition.* New York: Oxford University Press.

Mindfully.org. 2003. "FBI Seeking 2 Men in $2.5M Arson Spree against Calif SUVs." http:// www.mindfully.org/Heritage/2003/ELF -FBI-$2_5M-SUVs23aug03.htm. Retrieved 6/13/13.

Mission: Readiness, Military Leaders for Kids. 2010. "Too Fat to Fight." http://cdn.mission readiness.org/MR_Too_Fat_to_Fight-1.pdf. Retrieved 4/5/11.

Moore, John. n.d. "The Evolution of Islamic Terrorism." PBS *Frontline*. http://www.pbs.org/wgbh/pages/frontline/shows/target/etc/modern.html. Retrieved 5/14/13.

Morse, Jane. 2008. "Child Soldiers a National and Global Security Issue, Expert Says, April 8." US Diplomatic Mission to Italy. http://www.usembassy.it/viewer/article.asp?article=/file2008_04/alia/a8040801.htm. Retrieved 6/21/10.

Mufson, Steven. 2008. "A Crude Case for War?" *Washington Post,* March 16. http://www.washingtonpost.com/wp-dyn/content/article/2008/03/14/AR2008031403677_pf.html. Retrieved 4/24/13.

Murray, Sara. 2009. "Numbers on Welfare See Sharp Increase." *Wall Street Journal,* June 22. wsj.com: http://online.wsj.com/article/SB124562449457235503.html. Retrieved 2/10/10.

Nakashima, Ellen. 2007. "FBI Prepares Vast Database of Biometrics." *Washington Post*, December 22, http://www.washingtonpost.com/wp-dyn/content/article/2007/12/21/AR2007122102544.html. Retrieved December 22.

National Aeronautics and Space Administration. n.d. "Climate Change: How Do We Know?" Global Climate Change Evidence. http://climate.nasa.gov/evidence. Retrieved 6/12/13.

National Commission on Terrorist Attacks upon the United States (The 9-11 Commission). 2004. *The 9/11 Commission Report: Final Report of the National Commission on Terrorist Attacks upon the United States (9/11 Report)*. Washington, DC: US Government Printing Office. http://www.gpo.gov/fdsys/pkg/GPO-911REPORT/pdf/GPO-911REPORT.pdf. Retrieved 6/4/13.

National Committee on Pay Equity. 2002. "The Wage Gap by Education: 2001." http://www.pay-equity.org/. Retrieved 2/16/10.

National Counterterrorism Center. 2013. "Counterterrorism 2013 Calendar." http://www.nctc.gov/site/groups/index.html. Retrieved 6/11/13.

National Science and Technology Council Committee on Technology. 2006. Committee on Homeland and National Security Subcommittee on Biometrics. "Biometrics Frequently Asked Questions." http://www.biometrics.gov/Documents/FAQ.pdf. Retrieved 11/10/10.

Nature Conservancy. 2011a. "Climate Change Impacts: Higher Temperatures." http://www.nature.org/ourinitiatives/urgentissues/global-warming-climate-change/threats-impacts/higher-temperatures.xml. Retrieved 4/23/13.

———. 2011b. "Climate Change Impacts: The Rising Seas, Higher Sea Levels." http://www.nature.org/ourinitiatives/urgentissues/global-warming-climate-change/threats-impacts/rising-seas.xml. Retrieved 5/27/13.

New York Times. 2013. "Al Qaeda: Al Qaeda Chronology." (Multiple authors.) http://topics.nytimes.com/top/reference/timestopics/organizations/a/al_qaeda/index.html?inline=nyt-org. Retrieved 6/10/13.

Nielsen. 2012a. "The Cross-Platform Report: A New Connected Community." http://www.nielsen.com/us/en/newswire/2012/the-cross-platform-report-a-new-connected-community.html. Retrieved 4/9/13.

———. 2012b. "Social Media Report 2012: Social Media Comes of Age." http://www.nielsen.com/us/en/newswire/2012/social-media-report-2012-social-media-comes-of-age.html. Retrieved 4/9/13.

———. 2013a. "January 2013: Top U.S. Entertainment Sites and Web Brands." http://www.nielsen.com/us/en/newswire/2013/january-2013—top-u-s—entertainment-sites-and-web-brands.html. Retrieved 4/9/13.

———. 2013b. "Zero-TV Doesn't Mean Zero Video." http://www.nielsen.com/us/en/newswire/2013/zero-tv-doesnt-mean-zero-video.html. Retrieved 3/21/13.

Obesity Action Coalition. 2010. "Understanding Obesity Stigma." http://www.obesityaction.org/educationaltools/brochures/uoseries/understandingobesitystigma.php. Retrieved 9/20/10.

Obesity Society. 2010. "Obesity, Bias, and Stigmatization." http://www.obesity.org/resources-for/obesity-bias-and-stigmatization.htm. Retrieved 9/13/10.

Omelaniuk, Irena. 2005. "Trafficking in Human Beings." United Nations Expert Group Meeting on International Migration and Development. Population Division. Department of Economic and Social Affairs. United Nations Secretariat, July 8. http://www.un.org/esa/population/meetings/ittmigdev2005/P15_IOmelaniuk.pdf. Retrieved 5/6/13.

One Nation Online. n.d. "Internet for Everyone." http://www.freepress.net/files/IFE_Brochure.pdf. Retrieved 11/12/10.

O'Neill, Tom. 2007. "Curse of the Black Gold: Hope and Betrayal in the Niger Delta." *National Geographic Magazine.* http://ngm.nationalgeographic.com/2007/02/nigerian-oil/oneill-text. Retrieved 6/9/10.

Organization for Economic Co-operation and Development. 2011. "Health at a Glance 2011." http://www.oecd.org/els/health-systems/healthataglance2011.htm. Retrieved 5/29/13.

Otto, Mary. 2008. "Hidden Hurt: Desperate for medical care, the uninsured flock by the hundreds to a remote corner of Virginia for the chance to see a doctor." *Washington Post,* November 9. http://www.washingtonpost.com/wp-dyn/content/article/2008/10/31/AR2008103101756.html?sid=ST2010080204465. Retrieved 11/10/08.

Pachuari, R. K., and A. Reisinger (eds.). 2007. "Fourth Assessment Report, Climate Change—Synthesis Report." Geneva: Intergovernmental Panel on Climate Change. http://www.ipcc.ch/publications_and_data/ar4/syr/en/mainssyr-introduction.html. Retrieved 9/21/10.

Palmer, Brian. 2010. "Big Apple Is Watching You." *Slate,* May 3. http://www.slate.com/id/2252729/. Retrieved 11/1/10.

Pear, Robert. 2008. "Gap in Life Expectancy Widens for the Nation." *New York Times,* March 23. http://www.nytimes.com/2008/03/23/us/23health.html. Retrieved 10/4/10.

Pershing, Ben. 2009. "Groups Take Health-Reform Debate to Airwaves." *Washington Post,* August 5. http://www.washingtonpost.com/wp-dyn/content/article/2009/08/04/AR2009080401447.html. Retrieved 10/3/2010.

Pew Research Center Social and Demographic Trends. 2010. "How the Great Recession Has Changed Life in America: A Balance Sheet at 30 Months." http://pewsocialtrends.org/pubs/759/how-the-great-recession-has-changed-life-in-america. Retrieved 8/16/10.

Prager, Daniel, and Valerie Thompson. 2005. "Findings of the Millennium Ecosystem Assessment: How Do the Poor Fare?" World Resources Institute. http://multimedia.wri.org/wr2005/box2-1.htm. Retrieved 6/13/13.

Randall, Kay. 2005. "Generation 9/11." The University of Texas at Austin: Feature Story. http://www.utexas.edu/features/2005/generation/index.html. Retrieved 10/20/10.

Religious Tolerance.org. 2008. "Aftermath of the 9-ll Terrorist Attack: Why Do 'They' Hate the West?" Ontario Consultants on Religious Tolerance. http://www.religioustolerance.org/reac_ter13.htm#me. Retrieved 10/15/10.

Risen, James, and Eric Lightblau. 2013. "How the U.S. Uses Technology to Mine More Data More Quickly." *New York Times,* June 8. http://www.nytimes.com/2013/06/09/us/revelations-give-look-at-spy-agencys-wider-reach.html?emc=eta1&_r=0. Retrieved 6/9/13.

Ritzer, George. 2011. *The McDonaldization of Society 6.* Thousand Oaks, CA: Pine Forge Press.

Rothman, Barbara Katz. 1998. *Genetic Maps and Human Imaginations: The Limits of Science in Understanding Who We Are.* New York: W. W. Norton and Company.

Rucker, Philip. 2010. "TSA Tries to Assuage Privacy Concerns about Full-Body Scans." *Washington Post,* January 4. http://www.washingtonpost.com/wp-dyn/content/article/2010/01/03/AR2010010301826.html?sid=ST2010010301836. Retrieved 1/4/10.

Rummel, R. J. 2002. "Genocide." http://www.hawaii.edu/powerkills/GENOCIDE.ENCY.HTM. Retrieved 6/19/10.

Schoen, Cathy, Michelle M. Doty, Ruth H. Robertson, and Sara R. Collins. 2011. "Affordable Care Act Reforms Could Reduce the Number of Underinsured U.S. Adults by 70 Percent." *Health Affairs* 30 (9): 1762–1771.

Segal, David R., and Mady Wechsler Segal. 2004. "America's Military Population." *Population Bulletin* 59, no. 4 (December). Population Reference Bureau. http://www.prb.org/pdf04/59.4AmericanMilitary.pdf. Retrieved 5/14/13.

Siddiqi, Ayesha. 2011. "Kashmir and the Politics of Water," *Al Jazeera.* http://www.aljazeera.com/indepth/spotlight/kashmirtheforgottenconflict/2011/07/20117812154478992.html. Retrieved 10/22/13.

Singer, P. W. 2006. *Children and War.* Berkeley: University of California Press.

Skinner, E. Benjamin. 2008. "A World Enslaved." *Foreign Policy* 165 (Spring): 62–67.

Smith, Aaron. 2010. "Technology Trends among People of Color." Pew Internet: A Project of the Pew Research Center. http://www.pewinternet.org/Commentary/2010/September/Technology-Trends-Among-People-of-Color.aspx. Retrieved 11/12/10.

Sperling, Frank (ed.). n.d. "Poverty and Climate Change: Reducing the Vulnerability of the Poor through Adaptation." http://www.oecd.org/environment/cc/2502872.pdf. Retrieved 5/27/13.

Stein, Rob. 2010. "Sickle Cell Testing of Athletes Stirs Discrimination Fears." *Washington Post*, September 20. http://www.washingtonpost.com/wp-dyn/content/article/2010/09/19/AR2010091904417.html. Retrieved 9/20/10.

Sullivan, Meg. 2005. "Obesity Epidemic Overblown, Conclude UCLA Sociologists." UCLA Newsroom, November 15. http://www.newsroom.ucla.edu/portal/ucla/Obesity-Epidemic-Overblown-Conclude-6560.aspx?RelNum=6560. Retrieved 10/2/10.

Tamaki, Julie, Jia-Rui Chong, and Mitchell Landsberg. 2003. "Radicals Target SUVs in Series of Southland Attacks: Dozens Are Destroyed or Damaged." *Los Angeles Times*, August 23. http://articles.latimes.com/2003/aug/23/local/me-hummers23. Retrieved 5/17/13.

Turk, Austin T. 2004. "Sociology of Terrorism." *Annual Review of Sociology* 30: 271-286.

UN-OHRLLS. n.d. "About LDC's." http://www.un.org/ohrlls/. Retrieved 6/17/13.

UNAIDS. 2011. "AIDSinfo: Epidemiological Status." http://www.unaids.org/en/dataanalysis/datatools/aidsinfo/. Retrieved 5/10/13.

———. 2012. "Global Fact Sheet." World AIDS Day 2012. http://www.unaids.org/en/media/unaids/contentassets/documents/epidemiology/2012/gr2012/20121120_FactSheet_Global_en.pdf. Retrieved 5/10/13.

UNICEF. n.d. "Fact Sheet: Child Soldiers." http://www.unicef.org/emerg/files/childsoldiers.pdf. Retrieved 6/17/13.

———. 2005. "Convention on the Rights of the Child: Optional Protocols to the Convention on the Rights of the Child." http://www.unicef.org/crc/index_protocols.html. Retrieved 6/18/13.

———. 2010. "The State of the World's Children 2010: Child Rights." Table 5: "Education." http://www.unicef.org/rightsite/sowc/pdfs/statistics/SOWC_Spec_Ed_CRC_TABLE%205.%20EDUCATION_EN_111309.pdf. Retrieved 6/15/11.

United Methodist Women's Action Network. 2008. "Human Trafficking Fact Sheet." Women's Divison, General Board of Global Ministries. http://new.gbgm-umc.org/umw/resources/articles/item/index.cfm?id=360. Retrieved 6/15/12.

United Nations. 1948 (2000). "Convention on the Prevention and Punishment of the Crime of Genocide." December 9. http://un.org/millennium/law/iv-1.htm. Retrieved 11/18/10.

United Nations News Centre. n.d. "UN Releases First Report on Human Trafficking Photo Stories: Human Trafficking." http://www.un.org/apps/news/photostories_detail.asp?PsID=39. Retrieved 7/3/10.

United Nations News Service. 2011. "Cleaning up Nigerian oil Pollution Could Take 30 Years, Cost Billions—UN." http://www.un.org/apps/news/story.asp?NewsID=39232&Cr=pollution&Cr1=#. Retrieved 8/9/11.

United Nations Refugee Agency. 2012. "A Year of Crises: UNHCR Global Trends 2011." http://www.unhcr.org/cgi-bin/texis/vtx/home/opendocPDFViewer.html?docid=4fd6f87f9&query=global%20trends%202012. Retrieved 5/7/13.

United States Holocaust Memorial Museum. 2010. "What Is Genocide?" Holocaust Encyclopedia. http://www.ushmm.org/wlc/en/article.php?ModuleId=10007043. Retrieved 6/20/10.

Urban Institute. 2006. "A Decade of Welfare Reform: Facts and Figures." Fact Sheet. Assessing the New Federalism, June. http://www.urban.org/UploadedPDF/900980_welfarereform.pdf. Retrieved 6/6/12.

US Army. 2012. "Today's Women Soldiers." http://www.army.mil/women/today.html. Retrieved 6/18/13.

———. 2013. "Timeline of Terrorism." http://www.army.mil/terrorism/. Retrieved 6/11/13.

US Census Bureau. n.d. "Family Net Worth—Mean and Median Net Worth in Constant (2007) Dollars by Selected Family Characteristics: 1998–2007." http://www.census.gov/compendia/statab/2010/tables/10s0705.pdf. Retrieved 2/21/10.

———. 2010. "Table 2. Reported Internet Usage for Individuals 3 Years and Older, by Selected Characteristics: 2009." Current Population Survey, October 2009. http://www.census.gov/hhes/computer/publications/2009.html. Retrieved 11/12/10.

———. 2012a. "Historic Poverty Tables-People." Table 2: "Poverty Status by Family Relationship, Race and Hispanic Origin." http://www.census.gov/hhes/www/poverty/data/historical/people.html. Retrieved 3/27/13.

———. 2012b. "Income, Poverty and Health Insurance Coverage in the United States: 2011."

http://www.census.gov/newsroom/releases /archives/income_wealth/cb12-172.html. Retrieved 3/29/13.

———. 2012c. "Poverty Highlights." http:// www.census.gov/hhes/www/poverty/about /overview/. Retrieved 4/11/13.

———. 2013. "Poverty Thresholds." http://www .census.gov/hhes/www/poverty/data/ threshld/. Retrieved 4/11/13.

US Department of Defense. 2010. "Population Representation in the Military Services." Table 1: "Actual Endstrength by Service and Personnel Type, FY08–FY10." http://prhome.defense .gov/RFM/MPP/ACCESSION%20POLICY /PopRep2010/summary/Sect_I.pdf. Retrieved 6/18/13.

———. 2013. "U.S. Casualty Status." www .defense.gov/news/casualty.pdf. Retrieved 5/14/13.

US Department of Energy, National Human Genome Research Institute. 2010. "The Human Genome Project Completion: Frequently Asked Questions." http://www.genome.gov /11006943. Retrieved 6/11/13.

———. 2012. "Human Genome Project Information." http://www.ornl.gov/sci/techresources /Human_Genome/home.shtml and http:// genomics.energy.gov. Retrieved 6/11/13.

US Department of Health and Human Services. 2012. "The 2012 HHS Poverty Guidelines: One Version of the [US] Federal Poverty Measure. Weight-Control Information Network (WIN) Overweight and Obesity Statistics." http:// www.win.niddk.nih.gov/statistics/index.htm #b. Retrieved 5/10/13.

US Department of Homeland Security History Office. 2008. "Brief Documentary History of the Department of Homeland Security: 2001–2008." (Written by Elizabeth C. Borja, History Associates, Incorporated.) http://www .hsdl.org/?view&did=37027. Retrieved 6/3/13.

US Department of Homeland Security. 2011. "National Terrorism Advisory System Public Guide." http://mema.maryland.gov /Documents/ntas-public-guide.pdf. Retrieved 6/18/13.

US Department of Justice. n.d. "Identity Theft: What Are Identity Theft and Identity Fraud?" http://www.justice.gov/criminal/fraud /websites/idtheft.html. Retrieved 11/4/10.

———. 2011. "OJP Fact Sheet: Human Trafficking." Office of Justice Programs. http://www .ojp.usdoj.gov/newsroom/factsheets/ojpfs _humantrafficking.html. Retrieved 5/8/13.

US Department of Labor, Bureau of Labor Statistics, Division of Information Services. 2003. "Earnings by Educational Attainment and Sex, 1979 and 2002." TED: The Editor's Desk, October 23. http://www.bls.gov/opub/ted/2003/oct /wk3/art04.htm. Retrieved 5/26/13.

———. 2008. "Earnings of Women and Men by Race and Ethnicity, 2007." TED: The Editor's Desk, October 30. http://www.bls .gov/opub/ted/2008/oct/wk4/art04.htm. Retrieved 5/26/13.

———. 2009a. "Hours Spent Doing Unpaid Household Work by Age and Sex, 2003–07." TED: The Editor's Desk, August 6. http:// www.bls.gov/opub/ted/2009/ted_20090806 .htm. Retrieved 2/9/10.

———. 2009b. "Women in the Labor Force: A Databook (2009 Edition)." Labor Force Statistics from the Current Population Survey. "Report 1018 Introduction and Highlights." www.bls.gov/CPS/wlf-intro-2009.htm. Retrieved 2/8/10.

———. 2010. "Back to College." http://www .bls.gov/spotlight/2010/college/. Retrieved 12/2/10.

———. 2012. "Highlights of Women's Earnings in 2011." Table 1: "Median Usual Weekly Earnings of Full-Time Wage and Salary Workers, by Selected Characteristics, 2011 Annual Averages—cont'd." http://www.bls.gov/cps /cpswom2011.pdf. Retrieved 6/12/13.

———. 2012–2013. "Occupational Outlook Handbook." http://www.bls.gov/ooh/. Retrieved 11/8/13.

———. 2013a (last modified 5/22/13). "Employment Projections: Earnings and Unemployment Rates by Educational Attainment." http://www.bls.gov/emp/ep_chart_001.htm. Retrieved 6/12/13.

———. 2013b. "Median Weekly Earnings by Age, Sex, Race, and Hispanic or Latino Ethnicity, First Quarter 2013." April 19. http://www .bls.gov/opub/ted/2013/ted_20130419.htm. Retrieved 6/11/13.

———. 2013c (last modified 1/23/13). Table 2: "Median Weekly Earnings of Full Time Wage and Salary Workers by Union Affiliation and Selected Characteristics." http://www.bls .gov/news.release/union2.t02.htm. Retrieved 6/11/13.

US Department of State. 2010. "Trafficking in Persons Report 2010." Introduction: "10 Years of Fighting Modern Slavery." Office to Monitor and Combat Trafficking in Persons.

http://www.state.gov/j/tip/rls/tiprpt/2010/. Retrieved 5/6/13.

———. 2012a. *Country Reports on Terrorism 2011.* Chapter 6: "Foreign Terrorist Organizations." http://www.state.gov/j/ct/rls/crt/2011/195553.htm#imu. Retrieved 5/14/13.

———. 2012b. National Counterterrorism Center: Annex of Statistical Information. "Country Reports on Terrorism 2011." http://www.state.gov/j/ct/rls/crt/2011/195555.htm. Retrieved 5/14/13.

———. 2012c. "Trafficking in Persons Report 2012." Office to Monitor and Combat Trafficking in Persons. http://www.state.gov/j/tip/rls/tiprpt/2012/. Retrieved 5/6/13.

US Department of Transportation, Federal Highway Administration. 2013. "Highway Statistics 2011: State Motor Vehicle Registrations 2011." Office of Highway Policy Information: Highway Statistics Series. http://www.fhwa.dot.gov/policyinformation/statistics/2011/mv1.cfm. Retrieved 4/24/13.

US Energy Information Administration. 2011. "U.S. Primary Energy Flow by Source and Sector, 2011," Tables 1.3, 2.1b–1f, 10.3, and 10.4. Annual Energy Review. 2011. http://www.eia.gov/totalenergy/data/annual/pecss_diagram.cfm. Retrieved 3/23/13.

US Global Change Research Program. 2009. "Global Climate Change Impacts in the United States: 2009 Report." http://nca2009.globalchange.gov/. Retrieved 6/10/12.

US National Library of Medicine, National Institutes of Health. 2010. "Genetic Testing." MedlinePlus. http://www.nlm.nih.gov/medlineplus/genetictesting.html. Retrieved 11/8/10.

Washington Post. 2010. "Top Secret America: A *Washington Post* Investigation." http://projects.washingtonpost.com/top-secret-america/. Retrieved 6/3/13.

Weight Control Information Network. 2013. "Overweight and Obesity Statistics." http://www.win.niddk.nih.gov/statistics/index.htm#b. Retrieved 5/10/13.

Weiss, Rick. 2008. "Genetic Testing Gets Personal: Firms Sell Answers on Health, Even Love." *Washington Post*, March 25, A01.

Wilson, William Julius. n.d. "The First Measured Century." Interviewed by New River Media Hosted by Ben Wattenberg. http://www.pbs.org/fmc/interviews/wilson.htm. Retrieved 6/17/13.

World Bank. 2009. "Definitions of Fragility and Conflict." http://web.worldbank.org/WBSITE/EXTERNAL/PROJECTS/STRATEGIES/EXTLICUS/0,,contentMDK:22230573~pagePK:64171531~menuPK:4448982~piPK:64171507~theSitePK:511778,00.html. Retrieved 6/14/10.

World Conference Against Racism, Racial Discrimination, Xenophobia and Related Intolerance. 2001. "The Race Dimensions of Trafficking in Persons—Especially Women and Children." Durban, South Africa. http://www.un.org/WCAR/e-kit/issues.htm. Retrieved 6/14/13.

World Health Organization. 2010a. "Dispatch from Lithuania." http://www.who.int/hiv/mediacentre/lithuania/en/index.html. Retrieved 9/21/10.

———. 2010b. "Mortality and Burden of Disease" (Table 1) and "Health Expenditures" (Table 7). World Health Statistics 2010, Part 2: Global Health Indicators. http://www.who.int/whosis/whostat/EN_WHS10_Part2.pdf. Retrieved 9/16/10.

———. 2013a. "10 Facts on HIV/AIDS." http://www.who.int/features/factfiles/hiv/en/. Retrieved 5/10/13.

———. 2013b. "Life Expectancy: Life Expectancy by WHO Region." Global Health Observatory Data Repository. http://apps.who.int/gho/data/view.main.690?lang=en. Retrieved 5/10/13.

———. 2013c. "Obesity and Overweight: Fact Sheet No. 311." http://www.who.int/mediacentre/factsheets/fs311/en/. Retrieved 5/10/13.

———. 2013d. "Under-Five, Infant, Neonatal, Stillbirth: Rate by WHO Region." Global Health Observatory Data Repository. http://apps.who.int/gho/data/view.main.CM1300R?lang=en. Retrieved 5/10/13.

World Population Balance. n.d. "Population and Energy Balance." http://www.worldpopulationbalance.org/population_energy. Retrieved 6/12/13.

Zhao, Shanyang. 2005. "The Digital Self: Through the Looking Glass of Telecopresent Others." *Symbolic Interaction* 28 (3): 387–405. http://astro.temple.edu/~bzhao001/Digital_Self.pdf. Retrieved 11/12/10.

Zulfigar, Salma. 2010. "UNICEF and Partners Support Reintegration of Child Soldiers in Chad." http://www.unicef.org/infobycountry/chad_53771.html. Retrieved 5/28/13.

Index

About the Author

Roberta Goldberg is Professor of Sociology at Trinity Washington University. She has written about international adoption and labor organizing among women office workers. Her previous book is *Organizing Women Office Workers: Dissatisfaction, Consciousness, and Action*.